PATHWAYS TO POWER

NEW DIRECTIONS IN COMPARATIVE AND INTERNATIONAL POLITICS

Series Editors
Peter Merkl and Haruhiro Fukui

No Farewell to Arms? Military Disengagement from Politics in Africa and Latin America, Claude Welch

Comparing New Democracies: Transition and Consolidation in Mediterranean Europe and the Southern Cone, edited by Enrique A. Baloyra

The Rise and Fall of Italian Terrorism, Leonard Weinberg and William Lee Eubank

Comparing Pluralist Democracies: Strains on Legitimacy, edited by Mattei Dogan

Pathways to Power: Selecting Rulers in Pluralist Democracies, edited by Mattei Dogan

PATHWAYS TO POWER

Selecting Rulers in Pluralist Democracies

EDITED BY
MATTEI DOGAN

WESTVIEW PRESS • Boulder, San Francisco, & London

New Directions in Comparative and International Politics

This Westview softcover edition is printed on acid-free paper and bound in softcovers that carry the highest rating of the National Association of State Textbook Administrators, in consultation with the Association of American Publishers and the Book Manufacturers' Institute.

All rights reserved. No part of this publication may be reproduced or transmitted in any form or by any means, electronic or mechanical, including photocopy, recording, or any information storage and retrieval system, without permission in writing from the publisher.

Copyright © 1989 by Westview Press, Inc.

Published in 1989 in the United States of America by Westview Press, Inc., 5500 Central Avenue, Boulder, Colorado 80301, and in the United Kingdom by Westview Press, Inc., 13 Brunswick Centre, London WC1N 1AF, England

Library of Congress Cataloging-in-Publication Data
Pathways to power: selecting rulers in pluralist democracies/edited
by Mattei Dogan.
    p.   cm.—(New directions in comparative and international
politics)
  Includes bibliographies and index.
  ISBN 0-8133-7596-7
  1. Political leadership. 2. Cabinet officers. 3. Presidents.
4. Democracy. 5. Comparative government. I. Dogan, Mattei.
II. Series.
JF251.P38 1989
351.004—dc19   88-20814
                                                              CIP

Printed and bound in the United States of America

∞   The paper used in this publication meets the requirements of the American National Standard for Permanence of Paper for Printed Library Materials Z39.48-1984.

10   9   8   7   6   5   4   3   2   1

CONTENTS

List of Tables and Figures   vii
Preface   xi

    Introduction: Selecting Cabinet Ministers, *Mattei Dogan*   1

1   Career Pathways to the Cabinet in France, 1870–1986, *Mattei Dogan*   19

2   Presidential Personnel and Political Capital: From Roosevelt to Reagan, *Margaret Jane Wyszomirski*   45

3   Selecting Chief Executives in Norway and the United States, *Donald R. Matthews*   75

4   How to Become a Cabinet Minister in Italy: Unwritten Rules of the Political Game, *Mattei Dogan*   99

5   Junior Ministers and Ministerial Careers in Britain, *Donald D. Searing*   141

6   The Making of a Japanese Cabinet, *Hiromitsu Kataoka*   169

7   Pathways to India's National Governing Elite, *Richard Sisson*   181

8	Selection of Cabinet Ministers in Ireland, 1922–1982, *John Coakley and Brian Farrell*	199
9	Selection by Lot in Ancient Athens, *C. Fred Alford*	219
10	Irremovable Leaders and Ministerial Instability in European Democracies, *Mattei Dogan*	239

About the Editor and Contributors   277
Index   279

TABLES AND FIGURES

Tables

1.1	Number of newcomers in each cabinet, 4th Republic	22
1.2	Pathways to government by historical periods	24
1.3	Parliamentary seniority and number of governments served, French Third Republic	28
3.1	Norwegian governments, 1945–1985	77
3.2	U.S. presidential administrations since 1945	78
3.3	Positions held by leaders of major political parties in Norway, 1945–1985	81
3.4	Number of years in elective offices prior to becoming Norwegian party leader or U.S. presidential candidate	82
3.5	Number of years in elective public office before becoming party leader in Norway, by decade	83
3.6	Public offices held by Norwegian party leaders prior to achieving leadership position, 1945–1985	87
3.7	Occupation of U.S. presidential nominees and Norwegian party leaders, 1945–1985	89
3.8	Father's occupation of U.S. presidential nominees and Norwegian party leaders, 1945–1985	89
4.1	Italian cabinets during Christian-Democratic hegemony	102
4.2	Christian Democratic Party ministers and under secretaries of state, June 1945–August 1983	109
4.3	Public opinion survey about prime ministers in the Italian Republic, 1947–1984	135
4.4	Public opinion surveys about the functioning of the democratic regime, European Community Countries	136

5.1	Junior ministers: Attitudinal roles by age	145
5.2	Percent promoted to ministerial positions	166
6.1	Number of ministerial posts of LDP members of the House of Representatives	171
6.2	Occupational backgrounds of Japanese cabinet ministers	173
7.1	Regional distribution of the national governing elite in India, 1966–1980	185
7.2	Ministers' educational achievement, 1966–1980	185
7.3	Occupational distribution of ministers, 1966–1980	186
7.4	Time of ministers' first election to public office, 1966–1980	188
7.5	State government experience of members of councils of ministers, 1966–1980	191
7.6	Participation of future ministers in parliamentary committees, 1966–1980	192
7.7	Years from election to parliament to entry into Council of Ministers, 1966–1980	193
8.1	Irish governments, 1922–1982	201
8.2	Social characteristics of the Irish political elite and of the Irish population, 1922–1982	204
10.1	Parliamentary seniority before first appointment and length of ministerial career, French Third Republic, 1870–1940	244
10.2	Ministers and number of appointments, Czechoslovakia, 1918–1938	254
10.3	Austrian cabinets, First Republic, 1918–1933	258
10.4	Ministers and number of appointments, Austrian First Republic, 1918–1933	260
10.5	Ministers and number of appointments, Spanish Second Republic, 1931–1936	260
10.6	Ministers and number of appointments, First Portuguese Republic, 1910–1926	261
10.7	Ministers and number of appointments, Poland, 1918–1926	264
10.8	Index of ministerial mobility	268

TABLES AND FIGURES

Figures

1.1	Background to companionship and patronage under the Gaullist Republic, 1958–1974	26
3.1	Types of Norwegian governments, 1945–1985	81
3.2	Office-holding careers of presidential nominees in the U.S., 1945–1985	84
3.3	Leadership selection processes	91
5.1	Chain of command	157
8.1	Cabinets by age, 1922–1982	207
8.2	Cabinets by social class, 1922–1982	207

PREFACE

The research committee on political elites of the International Political Science Association has organized in recent years several panels on the recruitment of cabinet ministers in competitive democracies. Most chapters of this book were originally written for these panels; the others have been prepared or revised especially for this volume.

Over the years the IPSA research committee on political elites has also had on its agenda panels on "charismatic leadership and political idolatry," "party cadres and militants," "the political role of higher civil servants," "elite theory," and other issues, always manifesting a preference for the comparative approach. A number of publications have resulted from these meetings.

In the preparation of this book, I have been immensely helped by my colleague Dwaine Marvick (UCLA), who shared with me the responsibility for the various activities of the research committee. His precious help is warmly acknowledged.

Mattei Dogan

INTRODUCTION: SELECTING CABINET MINISTERS

Mattei Dogan

This book focuses on the selection process of cabinet ministers in a variety of democratic political systems. Rather than studying a few great political leaders, it surveys teams of rulers at the summit of the state apparatus. Only in two pluralist democracies, Australia and New Zealand, are ministers elected by Parliament; in the other thirty or so democracies they are appointed or co-opted by peers. Because the ministers are selected by the elected, and because they are of greater breadth of experience than the average parliamentarian, ministers are an elite within an elite. As a whole, the book reveals how this super-elite is chosen; because authors raise the same questions and deal with similar issues for the various political systems, the individual chapters are implicitly comparative.

Obviously, the recruitment patterns vary from one type of political system to the next. The road to power cannot be the same in a consociational democracy, where the parties play a crucial role, as it is in parliament-centered systems, where the selection process is located in the legislative committees; in a federal system like the United States, as in a centralized system like France; in a one-party-dominant system such as Italy, Japan, Ireland, and India, as in a majoritarian system such as Britain until recently. The chapters of this book discuss the variety of recruitment patterns in some of these political systems.

Cabinet building is the final goal of electoral competition in a parliamentary democracy, and the formation of a new government is a periodic but critical event in the political life of a nation. How ministers are chosen is therefore of prime importance. Despite the significance of this choice, constitutions and basic laws say little about the selection

of cabinet ministers. In most cases, there is simply an indication that the ministers are appointed by the chief of state on the proposal of the prime minister. Such simple provisions hide mountains of important political detail, the unwritten rules by which selections are made. Reading the texts of constitutions will not disclose these rules and criteria for minsterial recruitment; without being carved in stone, these rules are nevertheless well known by the most ambitious politicians. They are neither immutable nor rigid. It is precisely for this reason that they are not included in constitutional texts. Although understanding these rules helps one to understand better how the political system functions, this issue has not yet received the scholarly attention it deserves.

This lack of research is surprising in light of the importance and the generality of the topic. Among the thirty pluralist democracies in the world today, only one, the United States, does not have a real cabinet; in the United States, the cabinet secretaries do not constitute a collective decisionmaking body. In all other competitive democracies, even in the French presidential system, the cabinet is the key executive organ.[1]

APEX OF POWER

In contemporary competitive democracies, cabinet ministers are the heirs of the lords and barons of yesterday's aristocratic regimes. They are the most visible representatives of the ruling class; only entertainers capture media attention as often as cabinet ministers do. It is little wonder that so many ambitious politicians aspire to reach the visibility and fame of a cabinet minister. "It is like the zoo at feeding time," said the marquis of Salisbury, forming a cabinet in 1890. "It's been terrible. I have had people in here weeping and fainting," said Ramsay MacDonald, forming a cabinet in 1929. "At thirty-two I was a university professor, at forty-two a cabinet minister; for five years I was Federal chancellor and for a long time Federal minister. I have a beautiful life behind me. My ambition was early satisfied," said the great Austrian chancellor, Ignaz Seipel. Politics absorbed him so much that he confessed he had "never known any women" and "had seen them only in the streets." His biographer commented that Seipel's "background and his asceticism were precisely the reasons for his ambition" (Klemperer, p. 419). "At the age of eighteen, I made a wish that on my gravestone be inscribed: Here lies Louis Marin, French statesman" (written personal communication). Few people become cabinet ministers involuntarily, by accident. On the road to the apex of power, one has to be devoured by ambition, one has to desire to shine.

INTRODUCTION: SELECTING CABINET MINISTERS   3

Although these politicians share the same goal, there are many different ways they may achieve it. Studying these paths is important, because the course of a leader's career marks him at least as much as his social background. The experiences acquired in a party, in a parliamentary committee, or in high public administration has an unavoidable impact on the personal style and behavior of political rulers. Any typology must take into account the pathways that future ministers follow. A politician who has spent most of his time within a party faction does not present the same profile of experience and inclinations as that of his colleague who came through the upper levels of the administration, or of one who has had to demonstrate his competence in certain fields and his ability to compromise on difficult issues over the course of many years in parliamentary committees. The strategist and the planner, the orator and the expert, the theorist and the executive, have qualities and peculiarities that were fostered by the circumstances of their careers and the obstacles they have had to overcome. Consequently, the study of pathways promises to lead to the formulation of meaningful typologies, once we have a sufficient sample of national studies.

DEMOCRATIC TEAMS

In a democratic regime, there can never be a single ruler, notwithstanding the enormous power concentrated in the hands of the U.S. president, the French president (or alternatively the French prime minister), the German chancellor, the British or Indian prime ministers. Neither can there be too many, as C. Fred Alford discusses in Chapter 9 on democracy in Athens, where recourse to magistrates and boards of administrators was necessary. Democracies are ruled by teams, even when there is a single chief executive elected by universal suffrage. What Margaret Wyszomirski calls "political capital" (Chapter 2) is precisely the need to build a presidential team in Washington. The French president is also obligated to rule with the help of a team. François Mitterrand came to power in 1981 surrounded by the leadership of the Socialist party. In 1986, he was obliged to relinquish most of his power to another team, this time a conservative one. The British prime minister and the German chancellor personify executive power, but they need the support of the majority of the house of Commons or of the Bundestag and consequently have to build a ministerial team reflecting such a majority. In Japan, as Hiromitsu Kataoka writes: "It is the cabinet as a collective body, and not the prime minister, in which the constitution vests executive power. Every decision made in the name of the state and nation must be made by

the cabinet. . . . The prime minister . . . cannot decide anything officially without carrying his colleagues together with him. . . . Even a draft of his speech to the opening session of the Diet must be agreed to in cabinet meetings" (Chapter 6). The characteristics of these teams may vary, but the fact that power is held by a team is a constant.

Within the team, several circles should be distinguished. Of first importance is the inner circle, the "super ministers," as Lord Morrison of Lambeth called them, numbering between 4 and 8 leaders. The ministers of finance and of foreign affairs are almost always among them in every country. Some party leaders may play a role as crucial as that of the super ministers even if they do not formally belong to the government, as is the case in Italy or the Netherlands. A second circle would include all those ministers who formally belong to the cabinet and participate in its official meetings. The number in this group varies from country to country, without any systematic reason for the variation. For instance, in 1985 the U.S. cabinet had only 14 members, less than half that of the Australian cabinet (30), the New Zealand (39), and Canadian (31). The same year, there were 28 cabinet ministers in India, 26 in Belgium, 18 in Mexico, 19 in Israel, 23 in Britain, 21 in Denmark, 17 in West Germany, 16 in Finland. Obviously, the optimal size of the cabinet does not depend on the size of the country, a federal or unitary governmental structure, or other factors but reflects each country's history.

In many democracies, there is a third level of rulers below the cabinet, called secretaries or under secretaries of state, parliamentary secretaries, or, as in Britain and France, ministers outside cabinet or ministers-delegate. The size of this third circle varies even more than the size of the cabinet itself, but it tends to increase over time in many countries. The British government usually includes four times as many members outside the cabinet as cabinet ministers. In Bonn, the state secretaries and the parliamentary secretaries have been twice as numerous as the cabinet ministers since 1972 (in 1983, 43 compared to 23). In France, there have been more under secretaries of state than full ministers since the 1960s. In India, as Richard Sisson describes (Chapter 7), there is an important difference between the members of the Council of Ministers and the secretaries of state, who do not belong to this council. In other democracies the size of the government almost coincides with the size of the cabinet.

These circles create, within each government, a significant hierarchy. This suggests the questions, raised by all of the contributors to this volume, of how the patterns of selection vary according to the levels of this ministerial hierarchy. Naturally, the qualifications required of a candidate for a junior position are not the same as those for the

INTRODUCTION: SELECTING CABINET MINISTERS

position of full minister, and exploration of these differences will remain an important research topic in the study of the cabinet elites.

POOLS OF ELIGIBLES

The size of the cabinet is not the only aspect that matters. In order to understand the selection process, we need to look at the size of the pool of ministerial aspirants, the group of would-be ministers. Measuring the size of this pool is the first step for any comparative analysis of the selection pattern because, after all, the nature of the competition for ministerial positions is not the same if 30 rulers are to be selected from 300 aspirants or from 3,000. What are the main pools of eligibles, how large are these pools, and how does their importance vary over time? Much more research remains to be done before a full reply to these questions is possible.

A cabinet must have the confidence of a majority of parliament. When the prime minister builds the cabinet, his main concern is to obtain such a majority, and therefore he will choose most of the cabinet ministers from among parliamentarians. A basic feature of the selection of cabinet ministers everywhere except in the United States is the recruitment of most of the cabinet from among members of parliament. The skimming is done by peers, after a relatively long period of socialization in parliament. This permits some predictability: "Most ministers who will take office through the next decade are on the scene and well identified in Westminster," wrote R. E. Neustadt (p. 62). The arena of competitiveness is similarly closed in many other parliaments, since most future ministers have to pass through the parliamentary gate. Only in countries where there is a constitutional incompatibility between parliamentary seats and cabinet membership, as in the French Fifth Republic, the Netherlands, Norway, and the United States, does one find a significant number of ministers who have never sat in parliament; in Finland, too, on those occasions when it is impossible to crystallize a majority, the government may be composed primarily or entirely of "experts." Yet these countries, as well as Austria and India, are only partial exceptions, as many ministers nevertheless are drawn from parliamentary ranks.

The greatest exception is the United States, where the competition is so open that it is practically impossible to delineate in advance the pool of eligibles for cabinet positions and presidential staff. As astonishing as this may appear to a European observer, one president sent letters soliciting suggestions from everyone listed in *Who's Who in America;* another computerized the candidate lists; a third appointed a "talent hunt" group of prospectors. As Wyszomirski writes in Chapter

2, "the process of cabinet-making is the most personal and least institutionalized aspect of presidential staffing." But even in the United States, in some periods, many cabinet members were recruited in Congress: half in the period 1828–1860; 40 percent from 1860 to 1896; 20 percent from 1896 to 1932 (Hess, p. 115).

DEGREE OF COMPETITIVENESS

In the sixteen West European democracies, in Japan, Canada, Australia, New Zealand, Israel, and in the other parliamentary democracies, most ministers are recruited among parliamentarians. If the selection in some countries is almost totally restricted to this pool, a question becomes inevitable: What is the proportion of legislators who succeed in reaching governmental positions?

The chances for a newly elected parliamentarian to achieve executive power someday vary considerably from country to country. Within each country, they also vary from one epoch to another. These differences depend first of all on the size of parliament, which varies from nearly one thousand deputies and senators in Italy to one hundred in several small countries. The probability also depends on the size of the entire governmental team, from about one hundred in Britain to less than twenty in the Netherlands. Naturally, the larger the pool of eligibles and the smaller the size of the government, the harder it is to reach executive power, and vice versa.

Some parliamentarians are not really available for a ministerial job. First, there are those who are in opposition, who may amount to nearly half of the membership of the parliament. Others are too young or too old. Some are disqualified from appointment on personal grounds. As Richard Rose pointed out, "this means that a prime minister is left with a pool of potential ministers so small that he must give ministerial appointments or the status of PPS to half or more of all MPs who are not unsuited to receive an appointment" (Rose 1971, p. 402). Donald Searing also stresses in Chapter 5 that "the race is not as competitive as it seems." "In Ireland the near requirement of Dail membership dramatically limits the number of candidates for office: Fifteen ministers (or thirty, if junior ministers are included) are to be selected from an average of about eighty Dail deputies who constitute the parliamentary majority. If certain standards of ability and reliability are also demanded . . . it can be assumed that prime ministers' freedom in balancing cabinets . . . could be severely restricted" (John Coakley and Brian Farrell, Chapter 8). In other democracies, where the gap between the number of selected and the number of available politicians is higher, the selection is more competitive—except where one of the rules of the

INTRODUCTION: SELECTING CABINET MINISTERS

game is the promotion by rotation of the maximum number of parliamentarians to government, as in Japan.

The degree of competitiveness could be measured by comparing the number of those who are available to the number of those to be appointed. Is the degree of competitiveness higher and more efficient in the United States than in the parliamentary democracies? Contradictory hypotheses could be formulated because the empirical evidence is not yet sufficient.

Among those who are available, the probability of becoming minister depends also on the rules of the game. In some democracies the political class had adopted the principle that the majority of parliamentarians belonging to the governing party or coalition should be appointed at least once to governmental position. For instance, Kataoka reports that in Japan 43 percent of the Liberal Democratic members of the House of Representatives at the end of 1985 had served as ministers. In other countries, in contrast, the party leaders tend to reserve ministerial positions almost exclusively for themselves, leaving little chance to the average deputy. Many countries fall somewhere in between these extremes. Donald Searing writes that in Britain "the prospects for promotion to ministerial office are more than sufficient to entice the ambitious into apprenticeships and to keep alive their hopes." Searing elaborates this point with empirical evidence on the promotion of backbenchers to the position of junior minister and from there to the level of minister-not-in-the-cabinet, and finally to cabinet power.

An aspirant's chances of obtaining a position in government depend also on his political color, on the kind of horse he rides. In France, as discussed in Chapter 1, a premium has been offered to the parliamentarians who sat in the center of the political spectrum in the Third, the Fourth, and the Fifth republics. In Italy, the promotion of deputies and senators belonging to the dominant Christian Democratic party was much higher than for the other parties, except, as in France, for the small centrist parties.

One's personal competence, too, can greatly help one's chances. However, competence alone is insufficient. For that reason, the selection process has important consequences for the political system as a whole. More research into this important aspect of the topic is needed. It is clear that the competence of the chosen depends largely on the competence of the eligibles, and that the degree to which ministers are well qualified will therefore depend in part on the quality of the parliamentary pool. In exploring this issue, it will not be necessary to reopen the debate on the relative merits and defects of electoral systems based on single-member constituencies versus those based on proportional representation with rigid party lists. The Bundestag, which elects half

of its members by each system, does not make any distinction between the two categories in the selection of ministers.

FORMALIZATION OF INFORMAL RULES

Despite the wide range of democratic regimes, one can notice everywhere a kind of institutionalization of ministerial career ladders. The road to power is in fact a labyrinth through which ambitious politicians must find their way. They must learn the rules of the game, the unwritten prescriptions, and must learn how to behave among competitive peers and rival friends. In some countries the institutionalization of selection patterns is highly sophisticated and one has to admire the refinement of the procedures, obviously based on long collective experience.

Rules are informal rather than formal. One does not find them in documents but discovers them by talking to politicians, willing to unveil these rules to scholars, who are not perceived as political competitors. If everyone respects the rules of the game, it is as if the rules were institutionalized. Donald Searing says about junior ministers in Britain that "the climb has become highly structured as the ministerial career ladder has become institutionalized." They are as much institutionalized, even if in a different manner, in Bonn, Rome, Delhi, Tokyo, Oslo, or Dublin.

Rules tend to become more structured as a regime grows older, although one can perceive emerging rules even in new democracies such as Spain or Portugal. Longitudinal studies of the ways in which rules become more structured can tell us much about the development of a country's political system.

CHANNELS

The channels of ministerial selection can vary considerably. We find a particularly interesting channel in England, the shadow cabinet. These positions are important: "A place in a team that is widely regarded as a potential government, with an acknowledged role as the party's parliamentary expert in a particular subject, and with a formal title of spokesman or shadow minister, gives an MP a certain status in the eyes of backbenchers" (Punnett, p. 146). On the other hand, the filter of parliamentary committee and the mandarin ascent, so efficacious in the recruitment of French ministers, play a secondary or negligible role in the British two-party system.

In Germany, a political career normally starts and develops in the party and government of *Lander*. The federal system first decentralizes

the network of *cursus honorum* in the provinces and then concocts a geographically, religiously, and economically variegated federal government. Moreover, the German secretary of state is not a hybrid, half politician and half mandarin, like most of the French secretaries of state. He is exclusively a civil servant. As for the parliamentary secretary of state, who is a full politician, he bears a resemblance to the British junior minister.

In Italy (Chapter 4), ministerial selection operates according to well-defined, albeit unwritten, rules, which Christian Democratic leaders have observed with few exceptions since 1953. One cannot, for instance, become a full minister without first having been state secretary, nor can one become a state secretary without five years' seniority in Parliament, and so on. The most important of the dozen or so rules is the one that ensures the proportional representation in the government of the various factions and fractions of the dominant Christian Democratic party. This is done according to the distribution of mandates at the congress of this party, by means of a clear, if perhaps too simple, weighing: A full minister counts as much as three state secretaries. Such rules are virtually an unwritten paragraph of the Italian constitution. In contrast, the French Fourth Republic, with its more flexible and volatile political parties, never adopted such rules.

The mandarin ascent to cabinet positions has been well established in Sweden, the Netherlands, Finland, Austria, the French Fifth Republic, and elsewhere, in some cases for a long time. There is an analogy between the present French Fifth Republic and the German Second Reich and some countries with restricted suffrage. It is better, however, not to add here a diachronic dimension to our synchronic overview.

Another channel, the filter of parliamentary committees, is more generous in providing ministerial personnel in a fragmented party system with weak parties, where the parliament is necessarily the country's center of gravity, than it is in a party system with well-organized parties, where decisionmaking often takes place in party headquarters and contiguous spheres. In either case, the importance of the selection of ministers from among party leaders—what I call the party capillary—is well attested.

THE SELECTOR AND HIS LATITUDE OF CHOICE

Who selects ministers? Is there a single selector? If so, what is his latitude of choice? It is difficult to formulate a comparative view because theory and practice are not necessarily the same. In theory, a prime minister has the right to hire and fire ministers. In reality, there are many constraints on his choice. He has to appoint the more influential

leaders of his party, he might need to silence rival leaders of his party by including them in government, and he must reward supporters. The allocation of particular posts to specific individuals is the most difficult task that any new prime minister must resolve.

In Britain, "bargaining rather than command tends to be the characteristic feature of the relationship between prime minister and candidates for office far more frequently than is generally allowed" (Alderman, p. 109). The existence of "shadow cabinets" limits the freedom of the prime minister. In addition, senior ministers play a decisive role in the choice of junior ministers, and the chief whip is also an influential selector of junior positions.

The German chancellor is in practice elected by the parliamentary group of his party and of the coalition partner and, in the so-called chancellor democracy, several chancellors were in fact obliged to resign before the end of their parliamentary terms. In order to build a majority, he is forced, in choosing his ministers, to satisfy the demands of various party factions as well as regional and economic pressure groups. His freedom to choose the members of his cabinet is limited. Furthermore, "the appointments to the junior positions rest effectively with individual ministers and not with the chancellor" (Johnson, p. 55).

In the countries governed by coalitions, ministerial posts are allotted to the parties and factions in proportion to their parliamentary strength. Such a distribution is institutionalized in consociational democracies, particularly in the Netherlands, Belgium, Austria, and also in Italy and Norway. The parties "delegate" their representatives to government, so that the prime minister's latitude of choice is rather limited.

In Italy, for instance, the president of the Council of Ministers is only a primus inter pares. He plays the role of a coalition builder rather than of a selector of ministers. His role is analyzed in Chapter 4.

In Belgium, as in Italy, ministerial positions are calculated in "points," and the points are allotted to parties in proportion to their electoral strength; at the same time, linguistic parity is respected. The king plays a neutral role, although in a crisis situation his role would of course become crucial. He appoints an informateur, or formateur, who negotiates with the leaders of the parties and who may himself become the prime minister—unless he is obliged to propose some other leader. The king and the prime minister can influence the choice of some ministers for particular positions, but in the various phases of cabinet formation many leaders intervene as selectors-negotiators, especially the chairmen of the coalition parties: "The prime minister has little free scope" (Boeynaems, p. 482).

INTRODUCTION: SELECTING CABINET MINISTERS

In Austria during the Grand Coalition, the *Proporz* was the guiding principle in the allotment of government positions. The parties designated the ministers for "their" ministries. The power of the chancellor to nominate cabinet ministers "is strangely limited. It is one of the iron rules of Austrian coalition government to grant each party full autonomy in the selection of its cabinet members. In this respect the vice-chancellor, who comes from the junior party in cabinet, is a second chancellor. However, both have to take into account the intra-party realities and depend on a formal acceptance of their suggested cabinet members by the party executives" (Muller, Philipp, and Steininger, p. 4). Although elected by universal suffrage, the Austrian president has no power to choose the chancellor. The official leader of the major party has inevitably become the chief executive. Only in exceptional cases can the president discretely influence the choice of a few ministers. Rare exceptions are mentioned by competent observers; Karl Renner, for instance, is supposed to have rejected the renomination of a minister in 1949 because of the latter's alleged corruption.

A shadow cabinet has never been instituted in Austria. This is apparently because the parties are so well organized, at all levels of the hierarchy, that each party's national executive can play the role of shadow cabinet when in opposition. Nowhere in the Western democracies is the party apparatus such an important channel to cabinet positions as in Austria. It is for this reason that this country has the highest proportion of cabinet ministers without previous parliamentary experience: For only half of all ministers does the road to power pass through the parliamentary gate, whereas for the other half, it passes through the party gate.

As in Austria, Dutch parties make the actual ministerial appointments: "Prime ministers do not appoint ministers: appointments are formally made by the Queen, in practice they are the result of negotiations between the constituent parties. The prime minister cannot dismiss a minister" (Andweg, p. 17)

In Norway, as in Italy, Belgium, Austria, and the Netherlands, according to Donald Matthews, "the parties proceed to appoint people to their positions. The prime minister may or may not have some say in this matter. Per Borten learned of the membership in 'his' government by reading about it in the newspapers. Kaare Willoch insisted upon having some say" (Chapter 3).

In Japan, too, ministers are not selected by the prime minister, but by the factions. "The factions have prepared their own lists of prospective ministers" (Kataoka, Chapter 6), and each faction receives a number of ministerial posts according to its strength in the Diet. As

in Italy, each minister is loyal first to his faction and "is not, therefore, necessarily willing to follow the prime minister into the ditch."

Among democratic regimes, only one has a single powerful selector. The exception is not the United States, as can be seen from Chapter 2, by Margaret Jane Wyszomirski, which shows the complexity of presidential staffing. The exception is, instead, the French Fifth Republic after 1962. In that year, a referendum approved the election of the president by universal suffrage, creating what should be considered a superpresidential regime, a system where there is no equilibrium between powers unless the parliamentary majority is of a different color than the presidential majority (as was the case with the Chirac government between March 1986 and May 1988). In such a system prime ministers and ministers can be pulled out of a hat more easily than in other pluralist democracies. When the presidential grace descended upon Georges Pompidou, Raymond Barre, and Laurent Fabius, they were unknown by most French people, they were not leaders of political parties, and they were not prominent figures in French politics. The same can be said of many cabinet ministers and secretaries of state, whom the presidential choice brought from quasi-anonymity to the limelight overnight.

The choices have not necessarily been unwise. Retrospectively, it appears that the president was like the prophet anointing the young David. But in a democracy, there is no selection of rulers by divine inspiration. Charles de Gaulle knew Pompidou very well, as his principal collaborator during the "crossing of the desert," and then in the Elysée; Valéry Giscard d'Estaing had the opportunity to evaluate Barre's great competence; Fabius, chosen for his intellectual capacity, was for a time Mitterrand's dauphin. This anointing process may be more efficient than the election of the leader by parliamentary caucus: The selection criteria are not the same.

Pompidou, Barre, Fabius, and their homologues in other democratic systems represent a particular type of leader, the cognoscente, wise persons of expert knowledge. I would suggest that there are basically two types of ministers, these cognoscenti and the barons. The barons become ministers because of their retinue, like medieval lords who brought soldiers, horses, and money to the king. The cognoscenti do not impose themselves on the republican king but are chosen by him. This is a simple typology but a useful one, because the dichotomy can be found everywhere. It was not easy to avoid having Franz Josef Strauss in the German cabinet, while André Malraux in France had no political force behind him and represented no one but himself. Dozens of ministers belong to each of these types.

INTRODUCTION: SELECTING CABINET MINISTERS

The fact that, in all democratic regimes today except France, there is no great selector shows that the process of selecting cabinet ministers is structured, that there are patterns, rules, and procedures that represent the unwritten part of current constitutions and basic laws. Even the exception confirms the norm: There are gates, channels, pathways, patterns, and rules of selection even in the French Fifth Republic, as discussed in Chapter 1.

BINARY COMPARISONS

Given the paucity of empirical data about informal selection processes, one of the most fruitful research strategies is binary analysis (Dogan and Pelassy, pp. 112–116). In Chapter 3, Matthews provides a good example of how useful such a strategy can be. By comparing 47 Norwegian party leaders, from among whom the prime ministers were selected, to the 14 presidential candidates nominated by the Democrats and the Republicans between 1945 and 1985, Matthews shows that despite the contrast between presidential and parliamentary forms some basic analogies can be found in the selection process of U.S. presidents and Norwegian prime ministers. Matthews's binary comparison takes in consideration a series of parameters of the two political systems. The Norwegian prime minister is representative of other chief executives in multiparty systems. Matthews proposes four "ideal types" of leadership selection: apprenticeship, leadership choice, bargaining, and populistic choice. By using such ideal types, he greatly facilitates comparative analysis of ministerial recruitment.

Other binary comparisons can be drawn from the separate chapters on Italy and Japan. Nowhere is the sophistication of the game more impressive than in Italy and Japan. Take, for instance, the rule of seniority. In Japan, writes Kataoka, "every LDP [Liberal Democratic Party] member of the House . . . who had been returned eight times or more had been a minister at some time, without exception. . . . This suggests that a novice to the cabinet is normally chosen from the sixth return group and occasionally from the fifth. . . . The seniority of a member of the Diet is the result as well as a cause of cabinet service" (Chapter 6).

Factions also have well-defined roles in the recruitment of members of government in Italy and Japan. In these two countries, the center of gravity of the regime is Parliament, whose often fickle confidence is indipensable for governmental survival. Consequently, the ministers are recruited from the parliamentarians as they are organized into factions. The portfolios are distributed between the diverse factions of the predominant party (or of the majoritarian coalition) in proportion to

their importance in the party and in Parliament. The leader of each faction, not the prime minister, partitions the ministerial positions allocated to each faction. Choices are made according to criteria that, without being identical, respond to the same preoccupation in both countries: the establishment of rules to avoid conflict between competitors of the same party or the same faction.

In Japan, factions establish "waiting lists" based on seniority in Parliament and in the faction. Each aspirant has the opportunity of reaching the top of the list one day and when the government changes, of obtaining a ministerial position. The factions present candidates for governmental positions and the ministers are chosen from among these candidates. Ministerial positions are redistributed annually in order to maintain the factions' support of the government. Factionalism, which has deep roots in all sectors of Japanese society, animates the competition among aspirants to executive positions.

In Italy, as indicated in Chapter 4, one must sit in Parliament at least one entire legislative session—that is, one must have five years of parliamentary seniority—before becoming a candidate for a ministerial position. Promotion is made by steps, first to the rank of under secretary of state and only after that to the rank of full minister.

There is an important difference between the Italian and Japanese political regimes, with repercussions on ministerial selection. In Japan, the higher civil servants play an important role in the political decision process, constituting a counterweight to the influence of factions. In contrast, the higher civil service plays a secondary role in the Italian *partitocrazia*. A quarter of the Japanese ministers in the 1970s were recruited from among former higher civil servants, although some had also had a parliamentary seat. In Italy, in contrast, recruitment from the higher civil service occurs for only a handful, if we exclude university professors.

Another interesting binary comparison would be the elaboration of the differences and similarities in the roles of higher civil servants in the cabinets of Japan and the French Fifth Republic. A meaningful analogy could be drawn concerning the role of businessmen in executive office in the United States and Japan. Despite their common presidential foundations, the patterns of selection of cabinet members in the United States and in the French Fifth Republic are in vivid contrast. The systems of cooptation at the highest governmental level in India and Mexico present another example of an enlightening binary comparison. In the Indian and the Austrian federal systems, many ministers are selected from among the members of the regional state governments. What Richard Sisson (Chapter 7) says on this point about India could be partly applied to Austria. Two bilingual countries and consociational

democracies, Canada and Belgium, are also ideal cases for binary comparisons of ministerial selection patterns in segmented societies (see Gibson).

GENERATIONAL WAVES

The institutionalization of the selection process breaks down at moments of crisis. At the beginning of a new historical cycle, immediately after a war, a civil war, a revolution, or drastic change, a new team of rulers takes power. Everywhere in Europe, except unoccupied Britain and Sweden, a new political class emerged at the end of World War II; the same is true for Japan, and this also happened in the countries defeated in World War I. Many, if not most, of the new rulers after World War II were former resistance fighters, some having spent years in jail. The phenomenon appears with clarity in an entire generation of politicians in France and in Italy (see Chapters 1 and 4); an interesting comparison could be made between Eamon De Valera and the de Gaulle followers and comrades-in-arms. The accession to power of former resistance members is also documented in Chapter 7, on Indian elites, by Richard Sisson, and in Chapter 8, on Ireland, by Coakley and Farrell. Former resistance fighters came to power even in Germany and Austria. Nonetheless, certain unwritten rules for selection were formulated soon after the war in all countries, and after a period of time, the patterns of selection were again institutionalized. The same is happening now in Spain and Portugal, after the breakdown of the dictatorial regime and the emergence of a new class of politicians.

CONTRASTING SELECTION WITH RECRUITMENT BY LOT

We cannot conceive of a contemporary competitive democracy without a team of rulers. Organization implies oligarchy (in the etymological sense) and the state is the supreme organization. Even in ancient Athens, direct democracy produced such temporary teams of rulers. The founders of the first democratic regimes often cited ancient Athens, from the American Founding Fathers to European philosophers of the 18th century because it was the only historical example of democratic regime. Even today, there is frequent reference to the direct mass participation in ancient Athens. One way to understand the inevitability of teams of rulers in contemporary democracies is to look at this historical example. Chapter 9, by C. Fred Alford, gives us a sociological picture of the functioning of the Athenian democracy and of the random recruitment by lot of the officers in charge of various functions. It is

obvious that such a system of recruitment is possible only when the entity is limited in size. It is enough to visit Ephesus, the best preserved ancient city, to realize that the agora was in size the equivalent of the British, French, or Italian parliaments of today. The Athenian agora was certainly larger than the Ephesus agora, but it was not much larger than a U.S. presidential nominating convention. However, the comparison should not be pushed too far: People in the agora were meeting, not to chose a ruler, but rather to debate issues.

Although annual rotation avoided the development of oligarchical bureaucratic skills, there was nevertheless delegation of power for short periods. Issues could not be continually debated, and even in ancient Athens there were teams of administrators. As Alford shows, the administrative tasks were divided into hundreds of relatively simple job assignments, each held for only a year by magistrates, who were further organized into boards of ten. In the recruiting by lot, the ancient Athens democracy avoided elitist selection—but it could not avoid having a temporary executive team.

Given modern technology, direct democracy is again conceivable. In the United States, random recruitment of juries, by means of driver's license lists and voter registration rolls, already exists. Combining television, telephones, computerized voting machines, and the recruitment of two or three thousand citizens by random social security numbers, it would be possible—but this will only happen after tomorrow—to have a vote taken after a televised debate.

Such a system would be more or less the same as the opinion polls currently taken in all advanced democracies. In fact, we already have a kind of embryonic direct democracy with opinion polls, which have a very significant impact on the selection of candidates to various offices and on priorities on the governmental agenda. By combining television and opinion polls, the space of an enormous contemporary nation could be reduced to a kind of tele-doxa-agora. Yet as the case of Athens shows, even then we would need a team of rulers, a council of ministers.

GOVERNMENTAL CORE

After the first appointment to a government position, the selection process continues. Whenever there is a change of government, some outgoing ministers are not included in the ministerial team. Others are reappointed, either to the same position or to a higher or more influential position in the government hierarchy. Reappointment is a confirmation of the intitial selection, a new step in the political career. In many countries, most ministers have a brief ministerial career. For

Canada in the period 1867–1961, 28.4 percent of all ministers lasted no more than one year, and 15.5 percent lasted only between one and two years at their initial posts. In Canada, "a cabinet minister rarely entrenches himself in a post" (March, p. 77). In the Netherlands between 1848 and 1958—that is, for over a century—two-thirds of the ministers participated in only one cabinet and a mere 6 percent took part in four or more (Dogan and Scheffer van der Veen, p. 124). In Britain, reappointment is used as an important tactic, as Richard Rose related, "Frequent changes are a carrot to the ambitious, holding out hope of promotion to Cabinet, or promotion within Cabinet. Frequent changes are also a stick with which to punish ministers, threatening dismissal from office if the Prime Minister deems them a political liability" (Rose 1987, p. 79).

Reappointment, with or without promotion, is an essential aspect of ministerial selection, particularly in countries with high governmental turnover and frequent reshuffling. Chapter 10 analyzes the selection process in relation to ministerial instability, pointing out that an instability of cabinets can be accompanied by the maintenance in power of a small group of leaders, repeatedly reselected. Such a ministerial core represents a counterweight to the governmental instability and reflects a way of distinguishing between powerful ministers and ephemeral ministers.

* * *

How someone becomes a cabinet minister is in part an unknown and unintelligible process, in the sense that chance plays an important role. It is even possible to demonstrate that chance does exist, but chance is only part of the tale. It is the rest of the story that we seek to explore in this book.

NOTES

1. In Finland, Austria, Portugal, and Iceland, the president of the republic is elected by universal suffrage, but the constitution grants him or her limited powers. In these semipresidential systems, the cabinet is the central executive institution.

REFERENCES

Alderman, R.K. "The Prime Minister and the Appointment of Ministers: An Exercise in Political Bargaining." *Parliamentary Affairs* 29, no. 2, Spring 1976, pp. 101–134.

Andweg, Rudy B. "Centrifugal Forces and Collective Decision-Making: The Case of the Dutch Cabinet." Paper presented at the European Consortium for Comparative Research, Goteborg, April 1986.

Boeynaems, M. "Cabinet-Formation." *Res Publica* 9, no. 3, 1967, pp. 471–506.

Dogan, Mattei, and Dominique Pelassy. *How to Compare Nations.* Chatham: Chatham House Publishers, 1984.

Dogan, Mattei, and Maria Scheffer van der Veen. "Le personnel ministériel hollandais 1848–1958," *L'Année sociologique,* 1958, pp. 95–125.

Gibson, Frederick W. (ed.) *Cabinet Formation and Bicultural Relations.* Ottawa, Queen's Printer for Canada, 1970.

Hess, Stephen. *Organizing the Presidency.* Washington: Brookings Institution, 1976.

Johnson, Nevil. *Government in the Federal Republic.* Oxford: Pergamon Press, 1973.

Klemperer, Klemens von. *Ignaz Seipel. Christian Statesman in a time of crisis.* Princeton: Princeton University Press, 1972.

March, Roman R. *The Myth of Parliament.* Scarborough, Ontario: Prentice-Hall Canada, 1974.

Muller, Wolfgang, Wilfried Philipp, and Barbara Steininger. "The Selection of Cabinet Members in Austria," 1987 (unpublished manuscript).

Neustadt, Richard E. "White House and Whitehall." *Public Interest,* Winter 1966, pp. 55–69.

Punnett, R. M. "Her Majesty's Shadow Government: Its Evolution and Modern Role." In Valentine V. Herman and James E. Alt, *Cabinet Studies.* London: Macmillan, 1975.

Rose, Richard. "The Making of Cabinet Ministers." *British Journal of Political Science,* 1971, pp. 393–414.

———. *Ministers and Ministries. A Functional Analysis.* Oxford, Clarendon Press, 1987.

Weller, Patrick. "The Vulnerability of Prime Ministers: A Comparative Perspective." *Parliamentary Affairs* 36, no. 1, Winter 1983, pp. 96–116.

1
CAREER PATHWAYS TO THE CABINET IN FRANCE, 1870–1986

Mattei Dogan

From 1870 to 1986, that is, from Louis-Adolphe Thiers to François Mitterrand, 1,078 ministers, secretaries of state, and undersecretaries have succeeded one another to power, across three political regimes and 140 governments in France. (The Vichy government is not included.) How were these 1,078 personalities selected? In order to reply to such a question, we will trace the path by which the ministers came to power. According to the available documentation, there were three principal pathways: the partisan capillarity, the filter of parliamentary committees, and the mandarin ascent. However, success in one or another of these pathways implied, with few exceptions, previous parliamentary legitimation. In effect, among the 1,078 ministers, nearly 1,000 were recruited from among deputies and senators. It would be possible to count, for the entire period considered—116 years—about 8,200 parliamentarians. One out of every 8 of these exercised ministerial functions. Given these data, one can say that ministerial accession has been based on true selection.

The importance of each of these three pathways varied from one period to another, and these variations are the focus of my analysis. The three pathways were in competition. If one predominated, it was necessarily at the expense of the other two. The partisan capillarity prevailed in certain periods, such as under the Mitterrand presidency. The filter of parliamentary committees dominated during the second half of the Third Republic. The mandarin ascent became more important under Charles de Gaulle and still more important under Valéry Giscard d'Estaing.

My analysis refers to 631 ministers of the Third Republic; 227 of the Fourth Republic (20 of whom had survived from the third); 128 under the Gaullist Republic (including 29 survivors from the fourth); 95 appointed under Giscard d'Estaing (17 of whom had served before 1974); and 62 under the Mitterrand presidency until March 1986 (4 of whom had also served before 1981).

I am considering here a person's first appointment to a governmental position, without distinguishing between full ministers and secretaries or under secretaries of state, since the decisive moment occurs after similar processes in the two categories. But this distinction becomes essential for reappointments. It is necessary to indicate that among the 631 ministers of the Third Republic, 178 were under secretaries of state and never full ministers (except for a few who were elevated under the following republic). For the Fourth Republic, among the 227 ministers (see Table 1.1), 99 were only secretaries or under secretaries of state (and 36 others, first appointed secretaries of state, were later promoted as ministers). During the Gaullist republic, among 128 ministers, 24 were only secretaries of state, and 20 others who started in this position benefited later from a promotion to the higher rank.

My distinctions are an analytic necessity, but in the ascent of a politician, several factors intervene simultaneously or successively and, in most cases, cumulatively. It is rare that the achievements of a politician can be explained by a single factor. The real interdependence of factors is the major difficulty of analysis.

The turbulent history of France over a century obliges not only the historian but also the social scientist to distinguish several periods in order to analyze ministerial personnel (see Table 1.2). For the Third Republic, four periods can be identified: the republic of the dukes (1870–1877); the opportunistic republic (1878–1899); the radical republic (1900–1919); and the interwar period (1919–1939). For the Fourth Republic, it would be useful to distinguish the period of tripartism (1944–1947) from the later period of the third force, but such a differentiation would raise certain problems better avoided in this short analysis. A clear distinction must be made between the Gaullist republic and its successors, taking into consideration each presidency. In order to go beyond the historian's approach and to give sociological consistency to the analysis, we must proceed by groupings.

THE CRUCIBLE OF RESISTANCE

To the three pathways to power should be added a conjunctional pathway of primary importance. The predominant characteristic of the collective portrait of ministers of all political tendencies in the period

1945-1969 is the active participation to the Resistance movement during the war. During World War II a preselection occurred, a selection staggered in time and observable only in retrospect. The minister-former Resistant is a predominant figure in all twenty-four governments of the Fourth Republic and in the eleven years of the Gaullist reign. However, the ministers themselves were not fully conscious of this. The numerical preponderance of former Resistants among ministers was not remarked upon in the autobiographies and memoirs of the politicians of that time. It was not observed while it was happening. The phenomenon has been observed and reconstructed by the sociologist. The Resistance as a "greenhouse" of future ministers intervened in the selection process a long time before they received parliamentary legitimation and regardless of which pathway was later followed by the former Resistant when he became a politician. Because of the importance of the Resistance as greenhouse, the social recruitment of ministers of the quarter century following World War II appears to be, in a sense, of secondary importance.

Involvement in the Resistance did not necessarily imply ambition of making a political career. In any case, between engagement in the Resistance and appointment to government, many years passed, although some individuals went directly from the clandestine network of the Resistance to the political stage. It is in the crucible of the Resistance that most of the men who became political leaders were molded: 190 of the 227 ministers of the Fourth Republic, or 84 percent, and 69 of the 128 ministers of the Gaullist reign, 54 percent. Among these men there were deputies who voted in 1940 against the delegation of power to Marshal Philippe Pétain, deported persons, prisoners, civilians condemned to death by the Gestapo, founders of clandestine networks, commanders of the Free French Forces, chiefs of underground organizations, people sought by the Gestapo, fighters in the internal Resistance, civil servants dismissed by the Vichy government, members of the National Council of Resistance and of the provisional government in Algiers, members of the Consultative Assembly, chiefs of the Resistance in the colonies, and *chargés de missions* sent by General de Gaulle. In 1944, at the Liberation, the cadres of the Resistance became the cadres of political parties; consequently, the de Gaulle government was composed, in great majority, of former Resistants who had become official chiefs of parties overnight.

Was it visible in the 1950s, when precarious governments were constructed, that the selection of ministers was limited to the men ennobled before the rebirth of the democratic regime, that this selection was predetermined, staggered in time? Perhaps the prime ministers had the illusion that they were choosing the members of their cabinets

Table 1.1
Number of Newcomers in Each Cabinet, Fourth Republic (Ministers, Secretaries and Undersecretaries of State)

	Duration (months)	Communists	Socialists	Radicals	Popular Repub.	Moderates	Gaullists	Total new	Notes
De Gaulle	2	5	5	1	4	2	5	22	A
Gouin	5	3	7	1	3	0	0	14	B
Bidault I	7	2	4	1	4	0	0	11	
Blum	1	0	16	0	0	0	0	16	C
Ramadier	10	1	0	6	2	1	0	10	D
Schuman I	8	0	1	4	4	2	0	11	E
Marie	1	0	0	1	1	3	0	5	
Schuman II	8 days	0	1	1	2	0	0	4	
Queuille	13	0	0	4	0	4	0	8	
Bidault II	8	0	0	2	8	3	0	13	F
Queuille II	8 days	0	0	3	0	1	0	4	
Pleven I	8	0	1	0	1	0	0	2	
Queuille III	5	0	0	0	0	0	0	0	
Pleven II	5	0	0	4	2	5	0	11	G
Faure I	2	0	0	6	0	1	0	7	
Pinay	10	0	0	0	0	2	0	2	
Mayer	6	0	0	1	0	4	0	5	
Laniel	12	0	0	2	1	9	4	16	H

Mendès-France	8	0	0	7	1	9	6	23	I
Faure II	11	0	1	3	1	1	3	9	
Guy Mollet	13	0	8	7	0	0	0	15	
Bourges-Maunoury	7	0	3	11	0	1	0	15	
Gaillard	6	0	0	0	2	2	0	4	
Pflimlin	18 days	0	0	0	0	0	0	0	J
Total		11	47	65	36	50	18	227	

Notes:

A: Among the 22 ministers, 14 were veterans of the Third Republic or of the provisional government of August 1944 to November 1945.

B: Beginning of tripartism.

C: Homogeneous Socialist government.

D: Three Communists were excluded in October 1947 and replaced by 3 new ministers and 3 new secretaries of state.

E: Increase in the number of secretariats and under secretariats; among the 11 new men, only 4 were full ministers.

F: Resignation of the socialists on February 8, 1950, and of Pflimlin in December 1949, replaced by a few new men.

G: New legislature. Socialists retreat into opposition. Beginning of center-right phase.

H: "Integration" of a few former Gaullists and an increase in the number of secretariats.

I: New crystallization of the chamber and two reshuffles.

J: New legislature and 14 new secretariats of state with only 1 new full minister.

Table 1.2
Pathways to Government by Historical Periods

	Republic							
	Third				Fourth	Fifth		
	Dukes	Opp.	Rad.	Inter.		Gaul.	Gisc.	Mitt.
Crucible of Resistance	•	□	•	•	□	□	•	•
Parliamentary legitimation	□	□	□	□	□	-	-	-
Party capillarity	•	+	+	+	□	-	•	□
Filter of parliamentary committees	•	+	+	□	+	•	•	•
Mandarin accent	•	•	•	-	•	+	□	•
Co-optation	+	+	+	+	•	□	□	□

Key: □ : predominant
      + : important
      - : relatively important
      • : unimportant

Notes: Dukes: Republic of dukes, 1870-1877
       Opp.: Opportunistic republic, 1878-1899
       Rad.: Radical republic, 1900-1919
       Inter.: Interwar years, 1919-1940
       Fourth: Fourth Republic, 1945-1958
       Gaul.: Gaullist republic, 1958-1974
       Gisc.: Giscard's presidency, 1974-1981
       Mitt.: Mitterrand's presidency, 1981-1986 (first phase)

according to precise criteria responding to the political issues of the day. In fact, their latitude was limited, as the retrospective analysis demonstrated, by events and by behavior that were made manifest a long time before.

The Fourth Republic fell and the fifth was installed, but there were still men of the Resistance placed in command. Figure 1.1 illustrates the selection of the most important ministers of the de Gaulle regime among former Resistants. In effect, the names of those who are inside the so-called London circle were also those of the princes and barons of the Gaullist republic. When this regime was inaugurated in 1958, its rulers had already been potentially designated, with few exceptions. The former Resistants dominated the Gaullist decade.

Surely, the immense majority of the population had strong sympathies with the Resistance, but the truth is that less than 1 percent of French adults participated directly in clandestine activities against the enemy. Assuming that the 200,000 active members of the Resistance constituted a kind of sample of the whole adult population, and knowing that 1 percent of the adult population was university educated, we could then also assume that 2,000 of the Resistants had university educations. The proportion with university degrees was certainly higher among leaders than among members. Those men who possessed this double qualification, member of the Resistance and university graduate, represented 1/10,000 of the adult population (1 percent, Resistance members times 1 percent, graduates). By supposing that the proportion of graduates among Resistance leaders was twice as high as among persons who did not participate in the Resistance, we deduce that Fourth Republic ministers were recruited from an extremely restricted category that represented—just to give an idea—1/50,000 of the male population between twenty-five and sixty years of age. Paris had not yet been liberated when this preselection occurred!

It is also important to note that many of the former members of the Resistance who became ministers during the Gaullist Republic belonged to the exterior Resistance, whereas the majority of Fourth Republic ministers had participated in the interior Resistance. If Jean Moulin, leader of the interior Resistance, had survived, he would undoubtedly have become one of the dominant figures of the Fourth Republic. About forty former Resistance ministers of the Gaullist Republic had already been ministers or at least members of Parliament under the fourth. This fact brilliantly illuminates the impact of the Resistance beyond that of the changing of regimes. Many among them were in General de Gaulle's entourage in London or Algiers.

The preponderance of Resistance members among ministers diminished over the years but remained impressive even during Georges

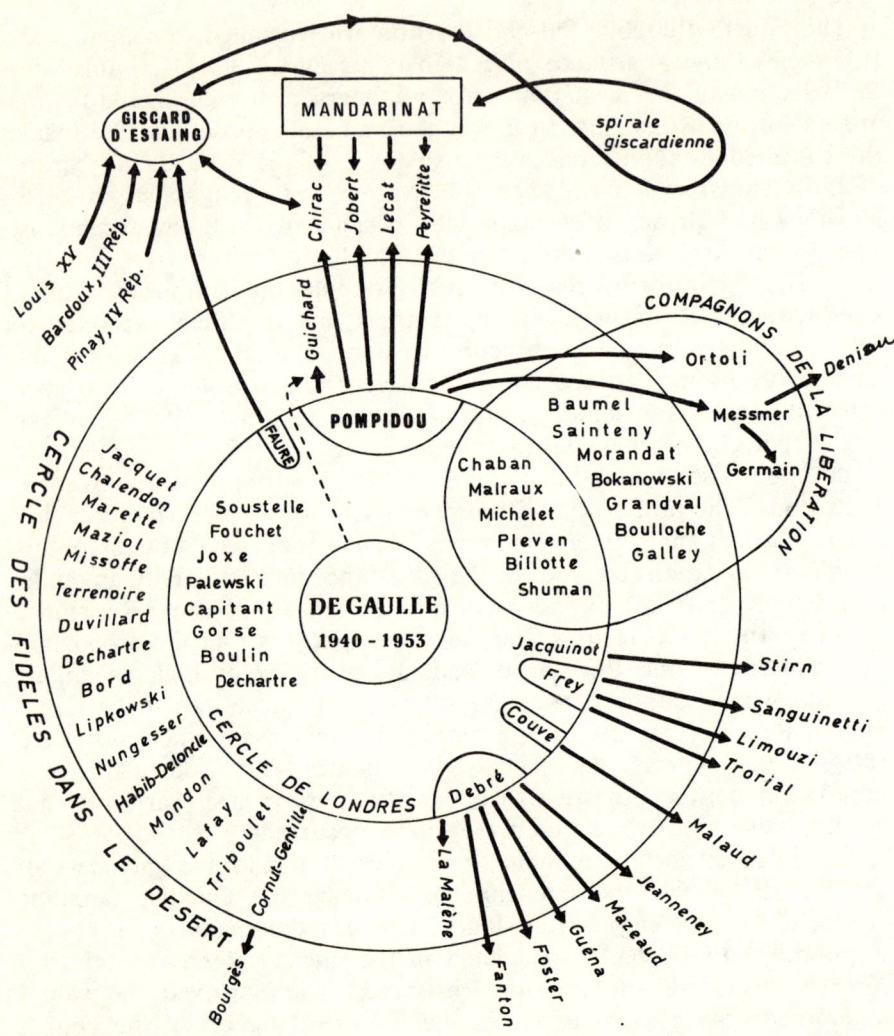

FIGURE 1.1
Background to Companionship and Patronage Under the Gaullist Republic, 1958-1974

Pompidou's presidency. Only after the appearance of younger faces following Giscard d'Estaing's election, thirty years after Liberation, did former members of the Resistance cease to dominate the political scene. Mitterrand was not too young to have participated in the Resistance; he joined the interior Resistance in 1941.

We observe a phenomenon similar to the Resistance at the beginning of the Third Republic: opposition to the empire before 1870. Those who had fought for the republic against Napoleon III were quite naturally found in the front ranks. Like the Resistance fighter of 1940–1944, those who opposed the empire could claim a certain republican legitimacy.

PARLIAMENTARY LEGITIMATION

A fact with profound significance for studying the selection of ministers comes to the fore. Of 631 Third Republic ministers, only 62 were chosen from outside Parliament, and most of those came from the military. Among the 227 Fourth Republic ministers, there were only 6 nonparliamentarians (de Gaulle, Léon Blum, André Malraux, Raoul Dautry, Yves Farge, and Bougenot). In spite of the constitutional prohibition against holding a ministerial office and a parliamentary seat simultaneously, 104 out of 128 ministers during the Gaullist republic held seats in Parliament at the time of their promotion to the cabinet. In other words, in order to become a minister, an aspirant had to have been consecrated by universal suffrage so as to acquire a kind of legitimacy. This legitimacy has not been explicitly invoked during the formation of cabinets. But in parliamentary regimes such as the Third and Fourth republics, in which Parliament was the center of gravity, only those who sat there could acquire the legitimacy necessary for promotion to the cabinet. This is a problem of parliamentary arithmetic: Under a parliamentary regime, a majority constantly has to express itself, and the prime minister must shape this majority. The best means to do this is to choose ministers from among the most influential parliamentarians.

The Chamber of Deputies and not the Senate gave the cabinet its investiture, even though the Senate contributed to the fall of some Third Republic governments. Quite naturally, ministers were preferably chosen from among deputies, rarely from among senators. Only 48 Third Republic ministers served exclusively in the Senate. Other ministers who had started their careers in the Chamber entered the government only after having passed through the Senate, as Georges Clemenceau did. Those men who switched houses between two cabinet

Table 1.3
Parliamentary Seniority and Number of Governments Served, French Third Republic (1870-1940)

Years between first election and first appointment	Number of Governments Served					
	1	2-3	4-6	7-9	9+	Total
Less than 4 years	70	54	39	14	15	192
5 or 6 years	34	34	13	9	10	100
7 to 14 years	69	63	33	17	10	194
More than 15 years	36	28	15	4	0	83
Non-MPs	38	22	2	0	0	62
Total	247	201	104	44	35	631

positions do not affect my analysis since it is restricted to first appointments as ministers.

If the selection of ministers occurs primarily within the Chamber of Deputies, the reason is that this body brings together the greater part of the most influential political elite. There were influential leaders elsewhere—in the Senate and at the head of certain parties and unions, pressure groups, or parapolitical organizations—but, in the final analysis, the Palais Bourbon was the forum. Only during the tripartite period after Liberation did the lower house lose its omnipotence to the benefit of the parties. A few years later another center of gravity, the presidency, was established.

The precariousness of cabinet positions contrasts with the longevity of most ministers' parliamentary careers. In effect, 122 Third Republic ministers sat in Parliament for more than a quarter of a century (40 of them sat for more than thirty-five years); 224 others sat between sixteen and twenty-five years; 100 sat between eleven and fifteen years; and 92 between six and ten years. Very few ministers, only 31 (5 percent), had short parliamentary careers—less than five years. This tally does not include the 62 nonparliamentarians.

However, the majority of these people entered a government shortly after having entered Parliament: 192 were appointed less than four years after their first election (see Table 1.3). This means, at least for the deputies, that appointments occurred during their first term. One hundred others were appointed during the fifth or sixth year of their parliamentary mandate. The 83 who had to wait a long time, more than fifteen years, before appointment to a government represent only

a small fraction of ministerial personnel: 14 percent (among them, the Socialists).

The paradox is that, two times out of three, the greater part of a parliamentary career occurred not before but after cabinet experience. Appointment as minister did not take place after a long parliamentary career, as in Britain during the same period or in Japan today. In fact, members of the British government between 1868 and 1958 had an average experience of fourteen years in the House of Commons when appointed (Willson 1959, 226). In France, entry into a cabinet did not depend upon parliamentary seniority. There is no significant relationship between seniority in Parliament and promotion to a cabinet, even if a clear distinction is made between full-fledged ministers and mere undersecretaries of state. Nevertheless, one limitation could not be circumvented: It was essential to have sat in the Chamber for two or three years in order to have any chances for promotion to a cabinet-level position. Once this condition was met, parliamentary seniority hardly came into play at all.

The classical relationship of cause and effect was reversed: Parliamentary seniority did not favor promotion to a cabinet; rather, participation in a cabinet seems to have brought about a prolongation of parliamentary careers for a long period after the last cabinet office. Former ministers succeeded better than the average deputy in getting reelected under universal male suffrage. Whereas 17 percent of the deputies of the Third Republic sat during at least five legislatures (twenty years), a good quarter of the ministers succeeded in sitting for that long; 59 percent of the deputies sat less than eight years, as contrasted with only 15 percent of the ministers (Dogan 1953, 331).

But the principal reason for this longevity in Parliament was refuge in the Senate. A third of the ministers, exactly 203, quit the Chamber of Deputies to fill more comfortable Senate seats, guaranteed for at least nine years. Few among them returned to a cabinet during their Senate mandates. More than half, 119 out of 203, continued sitting in the Senate between twelve and thirty years.

Not only were cabinet careers short and precarious, but also they came to an end so early that the rich political experience the deputy had gained still permitted many hopes, fed by cabinet crises. The number of former ministers that were in waiting increased in both houses. If one counts among the deputies ministers in office, former and future ministers, one sees the total rise from 59 for the 1876 legislature to 80 for the one beginning in 1885, to 197 in 1906, 139 in 1914, and 173 in 1928. Political loss of position, which occurred prematurely for most ministers, went along with a sometimes excessive prolongation of their parliamentary careers. This was certainly a source

of political frustration that increased cabinet instability, especially among those whose fortunes fell shortly after they had risen.

As a result of the election of the president by universal suffrage after 1965, parliamentary legitimacy has lost its primacy. Consequently, its importance in the choice of ministers has declined. However, the number of nonparliamentarians among the ministers, relatively high during de Gaulle's presidency, declined during Pompidou's. This temporary reduction is explained by the Gaullist party's preponderance in the National Assembly, the party to which the president himself was attached. Though his successor, Giscard d'Estaing, surrounded himself with a majority of nonparliamentarians, almost all of Giscard's ministers fought for a parliamentary seat in March 1978.

Legitimation by universal suffrage does not mean that a person instantly qualifies to be minister. The new deputies, even if they are prestigious in their original profession and already known by the influential leaders, must still make themselves known on the floor of Parliament. Parliamentary legitimacy is a necessary but not a sufficient condition either for becoming a minister or for returning to office as a minister. The hopeful can choose among three principal channels, which can cross each other, and which may have a cumulative effect.

THE FILTER OF PARLIAMENTARY COMMITTEES

By the filter of parliamentary committees I mean the sifting process that occurs among deputies or senators within the parliamentary committees to which they all belong. Contrary to party caucuses, these committees bring together parliamentarians from all sides. In the French political system, these committees have always played an essential role in legislative work and parliamentary activity. A committee's role is very different from that of a caucus. A committee is a miniature assembly, whereas a caucus contains only one party. The latter is preoccupied with strategy and ideology; the former accomplishes more concrete work: it negotiates, formulates, and reviews.

A parliamentary committee is both a place for apprenticeship and a forum. It teaches its members how to become statesmen. The committee is also the best place for someone to demonstrate skill and talents and to attract the attention both of colleagues and of members of the government; in the committee each deputy is surrounded not only by friends from his own party but also by representatives from the whole political spectrum. The committee is the best place to prove one's gift as a negotiator and conciliator, qualities much appreciated in a multiparty system. So the committee is the antechamber to higher office because it brings out the outstanding qualities of some of its

members. To be named committee reporter and to present a bill before the full assembly is a good opportunity for casting off the relative anonymity of the average deputy. To be elected committee president is to further increase one's chance of becoming minister someday. In effect, at any moment in the history of the republic, one could find that a large number of those who were committee presidents or reporters, sooner or later, were called upon to fill ministerial positions. Examples of this could easily fill several pages. Many ex-ministers, because of their prestige and influence, have become committee presidents. The proportions of future ministers and of ex-ministers among committee presidents depends upon the moment in history. There are more future ministers at the beginning of a period, more ex-ministers during the later phases. This is significant because the selection of ministers takes place in large part at the beginning of historical phases, such as just after wars.

The same does not hold true for committee reporters, who have often strenuous duties; the position of president has an honorary aspect. The differing nature of the positions is undoubtedly the reason for the preponderance of future ministers over ex-ministers among reporters. What is significant is the fact that ministers, at the time of their first appointments, receive either the ministerial department or the secretariat that corresponds to the committee for which they have been reporter. On the other hand, one can observe hardly any relationship between ministers' original profession and the ministerial department that they head. (This is partly explained by the preponderance among ministers of certain professional categories, such as lawyers and journalists.) The absence of such a relationship clearly indicates that experience and competence are acquired on a committee.

Not all committees are equally important. Those of foreign affairs and of finance were particularly desired by would-be ministers. Sometimes other committees were also attractive, for example, that of justice; but as J. Barthelemy wrote, "The Finance Committee is the dominant committee," since it designates not only a general reporter for the budget but also special reporters for each ministerial department. This committee holds the purse strings, a fact that led Barthelemy to say, "The general reporter of the budget is almost certainly a future minister" (Barthelemy 1934, 180, 279).

Ironical comments have often been made about the competence of ministers, but we can see the importance of competence in the work of the Finance Committee. The problem of competence is too often poorly formulated. The kind of skill needed by ministers is not specialization, that is, technical knowledge about a particular field, but rather the capacity to understand, judge, and evaluate problems and

to propose solutions. They must have oratorical skills or at least a capacity for persuasion. A parliamentarian will not necessarily make a good minister of public works just because he or she used to be a mining engineer. To stay with this example, most heads of this department were lawyers or professional politicians. One could say the same about the ministers of agriculture and almost the same about the others. However, departments are not assigned to ministers without consideration of their experience and interests that have been exhibited in parliamentary committees and most especially in the role of reporter.

These remarks are especially valid for the Third Republic after 1877. For the fourth, two phases must be distinguished. During the first one, the route through parties, to be analyzed in the following pages, played a decisive role in the selection of ministers. But from the moment the parties split up, parliamentary committees regained the effective role in the screening and selection they had had before 1940. As Parliament declined under the Fifth Republic, the committee filter dwindled to the point of drying up. The drying up of this channel had important consequences for the balance of powers. When ministers are extracted from Parliament, schooled and trained in the committees, they are quite naturally more sensitive to the requirements of parliamentary representation than other ministers selected from the higher civil service.

PARTY CAPILLARITY

The party channel includes two quite different and variously important realities, depending on the period. The first is simply one's geometrical position on the hemicycle of Parliament. This is a question of political label. The second is one's hierarchical position in the party: A person climbs up the party ladder before and after election to Parliament and, because of the eminent position this person has acquired in the party's hierarchy, qualifies as minister. These two realities must combine if he or she is to have a chance. Rising to the party's top does not suffice. The party must also be of the right coloration, that of the parliamentary majority.

Under the Fourth Republic, when the parties were relatively well organized, and especially during the third force period, the political label—Popular Republican (MRP), Socialist (SFIO), Republican Left (RGR), Democratic Union (UDSR), or any other—had less importance than the position held within the party. In fact, more than three-quarters of Fourth Republic ministers officially or unofficially held eminent party positions, shown by their titles or by their prominence in the mass media. In many circumstances, the importance of the

position in the hierarchy of the party is proven by the deals concluded at the time of the formation of a cabinet: The parties delegated their representatives to the government. During the first phase of the Fifth Republic (1958–1981), on the contrary, ministers were still chosen *from* a party but they were not delegated *by* the party and were not called upon because of the offices they held *in* the party. Promotion took place according to other criteria. Between 1981 and 1986 the president's party emblem was the same as that of the majority in the Palais Bourbon, and, consequently, party channels again became important.

The position in the parliamentary spectrum was a criterion in the selection of Third Republic ministers, at least until the Popular Front in 1936. The game of political labels became so subtle that it has no counterpart in other Western democracies. To classify deputies according to their political tendencies is difficult; to do so with ministers is risky, especially because some of them seemed like chameleons. Of the 427 ministers during the period from 1899 to 1940, from Waldeck-Rousseau to Pétain, I count 247 who belonged to various fractions and factions of the polymorphous Radical party. If, from among these 427, one excludes, on the one hand, the 35 nonparliamentarians and, on the other, the 36 Socialists, who, with few exceptions, came to ministerial office very late in 1936, one has to admire the dexterity of all shades of Radicals at keeping the helm in their hands. They were strategically placed in the parliamentary spectrum—in dead center, center-right, center-left, at the juncture of centers. Undoubtedly, they did not become ministers simply because they were so placed. Rather, some wormed their way into the center in order to improve their chances. The preponderance of radicalism is all the more remarkable inasmuch as the appearance of new parties on the left should have pushed radicalism to the right. Radicalism has always been able to blend in with centrism as an ideology, both in the Chamber and the Senate. (In twentieth-century French history, radicalism has meant centrism, as opposed to the U.S. usage in the sense of extremism.)

As for the 1870–1899 period, the possibility of simultaneously belonging to several groups made political identification quite problematic. Most ministers nevertheless came from the central section of the Chamber. Of a total of 247 ministers during this period, 65 could be classified on the radical left, 66 on the republican left, and 37 left of center, if we keep in mind that they were not geometrically far off center. Ambitious politicians who chose the wrong horse, regardless of their assets, could at the very most play brilliant roles in Parliament but not in the government; they constantly qualified for ministerial positions but never managed to capture one.

THE MANDARIN ASCENT

The pathways I have distinguished compete somewhat with each other. The prevalence of one necessarily goes against the two others. For instance, the party channel prevailed during some periods, the committee filter during others. The higher civil service, another reservoir of would-be ministers already operating during the second half of the Third Republic, was progressively revitalized under de Gaulle and, at the expense of the other two, still more under Giscard d'Estaing.

The higher civil service paves a political road that runs through a minister's staff. The mandarin who follows this channel first becomes a minister's assistant, in the position of counsellor, attaché, director, or head of the minister's staff, and only thereafter undertakes a truly political career. Membership on a minister's staff precedes parliamentary experience, seldom the opposite. Under the Third Republic's political system, when Parliament and the parties played an essential role in the selection of ministerial personnel, relatively few—less than 10 percent—had spent time on a minister's staff. By contrast, nearly half the ministers of the Gaullist Republic, 56 of 128, followed this channel. Of this half, 39 had first been assistants to ministers, then obtained seats in Parliament—often by electoral "parachuting"—before being finally promoted to cabinet positions. Only 17 others moved directly from the staff antechamber into such a position, thus bypassing the electoral step. Among the 39 with classical careers, 12 served as ministers or parliamentarians under the Fourth Republic, and 27 were newcomers who started in Parliament and in the government after 1958.

One of two Gaullist mandarin-ministers had belonged to the Resistance. After a thirteen-year eclipse during the Fourth Republic, eighteen Resistants entered government after General de Gaulle's return. Many of them were able to do without parliamentary legitimacy because they were endowed with another legitimacy, that of the Resistance.

The importance of the higher civil service in the selection of ministers after 1958 resulted from a series of circumstances. After his return, de Gaulle no longer headed a party in the traditional sense of the word. Inasmuch as the ministers were no longer chosen from leaders prominent in the party, they were selected from among senior civil servants. Under Pompidou's presidency, however, when Gaullism took the form of a large, well-organized party holding a majority in the assembly, priority was given to partisan recruitment, but not for long.

The election of Giscard d'Estaing as president consecrated more than ever before the mandarin channel: The top civil service furnished the majority of the 86 ministers during his presidency. We need not look

very far for the explanation. A young man, not the leader of a great party but independent and relatively isolated, came to power in a political system that forbade simultaneously holding positions in the cabinet and in Parliament, at a moment when the men of the Resistance were becoming scarce. Furthermore, the new president owed nothing to the Gaullist entourage, in contrast to his predecessor. In one stroke, one channel of preselection, Resistance, almost disappeared; another, which had been important before 1958, was impoverished—that of the party.

In the past, political heirs launched themselves directly into politics; but after World War II, they tended to pass through the higher civil service. Thus, political heritage, a channel for preselection that had so much importance at the beginning of the Third Republic, seems to have regained importance, but under a more techno-meritocratic form. Giscard d'Estaing himself symbolized this new variety of political heir.

Recruitment through the civil service could not develop without transforming the structure of the government, which has multiplied the number of state secretaries. In the two Jacques Chirac governments (1974–1976), for the first time in the republic's history, there were nearly twice as many secretaries as ministers. Two interpretations are possible: The number of state secretariats increased in order to appoint civil servants at their head, or the multiplication of state secretariats was deemed necessary for technical reasons, and top civil servants rather than full-fledged politicians were the privileged candidates for such specialized positions. Regardless of the initial reason, the fact of the matter is that this multiplication is related to the selection of a majority of state secretaries from among former higher civil servants. The monolithic nature of the presidency and the fact that Giscard was not indebted to a large party have undoubtedly favored such a selection. Since he had only partially to satisfy partisan demands, his choice naturally went to top civil servants, whom he appointed to secretariats.

One can now sketch a portrait of this new kind of state secretary. That person has neither party nor parliamentary experience and is assigned strictly defined duties. Even if he is wide-ranging, he is not asked to take a stand on general political problems. He is representative of neither a current of thought nor a political force. He owes his appointment entirely to the confidence that the president, or possibly the prime minister, has in him. As a consequence, the state secretary is in fact responsible not to Parliament but almost exclusively to the president. He incarnates no legitimacy of his own. His position resembles that of a high civil servant who heads his service but has a political orientation and, especially, direct relations with the political arena.

The state secretary is comparable to the senior minister outside the cabinet in the British government. The French secretary participates in cabinet meetings only on an exceptional basis but, like his British equivalent, is responsible for a ministerial department or part of it. Nevertheless, a fundamental difference separates them. Senior ministers are recruited from party men in the House of Commons, and they have rich parliamentary backgrounds. Most of the French civil servants who become secretaries of state were neither party men nor parliamentarians. The contrast in the recruitment, socialization, and cast of mind between these types is striking.

THE ULTIMATE STEP IN SELECTION: CO-OPTATION

A person can very well rise through these channels and become visible, but he is not yet a minister in title, only *ministrable*. A last step remains: sponsorship, even a kind of political godfatherhood, in the honorable sense of the French word *parrainage*. What is striking when one reads ministers' biographies is that this ultimate act in their careers is always a personalized choice. As an example of the many testimonies to be found in the literature about the importance of friendships in political life, I reproduce this passage: "The small apartment where Alain Targe lived in Verneuil Street was the preferred meeting-place for most of the young opponents who took the name 'Radical Democrats.' In particular, Brisson, Gambetta, Challemel-Lacour and Laurier, met together two or three times per week over dinner there. . . . This was a period during the lives of the five young men that was marked by friendship, enthusiasm and mutual devotion. This period always remained dear to them" (Porte 1939, xxvii). Fifteen years later these five friends simultaneously became cabinet ministers. A minister is not chosen simply because he is the reporter of the Finance Committee, but because he is Mr. So-and-so, who just happens to be this committee's reporter. The governor of the Bank of France cannot hope to be named minister because of his duties; personal relationships with leaders in office are a sine qua non for his appointment.

Except in the case of a crisis, any appointment at the top level of the state, regardless of the pathway followed, entails personal co-optation as a final step. The aspirant must inevitably be proposed and then accepted by the inner circle. In some cases the final selection is surrounded by mystery. The sponsors of those ministers whose careers have been the subject of detailed biographies are known. Biographies and autobiographies provide references about the importance of personal relationships in a ministerial promotion. One example from among many is Joseph Caillaux's memoirs (Caillaux 1942, 118–123).

CAREER PATHWAYS TO THE CABINET IN FRANCE

Republics pass away, recruitment channels change, the kinds of people appointed vary according to the relative importance of various channels, but the personalization of selection remains inevitable. From all evidence, ministers are not selected through anonymous competitions under either parliamentary or presidential regimes. The composite phenomenon that finally emerges is that of friendship-sponsorship-patronage-co-optation, which has nothing to do with nepotism, a very rare practice anyway at this high level. Even godfatherhood, like friendship, necessarily implies esteem and confidence.

Sometimes friendships have been woven in battle. Thiers, on the one hand, and Jules Simon, Cremieux, and Gambetta, on the other, were powerful patrons. Dufaure was the friend of Thiers and himself sponsored Ribot; Rouvier, the friend of Cremieux, also knew Gambetta, who himself backed de Freycinet, who in turn was the godfather of his former associate, Sadi Carnot, as Floquet was for Doumer. "The Great Ministry" of 1881 was "only a group of Gambetta's personal friends, young men from 36 to 46 years old, all politicians and exclusively politicians" (Soulie 1939, 288). Personal relationships were often born through work. Deschanel was Jules Simon's secretary; Flandrin, Alexandre Millerand's; Paul-Boncour, Waldeck-Rousseau's; Mandel, Clemenceau's; Pompidou, de Gaulle's; Laurent Fabius, Mitterrand's.

Léon Blum and Vincent Auriol were inseparable friends. More than half the Fourth Republic's Socialist ministers started their cabinet careers in a government presided over by a Socialist, in the governments of Blum, Gouin, Ramadier, or Guy Mollet. The same was true for men in the other parties (Popular Republican, Radical, Independents, etc.). Very often, prime ministers finally based their choices upon personal relationships, as in the Pierre Mendès-France cabinet.

Some other circles are not to be neglected. The Freemasonry backed Combes. Journalists advanced *papabili,* for instance, during the time of Sarraut and la *Depeche de Toulouse.* At la *Lanterne,* Clemenceau, the editor, worked with Rochefort and Viviani; Briand was a director. Millerand knew Clemenceau through journalism. The value of relationships woven outside of power and well before coming to power should not be underestimated.

But a minister's staff is the most strategic place for building relationships, friendship, sponsorship. A host of ministers came through that way. The phenomenon of co-optation takes on even greater importance under the presidential system, particularly with de Gaulle and Mitterrand. There are many similarities between these two presidents in the manner in which they promoted their faithful followers to government, despite the many differences between the two from other points of view.

SIMILARITIES BETWEEN THE GAULLIST AND SOCIALIST COMPANIONSHIPS

Like Moses, de Gaulle and Mitterrand have "wandered in the desert." The first endured isolation and alienation for thirteen years, between 1945 and 1958, and the second, twenty-three years, between 1958 and 1981. When these men were in the opposition, they built a community of followers, a companionship. The destiny of followers depended on the triumph of their leader's cause.

The Gaullist companionship was based on fidelity to a prestigious chief in spite of high tides and strong winds. Historical circumstances twice placed Charles de Gaulle at the head of state and thus entrusted him with the mission of promoting a new political order. This fidelity arose out of a short-lived charismatic phenomenon (Dogan 1965). It implied a personal tie between leader and led. Its effect was staggered over time, as was that of the Resistance.

Some companions had not participated in the Resistance; that depended on the individual's age. The elders of the Resistance were able to remain faithful during the "crossing of the desert," but a new generation sprang up to General de Gaulle's call after Liberation, men who were too young to have been able to enlist in the Resistance. Figure 1.1 illustrates the selection of the ministers during the first fifteen years of the Fifth Republic (de Gaulle and Pompidou presidencies). The second circle indicates the names of the men of the new generation who joined de Gaulle after the war and who remained faithful throughout the "crossing of the desert," (1947–1958) and who were promoted ministers after their leader's return to power. Most of them were chosen directly by him. Those who were promoted during the same period, but who did not enjoy the privilege of such personal ties, owed their appointments to an intervening patron; their names are written outside the circle.

When the Gaullist republic was inaugurated in 1958, most of the cabinet ministers had already been potentially designated. These designations were dependent on records of conduct dating, for some, from at least five years beforehand—before 1953—and for most, going back a quarter of a century. This entourage dominated the Gaullist decade.

If François Mitterrand decides one day to write a book on the subject "how I have chosen my ministers," he will involve himself in a very difficult literary genre, where it is not possible to tell the truth, the whole truth, without deceiving faithful friends and irritating rivals, and without getting in trouble with the historian of tomorrow. None of his predecessors have written such a confession. De Gaulle himself wrote only a few lines on this subject. In other countries, no president

or prime minister has really revealed the secret of his reasons behind choices of ministers. Here is what the impartial observer is tempted to say.

It is necessary to distinguish several categories among the ministers appointed between 1981 and 1986. First, the veterans: Mitterrand, as the Great Selector, offered a position as state minister to one of the few survivors of the Resistance and of the rulers of the Fourth Republic as well as a leader of the old socialist party (SFIO), and also a candidate for the presidency of the republic in 1965: Gaston Defferre, friend-rival, whose career was similar and parallel to Mitterrand's, but who was less fortunate. The president was generous with a defeated rival: Alain Savary, who had lost the leadership of the old Socialist party, thereby opening the road for Mitterrand. He has not been ungrateful to the former president of the Radical party Maurice Faure who, in order not to embarrass Mitterrand as candidate, retreated, willing or not, from the presidential elections in 1965. He offered a figurehead position to one of Pompidou's heirs, who had supported his candidacy from its beginning in 1981: Michel Jobert.

Among the fifty-eight new ministers, one can first observe four men without real political power who have made a nice career in academic life or as writers. The center-left allies constitute a small but visible group. They counterbalanced the presence of Communists in government. The manner in which the representatives of the Communist party were selected merits notice. The secret has been well kept, but I know from a reliable source that the president, by the intermediary of the prime minister, requested from the Communist party a list of names from whom he would select four. The party presented a long alphabetical list including not only all the members of the Politburo, but also a large number of members of the Central Committee (probably for the state secretariats). The four Communists were consequently chosen from outside rather than delegated by the party.

Among the Socialists, one notes first seven women, two or three of whom were on center stage. This number is probably higher than would have been obtained by free competition, because the proportion of women at various levels in the Socialist party hierarchy was relatively low. This deliberate promotion of women is not a new phenomenon but began with the previous president.

In order to understand the choice of ministers, the first task is to consult the organizational chart of the presidential campaign, on which Mitterrand had already been working in February 1981 "for several weeks" (Estier 1981, 77), and which included names from older lists: the friends of the Epinay Congress (1971), those of the Metz Convention (1979), those of the premature countergovernment (1967–1968), and the

older friends from the early 1960s when Mitterrand was almost a forgotten politician. The organization chart included about one hundred names. Not all have become cabinet ministers or state secretaries, since the *ministrables* were too numerous, but some obtained very interesting positions at the summit of the administrative state.

Among these excellencies, two groups are evident, the faithful friends and the rival friends, and between them a few hybrid cases. A majoritarian party is by necessity a rather heterogenous party, composed of factions and wings. The president had to reach a compromise with some of his older great rivals, beginning with Pierre Mauroy, who became prime minister, with Pierre Chevenement, and with Michel Rocard. It was wise to embark the last one onto the governmental ship, rather than leaving him free outside.

At a different level, it was necessary to satisfy those who held influential positions in the party hierarchy and those who had, sooner rather than later, joined the Mitterrand camp. About fifteen ministers and secretaries of state belong to this category, including Auroux and Chandernagor. There is also the category of those few selected directly by the prime minister. Satisfying these various currents was a relatively easy thing to do, according to the rules of the political game.

The circle of the true friends closed itself at the very moment of the electoral triumph. Their promotion was understood, perhaps promised in confidence. Only the date of their nomination remained uncertain. Some, among the greatest, had to be patient. These are the faithful companions, in the Gaullist sense of the word, during the very long Socialist "crossing of the desert." Among these true friends were Dumas ("I have been at his side for thirty years"); Beregovoy ("the total fidelity"); Hernu, Quiles, Quilliot, Mermaz, Joxe, Malvy, Mexandeau, and others. There were also privileged advisors for a long time: Badinter ("the perpetual friend"); Cheysson, Delors, Jack Lang, and Dreyfus, none of whom had held visible positions in the party hierarchy. There were also the "young wolves" such as Fabius ("the president's man") who became, in his own words, "the youngest prime minister in French history." As in the Gaullist companionship, this co-optation-friendship implied mutual confidence and respect.

If one limits the analysis to those who were forty-five years old in 1981, that is, those born before the Popular Front (1936), one can find in their biographies that the most noticable achievement of their political career, the significance of which appears only in retrospect, is their behavior in the various stages and circumstances, sometimes difficult and hazardous, of François Mitterrand's "long march" to the presidency, a march that was not always ascendant. It is necessary to go back fifteen years, if not twenty or more, in order to understand the reasons

of the promotion-reward. It is evident that in the selection of ministers, the personal friendship of the president weighed much more than the positions held in the hierarchy of the party.

The pool was partisan, but in its middle was the circle of personal friends. The selection was also made in terms of competence. Only a dozen cabinet ministers and state secretaries were dismissed for reasons other than the drastic change in political orientation in 1983-1984. Those eliminated for reasons other than political showed that they were lacking in one of the qualities required from a cabinet minister: judgment, competence, managerial spirit, discretion, or realism. Selection continues after the first appointment; if someone does not measure up to expectations, he or she is dismissed.

"It is not possible to found a political regime on the basis of the power of a single man," Mitterrand asserted to de Gaulle in 1958. In terms of recruitment of cabinet ministers, de Gaulle appears nevertheless to have been more open, more eclectic, then Mitterrand, at least until 1984.

One of the mechanisms of the French superpresidential system (which appears disequilibrated in comparison with the U.S. presidential system, where there are counterpowers: the Congress, the Supreme Court, federalism, the elected governors, the independence of the mass media, the influence of the newspapers) is the capacity of the president—selector-sorceror—to propel into the political forum "unknown" persons. De Gaulle discovered Pompidou, who "elevated" Chirac, Giscard pushed Raymond Barre forward, Mitterrand anointed Fabius, and Chirac unearthed Edouard Balladur. France was a nonhereditary monarchy until 1986 when, because of disparity between the presidential majority and the parliamentary majority, it finally became, twenty-eight years after the promulgation of the constitution, a semipresidential system. Then the prime minister, Chirac, instead of being a privileged selected politician, metamorphized himself into a Great Selector. In May 1988 the regime became again superpresidential.

AFTER QUITTING THE GOVERNMENT

The brevity and precariousness of the governmental experience of most ministers contrast with the sum of efforts deployed and energies spent in order to get a cabinet position. Few ministers had the possibility of building on solid foundations, and even fewer have left their names in history. To find fault with their capacities and skills would be vain. At the time when their ministerial careers terminated, the majority of Third Republic ministers were still in the prime of life: 373, or 60 percent, were less than fifty-nine years of age when they quit a gov-

ernment for the last time, with or without the hope of returning. The proportion is higher for the ministers of the Fourth and Gaullist republics. However, most of the ministers, of all historical periods, have succeeded in prolonging their parliamentary careers, some in the forefront of the stage, and most in the shadow, proud of being *anciens ministres* and to be addressed as *monsieur le ministre*. During the second half of the Third Republic, the postministerial parliamentary career went, for too many, along with the acquisition of positions on the boards of trustees of corporations. Thus, I have found nearly 100 of the 432 ministers from 1910 to 1940 in such positions, particularly during the period 1922–1938.

The contrast between the precariousness of most ministers' positions and the longevity of their parliamentary careers after serving in a government has important consequences for ministerial instability, since some of the frustrated former ministers easily tend to vote against those who "took their place." It is understandably difficult to confess these frustrations.

How many of these thousand ministers were what could be called professional politicians? Even those who served only for a springtime lived *for* politics and very often *from* politics, to use Max Weber's expression. Not only did most of them sit for a long time in Parliament, before or after their cabinet experiences, but they spent the essential part of their time in political or parapolitical activities long before their election. This was so even for those who continued to practice a profession, because the majority of them came from social strata, such as the senior civil service or journalism, that were close to politics, or else held jobs, such as practicing law or teaching, that very easily fitted in with political activities.

One more contrast, between the transient men and the stable nucleus should be stressed. This aspect is analysed—in a comparative framework—in Chapter 10 of this volume.

NOTE ABOUT THE SOCIAL PRESELECTION OF MINISTERS

In this chapter I do not discuss the social recruitment of ministers. The selection process is preceded by a preselection process, which occurs long before the selection itself and would require a rather long analysis. The most important element of this preselection process is education. The university has always played the role of a sieve for high political positions.

At any moment in the Third Republic, fewer than 1 percent of young people between eighteen and twenty-five years of age were taking

university courses. Among parliamentarians we find that 60 percent held university diplomas, as did 85 percent of the ministers. The 15 percent of ministers without university diplomas were either journalists, educated in the excellent schools that are the editorial staffs of newspapers, or individuals trained in a party's ranks. The fact remains that a fraction of 1 percent of the population furnished 85 percent of the ministers.

Half the ministers of the Third Republic, 315 out of 631, had studied law (54 of these 315 had also undertaken literary studies). However, the faculties of law received at that time only 2 per 1,000 of all French young people. This preponderance of legally trained persons gives rise to two possible interpretations: either that legal studies constitute a good preparation for a political career or that young persons with ambitions for undertaking such careers prefer orienting themselves toward law schools. Whatever the case, a preselection of ministers occurred a generation beforehand. Let us place ourselves at a given moment in 1880: We are among law students (who were not yet aware of it), from whom the majority of the ministers of the first decade of the next century would be recruited. At the turn of the century, the amphitheaters of law schools were the nurseries of ministers of the interwar period.

Under the Fourth Republic, this situation did not change: Nearly half the ministers, 109 out of 227, were trained in law; about 20 of them also held liberal arts degrees. As for the selective Ecole Polytechnique, the 85 ministers of the Third Republic and the 6 of the Fourth Republic who had graduated from it were mostly military officers, appointed especially as ministers of war. The small number of ministers trained in the sciences is noteworthy: only 9 from 1870 to 1940, to whom one can add 13 engineers (Dogan 1961, pp. 57–90).

The Ecole des Sciences Politiques trained most senior civil servants: There were 177 treasury inspectors in 1955, 225 members of the State Council or of the Audit Office. But this school produced few ministers during the Third Republic and only 16 Fourth Republic ministers. Under the Third Republic, the professors' training school, the Ecole Normale Supérieure, was more politicized than all other selective schools. It was the preeminent school for politicians, among whom were Jean Jaurès, Painlevé, Raymond Poincaré, Thomas, Edouard Herriot, and many others. Since 1945, however, it has been less productive of political personnel. For the privileged ones who graduated from these major schools, the principal difficulty seemed to be getting elected, one of the reasons for this being their residence in Paris. But once elected, they had a one-out-of-two chance of reaching the ministerial level. In fact, half the deputies who graduated from these schools became min-

isters. The political elite is thus not the fruit of spontaneous generation. It prepares itself long ahead of time—twenty, thirty, or forty years beforehand.

REFERENCES

Barthelemy, Joseph, *Essai sur le travail parlementaire et le systeme des commissions,* Paris, 1934.
Caillaux, Joseph, *Mes memoires,* vol. 1, *Ma Jeunesse orgueilleuse,* Paris, 1942.
Dogan, Mattei, "La stabilité du personnel parlementaire sous la IIIe République," *Revue Française de science politique,* no. 2, 1953, pp. 319–348.
_____,"Political Ascent in a Class Society: French Deputies," in Dwaine Marvick, ed., *Political Decision-Makers,* New York, 1961, pp. 57–90.
_____, "Le personnel politique et la personnalité charismatique," *Revue Française de sociologie* 6, July-September 1965, pp. 305–324.
_____, "Les filières de la carrière politique en France," *Revue Française de sociologie* 8, October-December 1967, pp. 468–492.
Estier, Claude, *Mitterrand President: Journal d'une victoire,* Paris, Stock, 1981.
Porte, Suzanne de la, *La République sous l'Empire,* Paris, 1939.
Soulie, A., *L'instabilité ministérielle sous la IIIe République,* Paris, 1939.
Viansson-Ponte, Pierre, *Les Gaullists, rituel et annuaire,* Paris, 1963.
Willson, F.M.G., "The Routes of Entry of New Members of the British Cabinet 1868–1958," *Political Studies* 7, October 1959, pp. 222–232.

2
PRESIDENTIAL PERSONNEL AND POLITICAL CAPITAL: FROM ROOSEVELT TO REAGAN

Margaret Jane Wyszomirski

The development of the American federal executive has been rather like that of the British Empire—both were characterized by a dearth of forethought and of clarity of purpose. Such "adhocracy"[1] is especially apparent in the foremost and most important component of the executive: the cabinet.

Collectively, the cabinet has been regarded as having great political significance, little organizational coherence or consistency, and variable policy influence. Historically (as well as currently), cabinet agencies have varied considerably with regard to importance, whether judged in terms of size, age, complexity, or programmatic responsibilities. Individually, the members of the cabinet exhibit an array of origins, abilities, and loyalties. Additionally, individual cabinet secretaries have performed a variety of roles with varying degrees of proficiency and have had quite disparate relations with their respective presidents. Yet, despite this intrainstitutional variability, cabinet appointments are publicly and politically regarded as the most important action of a new president.[2]

Given the cabinet's chameleon-like and diverse character, its study presents distinct conceptual difficulties. Indeed, as a political institution, the cabinet rests only upon the shifting sands of a "completely customary basis."[3] Moreover, attempts to analyze the staffing patterns of the cabinet have been hindered both by the ambiguity of the institution and the polyarchical bases for power—either political or otherwise—in U.S. society. Nonetheless, political recruitment and circulation may be analyzed productively by shifting the focus of concern away from the

cabinet as a political institution. As an institution, the cabinet is both discontinuous and variegated in terms of its personnel. It must, therefore, exhibit some other element of continuity. That element can be seen in the purpose of the institution.[4] At least since the rise of the modern presidency with Franklin Roosevelt (FDR), a major purpose of the cabinet has been to provide presidents with political capital. Each president requires political capital if he is to fulfill his roles and responsibilities as executive, as legislator, as policy designer and advocate, and as preeminent democratic politician. Although the cabinet is surely not the sole source of a president's political capital, it is nonetheless an important source.[5]

In addressing its primary purpose, the cabinet and its members are called upon to act in the following capacities, either singly or in combination:

- representative link
- political operations assistant
- departmental administrator
- expert policy adviser

The prospect for effective performance in each role can be associated with certain skills, experience, and other individual characteristics. If situational factors do not create hindering or countervailing conditions, then cabinet appointees who possess such qualities and qualifications should be assets to the president, increasing his political capital in terms of policy expertise, administrative competence, political skills, and/or political support. Ideally, cabinet secretaries will be able to augment the president's resources on more than one of these dimensions. Certainly it is logical to assume that presidents seek to maximize their capital accumulation by means of appointees who represent resources of more than one type.

It must be recognized that such political capital can be useful both in affirmatively advancing the president's agenda and in protecting his balance of resources from unnecessary depletion through error or mischance. Such "preventive assistance" would include using political skills to help keep congressional-executive relations cordial so as not to prejudice prospects for positive cooperation. It would also include the use of administrative skills to conduct departments in such a way as to avoid unnecessarily burdening the president. These preventive contributions to the president's political capital are rather like tax exemptions: Their impact is "measurable by contrast to what the consequences (or costs) might have been if the situation were otherwise."[6]

Using the concept of political capital to orient an examination of cabinet recruitment and circulation reveals a number of both long- and short-term patterns. For example, the varieties of political capital that the cabinet members can provide are not of fixed or equal portions. Rather, the relative portion of different kinds of political capital acquired through cabinet recruitment varies both with time and with specific cabinet position. Circulation patterns can also be discerned and related to such factors as the ideological distinctiveness of the president's political philosophy, the character of a president's requirement for the loyalty of his "lieutenants," the impact of other interacting political institutions, the influence of partisan differences, or the effect of circumstantial elements (such as whether it is a first or a second term for a given president, or whether it is the term of the in-term successor president).

Noteworthy with regard to circulation patterns is the apparent increase of administrative capital and the decrease of political skills and support capital that distinguishes initial cabinet appointees from their replacements and first-term cabinets from second-term ones. Additionally, turnover rates and patterns do not vary consistently throughout the cabinet; that is, the costs of replacements (especially in terms of administrative and expertise capital) are frequently minimized by patterns of internal promotion. On a more general level, one can see the trend toward an increasingly deinstitutionalized cabinet. The concomitant weakening of institutional boundaries between the cabinet and the Executive Office of the President (EOP) is clearly indicated by the increasing frequency of personnel circulation between these two presidential organizations.

The analysis will open with a historical survey of structural variation within the cabinet and of broad trends in personnel recruitment and circulation. It will then present an administration profile of the cabinet recruitment processes and patterns of each of the presidents from Franklin Roosevelt to Ronald Reagan. Next, it will discuss in detail the capital considerations that have characterized cabinet recruitment with regard to the political skills and political support assets of appointees. Finally, a brief concluding section will discuss the changing role of the cabinet in the modern American presidency.

THE CABINET: STRUCTURAL CHANGE AND CONTINUITY, 1933-1985

U.S. presidents have always had cabinets and probably always will. During the fifty-two years that separate Franklin Roosevelt's inauguration in March 1933 from the reinauguration of Ronald Reagan in

January 1985, the cabinet has experienced both notable changes and continuities.

Most fundamentally, what constitutes the cabinet has changed. The list of executive departments that cabinet officers head today is both different and expanded from what it was in Roosevelt's day. Although through much of the past half century the cabinet's size has hovered at ten, during the Harry Truman years it dipped to nine following the consolidation of the Departments of War and of Navy into a single Defense Department (1947). With the creation of the Department of Health, Education, and Welfare (HEW) in 1953, the number returned to ten. (HEW was reorganized and renamed the Department of Health and Human Services, or HHS, in 1979.) Beginning in the mid-1960s, a number of new executive departments were created, eventually increasing the cabinet's size to thirteen in 1985. These new departments include the Department of Housing and Urban Development (HUD) (1966), the Department of Transportation (1967), the Department of Energy (1977), and the Department of Education (1979). In addition, one department was transformed into a government corporation and transferred out of the cabinet (the Post Office Department, in 1970).

In a broader sense, the potential size of the cabinet has also been increased by the creation and inclusion of executive positions that carry cabinet rank but do not involve jurisdiction over an executive department. These may include the United Nations ambassador, the directors of the Central Intelligence Agency and of the Office of Management and Budget, and the special trade representative. Various presidents have, at different times, also extended cabinet status to other officials. For example, it is occasionally accorded to select EOP personnel such as Edwin Meese, who served as counsellor to the president during Reagan's first term or to John Foster Dulles, when he served as special consultant to President Dwight Eisenhower (DDE) in 1959. Similarly, during FDR's wartime administration the director of the Office of War Mobilization was considered to be of cabinet rank. Because none of these offices existed for the entire period under examination and because they are more appropriately treated as part of the EOP, these offices and their appointive heads have not been included in this discussion.

Although all executive department heads are part of the president's cabinet, all cabinet secretaries are not equally influential, nor do they all head agencies that preside over similar types of policy. Instead, the cabinet may be divided along two dimensions: influence and functional policy responsibility. According to influence, there are "inner" and "outer" cabinet departments.[7] Inner departments are vested with high priority responsibilities that bring their secretaries into close, continuing, and influential contact with the president. These have generally

included the Departments of State, Defense, Treasury, and Justice. Occasionally, as certain policy topics assume special priority in specific administrations, one or more of the other departments may temporarily assume inner status (for example, HEW during the early years of Lyndon Johnson's Great Society initiatives or the Department of Energy during the early part of the Jimmy Carter presidency).

All other cabinet offices (interior, post office, agriculture, commerce, labor, HEW, HUD, transportation, and education) can be seen as usually occupying outer-cabinet status. Such outer departments are likely to be engaged in policy responsibilities that are not presidential priorities. They are also likely to experience unremitting competitive partisan and interest group pressures, to be subject to serious congressional oversight, and to administer programs that involve a considerable necessity for intergovernmental cooperation. In other words, outer-cabinet secretaries are likely to have distanced and sporadic contact with the president and to be drawn into assuming perspectives and priorities other than those of the chief executive. Consequently, such secretaries are often regarded as advocates of special interests rather than as the president's emissary to those constituencies. Furthermore, the programs of these departments are likely to involve considerable political controversy and, with that, the potential for political risk and costs for the president. Thus, these departments and their heads are pulled centrifugally away from the president since they are perceived as being unlikely to increase a president's resources and reputation but quite capable of diminishing them.

Although inner- and outer-cabinet groupings were evident during the Roosevelt years, their composition differed from what has come to be considered typical. During his first term, FDR's inner cabinet seemed to include only the secretaries of agriculture and labor. These officials administered key relief programs for groups that were critically affected by the domestic crisis. Hence they do conform to the pattern that inner-cabinet officers are those with high-priority policy responsibilities. What is unusual was the exclusion of all of those officers who are today considered to be likely candidates for inner-cabinet status. In this regard, FDR's first two terms were an anomaly. During his third term and in each cabinet thereafter, at least one, if not all, of the secretaries of state, defense, treasury, and justice had inner-cabinet status.

Moreover, although each department presides over a mix of policy concerns, cabinet departments can, nonetheless, be subdivided according to differences in type of functional policy responsibility. Using this dimension, one finds that there are three types of cabinet departments: those with a national policy responsibility, those with constituency-oriented policy concerns, and those that address issue-area concerns.[8]

National policy departments are those that manage comprehensive national concerns such as diplomatic relations, defense, finances, and legal affairs, or the Departments of State, Defense, Treasury, and Justice. These departments typically handle the kinds of public affairs that the founding fathers seemed to envision as comprising the major duties of a national executive.

Constituency-oriented departments deal with the concerns of a more particularized clientele and have usually been established at the insistence of an organized interest group. This subcategory includes the Departments of Agriculture, Commerce, Labor, and Education. The secretaries of such departments are frequently seen as advocates of their constituency's interests within the president's councils.

In addition, two other departments were originally established as national policy departments but evolved into constituency-oriented ones. Originally the Post Office Department was charged with maintaining a national communications service. During the 1830s, it acquired a second and constituency-oriented purpose of administering political patronage for the president's party. Thus, the postmaster general came to be regarded as the primary dispenser of the "spoils of victory" to the president's loyal partisans. Similarly, the Interior Department, established in 1849, had been created as a "home office," responsible for territorial governance, national highways and canals, and Indian affairs. Because these responsibilities were concentrated in the western sections of the country, the department gradually assumed the role of spokesperson for and protector of western regional interests. Thus, both the Post Office and the Interior departments evolved into constituency-oriented departments with the postmaster general concerned with a partisan constituency and the interior secretary with a geographic one.

Issue-area departments are those agencies that have been created to deal with complex and problematic issue areas. Generally these issue areas have reached a crisis level and are therefore deemed to demand the status and coordinated attention that can only be accorded by cabinet stature. These departments include HEW (now HHS), HUD, and Transportation.[9] The empowerment of each has occasioned intense political controversy, usually of an ideological cast. The creation of these departments is usually the expression of an active administration expanding into a domestic problem area.

The secretaries of each kind of department seem to be naturally associated with a particular role: National policy department heads tend to be presidential policy advisers, constituency-oriented-department secretaries tend to be representative links, and the heads of issue-area departments tend to be administrators. Additionally, all may be expected to provide at least preventive political assistance. However,

each may also be called upon to provide positive political assistance for particular items on the president's legislative agenda.

Finally, an overarching and subtle change has occurred pertaining to what constraints operate upon the "availability" of potential cabinet members[10] and upon the impediments to retaining incumbent cabinet secretaries. In FDR's day, the availability of preferred nominees was most frequently limited by considerations of ill health or by hesitation to forgo the prerogatives of elective office (particularly that of accrued seniority in Congress). Similarly, poor health or the desire to seek elective office were frequent factors limiting the retainability of cabinet members during the Roosevelt, Truman, and Eisenhower presidencies.

Roosevelt cabinet secretaries, George Dern and George Swanson, died in office, while Secretaries Harry Woodring, Cordell Hull, and Harry Hopkins all cut short their tenure because of poor health. Similarly, Truman's secretary of labor, Lewis B. Schwellenbach, died in office, while failing health limited George C. Marshall's service as secretary of state and later as secretary of defense. During Eisenhower's presidency, Secretary of State Dulles was forced to resign shortly before his death in 1959.

In terms of elective ambitions, both Naval Secretary Charles Edison and Agriculture Secretary Henry Wallace resigned at the end of FDR's second term to run for office, succeeding in becoming the governor of New Jersey and the vice president, respectively. Truman's secretary of agriculture, Clinton Anderson, resigned in spring 1948 to seek a Senate seat (and thereby add to the appeal of the national Democratic ticket in New Mexico). Similarly, Douglas McKay resigned as Eisenhower's first secretary of the interior to seek the Republican nomination for U.S. senator from Oregon and, in the process, to win a popular endorsement for the administration's power and resource development policies.[11]

The John F. Kennedy (JFK) administration marked a change in these availability and retainability factors. Between the 1960s and the mid-1980s only one cabinet secretary resigned because of serious health problems (Alexander Trowbridge, Johnson's secretary of commerce) and none died in office. Kennedy's Secretary of HEW, Abraham Ribicoff, was also the last cabinet secretary in the twenty-five years before 1986 to resign from the cabinet to campaign for high elective office (he succeeded in becoming U.S. senator from Connecticut in the 1962 election). Not until Jimmy Carter in 1977 did a modern president make more than a token effort to recruit incumbent elected officials: His initial cabinet appointees included incumbent Representative Robert Bergland and House Budget Committee Chairman Brock Adams, as well as incumbent Idaho governor Cecil Andrus.

Indeed, since the Kennedy administration, there seems to have been a tendency to recruit former elective politicians such as Orville Freeman and Luther Hodges (JFK), Donald Rumsfeld (Gerald Ford), Margaret Heckler and James Edwards (Reagan). Recent presidents have also tended to appoint elective officials whose tenure in office was "numbered," either by personal choice (for example, William Saxbe had announced his intention to retire at the end of his first Senate term before Richard Nixon appointed him attorney general in 1974) or by political circumstance (for example, governors such as John Volpe, George Romney, and Andrus had already been reelected to second terms and were facing practical and formal limits on their future statehouse tenures at the time they were recruited into the cabinets of Nixon and Carter). Clearly such former and departing officials are attractive executive recruits because they possess political skills and are relatively available. Nonetheless their potency as political allies is compromised because their independent political support base is likely to be outdated or eroding. Thus, the political capital to be gained from such appointees must be discounted accordingly. Similarly, the increasingly rare incidence of incumbent cabinet secretaries seeking (and winning) major elective offices (especially as senators or governors) has also diminished the opportunity of presidents to move appointive cabinet personnel into elective positions where they might prove to be helpful political allies in Congress or in the states.

Concurrently, the postwar period has seen the availability of potential cabinet personnel become increasingly constrained by economic considerations. Frequently, possible nominees have been reluctant to comply with stringent disclosure and conflict-of-interest requirements or unwilling to endure a substantial cut in pay that accepting a cabinet position would impose upon them.[12] Similar economic factors have also tended to limit the retainability of cabinet secretaries. Some individuals, particularly wealthy businessmen serving in Republican administrations, have been unwilling to leave their private financial affairs relatively untended or in blind trusts for more than two years. Hence financial considerations have contributed to cabinet instability and turnover since the Eisenhower administration.[13] Alternatively, other cabinet members choose to resign after only a short time in office so as to enhance their "marketability" as influential lobbyists while their administrative colleagues remain in office. This practice would include former Reagan cabinet secretaries Andrew Lewis and Richard Schweiker, both of whom resigned to take six-figure-salary positions in the private corporate sector. It has been even more prevalent among former

Reagan administration White House staff members such as Michael Deaver, Richard Allen, and Lyn Nofziger.

Historically, retainability of cabinet members has sporadically been affected by policy disagreement. Although this is common in most political systems, it generally takes the form of a resignation in protest by a cabinet member.[14] Such resignations, however, seldom occur in the United States.[15] More frequent in the U.S. situation is the presidential dismissal of a cabinet member who disagrees with the president's policy agenda in deed or in spirit. Such dismissals may take a variety of forms.

1. The face-saving, regretfully accepted resignation is generally used to fire the head of an inner-cabinet department such as defense or state. Examples include the 1975 "resignation" of James Schlesinger as President Ford's secretary of defense, the 1947 "resignation" of James Byrnes as Truman's secretary of state, and the 1983 "resignation" of Alexander Haig as President Reagan's secretary of state.

2. There can be a forced resignation followed by transfer to another post. Examples include Truman's reassignment of Secretary of State Edward Stettinius as United Nations ambassador or Reagan's transfer of HHS Secretary Margaret Heckler to become U.S. ambassador to Ireland.

3. A mutually agreed upon decision to part company can occur during the interim between the reelection and reinauguration of an incumbent president. This was the case with FDR's acceptance of Secretary of War Harry Woodring's resignation in June 1940; with Nixon's failure to retain Secretary of Transportation John Volpe or HUD Secretary George Romney beyond 1972; and with Reagan's willingness to see Education Secretary Terrel Bell resign at the end of 1984.

4. There can be an outright firing. Such instances are infrequent because they invariably diminish a president's political capital as well as incur additional political costs. Nonetheless, cabinet members have been explicitly fired, including Truman's dismissal of Secretary of Interior Harold Ickes in February 1946 and of Secretary of Commerce Henry Wallace in September 1946; Nixon's highly publicized firings of Interior Secretary Walter Hickel in November 1970 for disloyalty and of Attorney-General Elliot Richardson in October 1973, for insubordination. In addition, Carter's July 1979 Camp David Massacre involved the firing of HEW Secretary Joseph Califano and Treasury Secretary Michael Blumenthal as arrogant, uncooperative, and disloyal.[16]

CABINET RECRUITMENT: ROOSEVELT THROUGH REAGAN

The process of selecting presidential appointees (including cabinet members) has undergone important changes during the past half century. Although cabinet recruitment has become part of a more institutionalized staffing system, it nonetheless retains strong idiosyncratic and personalistic aspects. Post-World War II presidents have developed (and increasingly rely upon) elaborate personnel recruitment and talent-scouting systems to fill specialized administrative and subcabinet positions.[17] Nonetheless, they have preferred to manage cabinet appointment processes more directly. Hence the process of cabinet making is one of the most personal and least institutionalized aspects of presidential staffing.

Within this apparent commonality, however, presidents have followed notably different staffing approaches to achieve significantly different results. Roosevelt himself consulted widely to gather the names of potential appointees, made his own lists, and used unofficial aides to negotiate both with serious prospects and with politically influential pending rejects. Generally FDR seems to have begun with a fairly clear notion of which individuals he wanted (and perhaps needed) to recruit and of what characteristics and/or interests he wanted represented prominently in his administration.

FDR's staffing procedures exhibit both intimate presidential involvement and strong partisan considerations. In part, this relates to the state of two other political institutions—the presidency and political parties. As there was no official Executive Office of the President until 1939, Roosevelt could not turn to a White House staff to administer a personnel recruitment system. Hence his personal involvement in all stages of the staffing process was necessary. Conversely, in an era when political parties were still vital, FDR could and did rely more heavily than his successors on the leaders and good offices of the party to assist in the recruitment of political executives.

Roosevelt's initial cabinet was rich in political skills and representative capital. It included three elective politicians, four Democratic party leaders, and two Progressive Republicans who had campaigned for him in 1932. Furthermore, Henry Wallace was also an influential farm representative and an agricultural expert, while Frances Perkins was a precedent-setting (although symbolic) representative of the relatively newly enfranchised women's constituency. Cabinet membership was quite stable during FDR's first and much of his second term, thus allowing the cabinet to acquire considerable administrative capital. Administrative capital was further augmented by replacement appoin-

tees who were frequently promoted from the assistant or under secretary level. For his unprecedented third, wartime term, Roosevelt made an audacious bid for additional political capital by recruiting two leaders of the opposing Republican party as secretaries of the prestigious and important Departments of War and Navy.

Presidents Truman, Johnson, and Ford all inherited cabinets from their predecessors and faced the initial task of assessing cabinet carryovers, deciding whom they wanted to retain and ascertaining who wanted to leave office. Each of these presidents liked politics and had a well-developed sense of political calculation. Each also perceived a clear need to establish his own administration while maintaining continuity with that of his predecessor. Thus, each of these presidents bowed to political expediency in making or postponing their initial cabinet changes during the transitional phase of their presidency. For Truman and Johnson, the freedom to construct cabinets that were truly their own did not occur until after each had won election to the presidency in his own right (1948 and 1964). Since Ford was defeated in the 1976 election, he never exercised that prerogative. He did, however, have many opportunities to fill vacancies left in the wake of the crumbling Nixon administration.

Eisenhower had little experience with elective office, apparently little taste for political patronage, and a relatively limited civilian acquaintanceship network. Hence he delegated much of the recruitment effort to Republican power broker Herbert Brownell and to General Lucius Clay, a military colleague whose judgment of people the president trusted. Cabinet appointments were designated unusually quickly and with little consultation from leading congressional Republicans or the leadership of the Republican National Committee. Indeed, political concerns, both as to process and to the qualifications of appointees, were not the Eisenhower priority. Rather, administrative capability took precedence.

For those presidents elected by very narrow electoral margins, the need to acquire additional political capital is critical. Yet the very precariousness of their position may prompt such presidents-elect to be cautious about incurring the costs of new political alliances and make them suspicious of individuals who are not already known adherents. Thus, Presidents Kennedy, Nixon, and Carter faced the paradox that although their narrow electoral victories made the need for additional political capital a crucial necessity, those same electoral conditions constrained their willingness and ability to assume the political costs or risks required to acquire that political capital through an entrepreneurial cabinet appointment strategy.

Close-contest presidents have apparently tried to address this paradox through three staffing options. These include: attempts to expand political resources by recruiting political allies who can command political skills and support; accumulation of expertise capital in the hope of attracting new support to what is anticipated to be an attractive and well-designed policy agenda; or appointment of managers to implement an administrative strategy of presidential control and accomplishment. In part, which of these options a president selects will depend upon his personality and his opportunities. A president who is personally self-confident, who likes politics, and who is willing to bargain is likely to follow the first option. Although this strategy is likely to require the president to exercise considerable political skill to negotiate personally for the support of allies, it also seems to add to his political capital and hence improve his chances for effectiveness in office. Because this strategy poses particularly unwelcome costs and risks for a narrowly elected president, it may be a more appealing strategy for presidents elected with a more substantial margin of support, such as Roosevelt in his first and third terms of office.

Alternatively, a president with less self-assurance or who has an intellectual rather than a political sense of confidence may opt for the second course. The same may apply for those presidents who have little taste for politicking or who feel, either on the basis of principle or political precariousness, that they will not or cannot bargain for support. Rather they must attempt to persuade others by the sheer merit of their proposals. Hence such presidents may follow an expert recruitment strategy.

Finally, presidents lacking a basic sense of self-confidence may be suspicious of both politicians and experts; hence they may recruit administrators in an attempt to minimize both their potential political alliance costs and the risks of potentially disloyal or independent-minded allies and/or experts. Of these three options, Presidents Kennedy and Carter seem to have adopted the expert recruitment strategy with touches of a political alliance approach. In contrast, Presidents Nixon and Reagan opted for the administrative staffing strategy[18] combined with elements of a political strategy.

JFK's personnel recruitment system emphasized a search for the "best and the brightest" along with the recognition that his very narrow electoral victory required efforts to broaden his base of political support. A recruitment system dubbed Talent Hunt was organized to locate, screen, and recommend possible appointees. At the cabinet level, Kennedy was actively involved in soliciting information on prospective appointees and interviewed many of the candidates personally. The result was a cabinet of "safe" appointees keyed to providing "preventive

assistance" politically as well as a modicum of administrative and expert capital.

Richard Nixon, elected by a mere plurality of 43 percent of the popular vote and facing opposing Democratic majorities in both houses of Congress, was both politically more precarious than Kennedy and personally less self-assured. Hence he tried to minimize the risks of possible unpredictability or undependability by selecting individuals who were known by him personally or known to him from prior service in the Eisenhower administration. Most of those individuals had demonstrated administrative ability in the private and/or public spheres. In addition, Nixon appointed four elective politicians—Hickel, Melvin Laird, Romney, and Volpe—who possessed political skills and served as representatives of the liberal wing of the Republican party. Lastly, President Nixon seems to have regarded expertise rather than representative capital as a better staffing investment (more dependable and less politically costly) in selecting secretaries for the constituency-oriented departments. For example, an agricultural economist rather than a farmer came to head the Agriculture Department (Clifford Hardin), and an industrial relations and economics professor was chosen as secretary of labor (George Shultz) rather than a union representative. Only one appointee—William Blount, who lasted only eleven months—had substantial links to a political interest group (he had been president of the U.S. Chamber of Commerce).

Jimmy Carter, like Kennedy, also sought the best, but defined merit largely in terms of expertise, rather than as preventive assistance. Furthermore, Carter had campaigned as a political outsider who was highly critical of the Washington establishment and who was intent upon recruiting a new generation of leadership. Although he was narrowly elected, this circumstance did not prompt Carter to employ a coalition-building strategy of cabinet recruitment. Instead he allowed his personal distaste for political expediency to reinforce his view of the 1976 election as a personal triumph that evoked little sense of obligation to reward with high office those political interests that had contributed to his electoral coalition. Thus, Carter's cabinet recruitment process became something of a cross between the styles of Eisenhower and Kennedy. Like Eisenhower, he largely eschewed the counsel of party leaders in Congress and at the national committee. Like Kennedy, he was intimately involved in finding the most qualified person for each position. Additionally, Carter wanted cabinet secretaries who would be both capable advisers and who would be compatible with others in their policy areas.[19] The resultant cabinet exhibited considerable advisory expertise but was deficient in administrative, political, and representative resources.

In contrast to most other presidents, Reagan delegated much of the initial name gathering and the screening responsibilities to others, particularly his "kitchen cabinet" and White House staff.[20] When all these preliminary hurdles had been cleared, President Reagan was presented with a list of three to five prospects for each cabinet office. In most cases, the president made his choice from this list.

Like FDR, Reagan had some clear ideas about what he wanted in cabinet appointees. He "wanted officers who would be 'managers of the national administration, not captives of the bureaucracy of special interests in the department they were supposed to direct'"[21] and who "shared his belief in Cabinet government."[22] He was also said to "want some new faces . . . not just . . . a rehash of people who've already been there."[23] He was also interested in finding a woman, a black, and perhaps a Democrat.[24] Furthermore, as Reagan was intent upon a new and more conservative ideological course and was stylistically inclined to delegate significant authority to cabinet officers, philosophical compatability or loyalty was a key recruitment criterion.[25]

The circumstances of Reagan's electoral victory also affected his cabinet staffing pattern. First, having won the 1980 election by a substantial popular vote margin, Reagan saw little need to expand the electoral coalition for governing purposes. Second, Reagan personally had been the focus of considerable positive and negative comment during the campaign. These concerns ranged from his affable congeniality and effective communications skills to his age and questionable job qualifications. Such a personalistic campaign focus, combined with the decisive electoral results, minimized the likelihood that Reagan would make any "celebrity" appointments to his cabinet. Rather he would prefer to retain center stage himself.

Consequently, Reagan's initial cabinet appointments were rich in administrative skills and predominantly of a conservative ideological cast, especially with regard to policy issues that fell within their specific departmental jurisdictions. Expertise was in relatively short supply. Political skills were also relatively scarce but were concentrated in departments involved in matters high on the president's policy and legislative agendas. Finally, the representative capital of the first Reagan cabinet was minimal and merely symbolic.

CAPITAL CONSIDERATIONS

Presidential appointees can be an important source of political capital. Four types of political capital have been identified: policy expertise, administrative competence, political operations skill, and political interest group support. A comprehensive analysis of patterns of presi-

dential capital accumulation of all four types of capital during the past fifty years is beyond the scope of this paper. Instead the preceding president-specific profiles have presented a general sense of how these combined and patterned in each presidency. What follows are the analyses of a selection of important patterns pertaining to the most explicitly political types of political capital.

Political Skills

Such skills are best acquired and polished through active engagement in public affairs. This may be done from authoritative bases or from informal ones. Authoritative bases may include tenure as the member of a legislature or as a political executive who has dealt with the legislature, such as a governor or a big city mayor or as the director of a major federal agency that has had extensive contact with Congress. Informal experience is most likely gained through experience as a lobbyist for an interest group. The different routes toward acquiring these political skills might be considered as the "insider" and "outsider" routes, respectively.

Given the necessity for collaboration between the president and Congress, skills pertaining to the legislative process are highly valuable. It seems logical to assume that those who have acquired these skills via the insider route are likely to have additional qualitative advantages over outsiders in that the insiders have established reputational and social networks that they can draw upon and that enhance their credibility with other political officials. It therefore follows that congressional representatives are the most valuable source of political skills, that the utility of nonfederal elected executives may be limited by their relative unfamiliarity with the specifics of the national political scene, and that outsiders may have considerable skill but comparatively little independent legitimacy for its exercise. Thus, to maximize their investment in political skills capital, presidents would be wise to recruit members of Congress and, secondarily, governors. Furthermore, incumbent officials are likely to carry greater cachet than former officials, with the utility of their social networks and legitimacy declining in proportion to the length of time out of office and the circumstances under which they left office. Conversely, this utility would increase according to their institutional position and seniority (for example, as chairman of a congressional committee or as governor of a major state).

During the past five and a half decades, Democratic presidents have sought such political capital with more consistency than have Republican presidents. For example, in an unlikely pair, FDR and Carter had the most success in recruiting prestigious congressional incumbents.

FDR recruited Senate committee chairmen Cordell Hull and George Swanson in 1933. Later he brought in Henry Stimson and Jesse Jones—two highly respected federal executives known for their ability to work with Congress. Carter initially recruited the chairman of the House Budget Committee and later appointed Senator Edward Muskie as a replacement secretary of state. Additionally, Carter also appointed one incumbent congressman, one governor (of Idaho), and two big-city mayors.

Although other Democratic presidents sought to recruit politically skilled individuals, they followed less prestigious patterns. Truman generally settled for former members of Congress who had gone on to federal judgeships, such as Schwellenbach, Vinson, Byrnes, or McGranary. He supplemented these with the acquired skills of a number of experienced federal administrators. JFK mixed one relatively junior representative with three governors (one an incumbent and the other two not), and a big-city mayor. Even though these appointees were quite successful in terms of preventive political assistance, they were less able to move Kennedy's policies through Congress to enactment. Lyndon Johnson (LBJ) paid surprisingly scant attention to political skills among his cabinet personnel, retaining only two of Kennedy's original political appointees but recruiting none himself. Perhaps, given Johnson's own considerable political skills, he felt little need for additional political skills among cabinet members.

In contrast, Republican presidents have made fewer and weaker efforts to use cabinet appointments to increase their political skills capital. Throughout his eight years in office, Eisenhower only had the services of an interim-appointed, former senator (Seaton at interior) and two governors (Christian Herter—Massachusetts and Douglas McKay—Oregon). Nixon also tended to tap governors as his initial appointees (Volpe, Romney, and Hickel), as well as selecting Representative Melvin Laird. Later, Nixon brought in former Texas Governor John Connally, retiring junior Senator William Saxbe, and incumbent Representative Rogers Morton. Although the total number of politicians in the Nixon administration looks impressive, this belies the record of their performance. Both Saxbe and Morton were brought in to attempt political damage control. Governors Romney and Hickel apparently used their political skills to work for policies *not* high on the president's agenda and thus came to be regarded by the president as political liabilities rather than assets. Thus, the net political advantage of these appointees was considerably less than it might appear. Finally, Presidents Ford and Reagan each recruited only one legislator. Ford tapped his former House colleague Donald Rumsfeld, and Reagan recruited incumbent Senator Richard Schweiker.

A possible explanation for the infrequency with which Republican presidents appoint members of Congress or governors into their cabinets may be in the relatively small recruitment pool of such individuals. For the past fifty years the Republicans have been the minority party. As such, Republican presidents have fewer elected partisans to consider for executive appointments. For example, in 1966 only seventeen states had Republican governors and in 1981 only twenty-one states did. Thus when Presidents Nixon and Reagan came to office there were relatively few Republican governors to select from and even fewer who had served long enough to be available for federal office. Similarly, the Republicans have held majorities in either houses of Congress for only eight of the past fifty-two years. Thus there are fewer Republican members of Congress for Republican presidents to recruit and few of those will have had the opportunity to have exercised leadership as committee chairmen. Furthermore, as Republican capture of both houses in 1952 and of the Senate in 1980 coincided with the election of new Republican presidents, many Republicans in Congress in those years were essentially unavailable for cabinet office because they were only just assuming the powers and prerogatives of seniority and majority control.

Of course, an alternative source of political skills has historically resided in the political parties. Indeed party functionaries, even if they have never held elective office, are likely to be adept political operants. However, their practice in coalition building has often been gained through activity in nomination and campaign politics rather than in governance. Virtually every president has recruited such political operants into the cabinet, with the campaign director, the party chairman, or the party campaign finance chairman being most frequently rewarded with cabinet office.

Historically, the postmaster generalship went to one of these party officials (for example, James Farley [FDR], Robert Hannegan [HST], Arthur Summerfield [DDE], and Lawrence O'Brien [LBJ]). Additionally, modern presidents have sometimes appointed such campaign supporters to inner-cabinet posts (such as Lovett to defense [HST], Robert Kennedy [JFK] and Herbert Brownell [DDE] as attorneys-general). One must, however, note that in a period of declining political parties and of increasingly individualized campaigning, the political skills gained in party positions are likely to be particularly attuned to the mobilization of electoral coalitions rather than readily transferable to the task of assembling and maintaining governing coalitions.

The decrease and diminution of political skills capital in the cabinet has been erratic and subtle; the significance of this change is nonetheless apparent. A growing chorus of observers and critics has pointed to the

difficulty presidents have in forming "a government"[26] or in converting their electoral coalition into a governing one.[27] Whereas some attribute this problem to split partisan control of the institutions of Congress and of the presidency (for instance, during the Nixon, Ford, and Reagan years), it is equally true that Kennedy and Carter fared no better with solid Democratic party control of both Congress and the White House. Conversely, Presidents Truman and Eisenhower seemed to have dealt effectively with opposition-controlled Congresses. Thus, awareness of a less politically efficacious presidency with regard to Congress seems to coincide with the noted decline in the political skills capital available in the cabinet. Although not the sole cause of this worsening performance, changes in cabinet recruitment patterns certainly seem to be a contributory factor.

Aside from the frequency and the potency of political skills in the cabinet, anecdotal evidence indicates that the advantageous use of such resources has declined. For example, recent presidents seem highly prone to firing or losing skilled politicians-turned-cabinet-members. Conversely, one encounters frequent references to bad congressional relations as a reason for the turnover of cabinet personnel.

The decline of political skills capital in the cabinet has, no doubt, been affected by the expansion of political advice and assistance available within the EOP. Since the establishment of a White House staff, it has been customary for presidents to move key campaign aides into staff positions. With the proliferation of agencies within the EOP as well as the growth of the White House staff, presidents have had many opportunities to retain and reward campaign assistants with staff jobs. Indeed, campaign chairmen were appointed to senior White House staff positions by Kennedy and Carter, whereas both Carter and Reagan appointed the national party chairman as EOP special trade representative.

Within the White House staff a special office for congressional liaison was initiated by President Eisenhower and maintained and expanded by subsequent presidents. Thus it would appear that presidential staff agencies have become a locus of political skills capital rather than the cabinet. Such presidential staff resources are not, however, completely comparable substitutes for political allies in the cabinet. First, the skills of many such campaign assistants are geared to electoral politics rather than governance; the newer breed of political operants tends to be candidate centered and politically dependent upon a specific president, in contrast to the older type that was more politically independent and party centered. Second, the White House Congressional Liaison Office, unlike cabinet politicians, seldom adds to a president's political capital; rather, its staff assists him in utilizing already available resources when

he deals with Congress. Indeed, the existence of such an office does not guarantee that it will function successfully. For example, President Carter's congressional assistants were notorious for their ineptitude and consequently for diminishing the president's political capital.

Political Support

It is commonly held that "the chief significance" of the cabinet is that it "offers an opportunity for consolidating political strength through a coalition of leaders whose adherence brings the strength of their political following to the administration."[28] During the past fifty years, however, there has been a decreasing tendency to recruit actual political leaders who can command either partisan or constituency support. The decrease of partisan leaders is, in part, related to the declining incidence of former elected officials with their attendant political skills. But it is also due to the increasing tendency (and indeed necessity) of presidents to seek support beyond their own party base. Hence most modern presidents have deviated from the historic norm of partisan purity when appointing their cabinet. Perhaps the most common strategy has been to appoint representatives of "opposition" party factions that have already begun to shift their allegiance. For example, FDR's appointments of Progressive Republicans, Henry Wallace and Harold Ickes, were meant to confirm both their personal and their constituency's support during the 1932 election campaign. Similarly, the appointments of Oveta Culp Hobby and Robert Anderson brought nominal Texas Democrats into Eisenhower's administration when he was seeking to consolidate the electoral support of moderate Southern Democrats who had voted for him in 1952 and 1956. Richard Nixon sought to appeal to the same geographic constituency with his appointment of a Democrat and former governor of Texas, John Connally.

From a different perspective, Connally's 1971 appointment also illustrates the importance of timing in announcing such cabinet replacements. Thus, Connally's appointment was part of Nixon's 1972 campaign strategy to gain support from the traditionally Democratic southern states. Likewise, FDR's June 1940 appointments of a former Republican secretary of state and of a former vice presidential nominee were intended to attract bipartisan support for his unprecedented bid for a third term. Similarly Ford's appointments of Southern Democrats William Usery and F. David Mathews were part of the long-term Republican campaign to realign the support of Southern Democrats and of the pending Ford campaign to win southern votes in 1976.

Again, a subtle shift in the potency of such partisan representative capital must be noted. Beginning with Eisenhower, the tendency has

been to seek to appoint *nominal* members of the opposition party rather than leaders within the opposition. Both Hobby and Anderson were active in Democrats for Eisenhower, but this represented a candidate-centered group rather than an enduring partisan realignment. Kennedy appointed registered Republicans, Douglas Dillon and Robert McNamara; these gentlemen were not party leaders or spokesmen but rather symbolic representatives of the opposition party. Johnson's appointment of Republican foundation executive, John Gardner, was of a similar cast. Ford appointed not only symbolic Democrats like Usery and Mathews but also the avowed independent Edward Levi and the apparently nonpartisan Henry Kissinger. Finally, Carter appointed veteran Republican administrator James Schlesinger to serve as his first energy secretary.

A related development indicative of an era of shifting partisan allegiances concerns the recruitment of former members of the opposition party who have switched party identification shortly before being appointed or soon after appointment. This phenomenon is especially noteworthy within Republican administrations. For instance, Democrats-turned-Republicans include Secretaries Hobby and Anderson of the Eisenhower administration; and cabinet members Blount, James Hodgson, and Connally in the Nixon administration. President Reagan and his first UN Ambassador Jeane Kirkpatrick are themselves well-known ex-Democrats. With the exception of Progressive Republicans-turned-Democrats Wallace and Ickes of Roosevelt's presidency, none of the Republicans in Democratic administrations underwent such conversions.

Aside from partisan representatives, political support capital can also be accumulated through the appointment of interest group representatives. Indeed, this would seem particularly appropriate among the nominees to head the constituency-oriented Departments of Agriculture, Commerce, and Labor. Indeed there is strong precedent for the recruitment of just such representatives at Agriculture and Labor, although interest group leaders can be placed in any cabinet position. Here again it would seem that presidents have had an increasing tendency to discount the potential value of such appointments by selecting instead symbolic representatives or special interest administrators.

The trend toward special interest administrators rather than leaders is perhaps most clearly seen at two of the historic clientele departments. For example, while each secretary of agriculture is expected to own a farm and figuratively "to have dirt under his fingernails," Henry Wallace (FDR) may have been the last actual agricultural leader to head the department. Since then, the secretaries have generally been state or national agricultural administrators (for example, Claude Wickard [FDR],

Ezra Taft Benson [DDE], Charles Brannan [Truman], and John Block [Reagan]) or academic agricultural economists (Clifford Hardin [Nixon], Earl Butz [Ford]). Occasionally a former member of Congress who had served on food or agriculture committees (Clinton Anderson [Truman], Robert Bergland [Carter]) has been recruited to this post. Whereas such appointees are usually acceptable to the farm constituency, it is clear that they function as the president's spokesman to farmers rather than as farm-leader-as-member-of-the-administration. At least one recent secretary of agriculture was actively opposed by farmers upon his nomination (Earl Butz).

Somewhat similarly, the secretaries of labor display a rather paradoxical pattern, with union leaders often recruited by Republican administrations while Democratic presidents tend toward naming labor lawyers and mediators. FDR started this line of nonlabor leaders with the appointment of Frances Perkins. Truman followed with Lewis Schwellenbach, a former senator who would stay clear of the then-current factional struggles within labor; he was succeeded by a former mayor who had good ties to labor (Maurice Tobin). Kennedy first appointed labor lawyer Arthur Goldberg; then he (and later Johnson) turned to lawyer and labor negotiator Willard Wirtz. Carter tapped an academic labor economist who had served on a number of governmental advisory commissions concerning manpower issues (F. Ray Marshall). Thus the Democrats, long identified as the party of the worker, did not appoint a single labor leader to head the Labor Department during the fifty year period before 1986.

In contrast, Republican presidents have named nearly as many union leaders as industrial management specialists to this post. For example, Eisenhower's first labor secretary was Martin Durkin, a Democrat and the president of the United Association of Plumbers. Similarly, Nixon recruited Peter Brennan, who was also a Democrat and the head of the Building and Construction Trade Council of Greater New York, while Ford selected International Association of Machinists activist, William Usery. Since the tenure of all these recruits has been short and relatively stormy, one may question the ultimate utility of what is clearly a bold bid to attract unorthodox coalition partners. Alternatively, other Republican labor secretaries have been industrial relations experts and administrators, such as James Mitchell, George Shultz, James Hodgson, John Dunlop, and Raymond Donovan. Thus, with the exception of gestures to demonstrate an "above politics as usual" style (as with Eisenhower's appointment of Durkin) or to woo electoral support in an upcoming election (Usery), the labor secretaries have been only symbolic representatives of their nominal constituency and

therefore could bring little additional political support capital to the presidents who appointed them.

Minority interests have also come to be represented in the cabinet, though these appointees have been rare, tended to cluster in issue-area departments, and to occupy outer-cabinet influence status. During the period from Roosevelt to Reagan, eight women have been named to the cabinet, six of these since 1975. Four of the nine presidents from FDR to Reagan have not appointed even one woman to their cabinets, whereas the two most recent presidents (Carter and Reagan) have each named more than one. Thus, female cabinet members account for a mere 4 percent of all secretaries who have served since 1933, and 11 percent of those who have served in the decade preceding 1986. These figures indicate both the persistent underrepresentation of women in the highest councils of government as well as recognition of their growing political significance in modern U.S. society. Nevertheless, none of the appointees could be considered to be representatives of women in any politically organized sense. Rather, they were symbolic representatives of their gender constituency. As such, they added little in actual political support capital to the administrations for which they were recruited. Indeed, most were appointed for a complex of reasons and attributes of which their gender was a contributory, rather than a decisive, factor.

For example, FDR had wanted a woman in his cabinet. He also needed a competent labor administrator but did not want a union leader. In Frances Perkins, he found the combination of characteristics that he sought. From a different perspective, Oveta Culp Hobby (HEW, 1953-1955) and Patricia Harris (HUD, 1977-1979; HHS, 1979-1981) were recruited for the political support they commanded rather than for the interest group they merely symbolized. Hobby had helped bring many Texas Democrats into Eisenhower's winning electoral coalition, and Harris was a respected civil rights activist and a black Democrat.

Other considerations of symbolic politics entered into the appointments of Elizabeth Dole (Transportation, 1981-1986) and Margaret Heckler (HHS, 1983-1986). President Reagan's midterm selection of these women marked an attempt to bridge the "gender gap" as well as to enhance party unity and to cushion an electoral defeat.[29] In another instance, it was widely rumored that President Carter's 1979 appointment of Shirley Hufstadler as head of the new Department of Education was a step toward her eventual appointment to the Supreme Court. Juanita Kreps, a Duke University labor economist named as commerce secretary (1977), may be considered a counterclientele appointment made to mute the voice of business in the Carter administration.[30] Only Carla Hills (HUD, 1975-1977) was apparently selected for little

reason other than that she was female and that President Ford's wife had convinced him that there should be more women in high government positions. Finally, it must be noted that both the utility and influence of these women were limited by factors other than political support capital. Virtually none had experience in electoral office and hence had had little opportunity to acquire proficient political skills. Only Margaret Heckler had successfully run for elective office, while Patricia Harris had gained some experience in party politics. Conversely, Perkins, Hobby, and Dole had seen prior service as appointive public administrators but none of them at the agency they were to head. Furthermore, none of the female cabinet members could make a strong claim to substantive expertise in their areas of responsibility. Thus, these individuals possessed few administrative, expertise, or political assets that might have enhanced their utility to or influence with the president.

Additionally, women secretaries have rarely been positioned to become part of a president's inner circle, either by personal friendship or by appointive position. Of the eight female cabinet members, only Frances Perkins could be considered a presidential confidant or the head of a department central to the president's policy agenda. None of the others could claim a close personal relationship with her president. Each of these seven was appointed to head a department that was low among or antagonistic to the president's priorities or else was newly established and beset by the problems of bureaucratic birth. In other words, female cabinet appointees have seldom added substantially to a president's political capital and have rarely exercised significant influence within an administration.

Even fewer blacks and no Hispanics have been appointed to the modern cabinet. Lyndon Johnson was the first president to appoint a black, naming Robert Weaver to head the new Department of Housing and Urban Development. Weaver was a Harvard-trained economist who had served as a New Deal agency adviser on minority affairs and later as a New York City housing administrator and as head of the federal Housing and Home Finance Agency. With the exception of Nixon, subsequent presidents have each named one black to their cabinets: William Coleman, Jr. (1975–1977), Patricia Harris (1977–1981) and Samuel Pierce (1981–1986). Each of these has been appointed to head an issue-area department responsible for programs of particular importance to minorities. Most frequently, this post has been the Housing and Urban Development Department (Weaver, Harris, and Pierce). In addition, Coleman, a respected transportation lawyer, headed the Transportation Department; Patricia Harris served at HHS as well as at HUD. The Department of Transportation and HHS both admin-

ister programs of importance to inner-city and low-income minority citizens.

As interest group representatives, Harris and, especially, Coleman brought considerable political capital to their appointing presidents. Harris, in addition to being a symbolic representative of women, had been active in Democratic party circles on civil rights issues. Whereas both Weaver and Harris might be considered well educated, successful, and prominent members of the black community, neither had the constituency stature of William Coleman. Educated at Harvard School of Law, then a law clerk to Supreme Court Justice Felix Frankfurter, Coleman had coauthored the brief for the hallmark desegregation case of *Brown v. Board of Education* in 1954. In 1971, he was elected president of the National Association for the Advancement of Colored People (NAACP) Legal Defense and Education Fund. In recruiting Coleman (who was also a lifelong Republican), President Ford gained considerable political support capital from an interest group that seldom identified with the modern Republican party. Reaching out to blacks (and women) through executive appointments was but one of the many efforts made by President Ford to help restore legitimacy and public support for the discredited government he had inherited in the wake of the Watergate scandal and President Nixon's resignation.

In contrast, the Reagan administration gained little political capital from the appointment of Samuel Pierce in 1981. A New York labor lawyer who had served in the prior Republican administrations of Eisenhower and Nixon, Pierce was no minority leader and did little to improve relations between the Reagan presidency and black Americans.

SOME FINAL OBSERVATIONS

Preceding sections have examined internal and historical variations in the staffing of the president's cabinet from 1932 to 1986. Despite its discontinuous character, the cabinet has persistently functioned as a mechanism and resource of presidential governance. Cabinet personnel have been treated herein as bearers of political capital that may add to a president's capacity to govern. Although the discussion has focused on capital of the political skills and political support variants, even this limited focus is suggestive of broad aspects of the evolution and problems of the modern presidency.

The scarcity of experienced politicians as well as of interest group leaders illustrates one way in which the quest for managerial control by the chief executive has hindered the presidency as a political institution. Indeed, the evidence suggests that the cabinet has atrophied as a political institution whose members are skilled political operants and/

or potent political allies. Rather, the political qualities of cabinet personnel have become virtually residual. Constituency representatives are merely symbolic (not actual) group leaders, and politicians who have lost or are losing their political base are more frequently recruited than those who can command their own independent power base. Although this tendency deprives presidents of certain political assets, it nonetheless has the virtue of producing cabinet secretaries who are likely to be dependent on and therefore relatively controlled by presidents. Because this is in contrast to the historic independence of self-sufficient politicians who served in earlier cabinets, the trend toward technocrats can be viewed as a move toward more manageable bureaucracy.

Since the 1937 Brownlow Commission's declaration of the president as the managerial head of the executive branch, presidents have sought to realize and exercise control over the so-called fourth branch of government—the bureaucracy. Theoretically, cabinet officers were to be a president's chief field officers in exercising this control. As administrative control became an increasingly important presidential goal, presidents have sought greater managerial resources to employ toward its achievement. Hence cabinet recruitment in the postwar period has come to emphasize the accumulation of administrative capital. Concomitantly, cabinet recruitment has de-emphasized those political assets that might incur bargaining costs if the president were to secure political alliances with other elective, factional, or interest group leaders.

A second modern development has cast the president as the chief policy designer—a role that requires expertise in such a variety of fields that it is beyond the capacity of a single individual. In many ways, the growth of the Executive Office of the President can be explained as the cumulative effect of repeated efforts to provide presidents with the expert resources needed to function as chief policy designer. The Council of Economic Advisers, the National Security Council staff, and the Office of Science and Technology Policy are each prominent examples of new institutional assets available to presidents requiring diverse expertise capital. Similarly, the search for expertise capital has carried into cabinet recruitment as presidents have sought technocrats rather than political allies. Indeed, the search for technocrats, such as labor, industrial, and agricultural economists, may have been pursued at the cost of seeking political allies, particularly with major political interest groups.

In sum, these two related trends are illustrative of and contributory to one of the central paradoxes of the modern American presidency. Against enormous structural and customary impediments, presidents have enhanced their managerial control of the executive branch and with it gained significant influence over the direction of public policy.

This managerial gain has apparently been realized at the cost of the capability to govern effectively. As one recent commentator noted, presidents form "administrations" rather than "governments."[31] But in a political system of separate institutions sharing power, it is only "governments" that have both the capacity and legitimacy to govern.

NOTES

1. The term *adhocracy* is one that Roger Porter used to refer to an informal and changing policy organization system that characterized the Carter administration and that tends to neglect the need for overall policy coordination. See Porter's *Presidential Decision-Making: The Economic Policy Board* (New York: Cambridge University Press, 1980). Also see Graham Allison's use of the term in a discussion of the cabinet in "An Executive Cabinet," *Society*, July/August 1980, pp. 41–47, especially p. 44.

2. Samuel Lindsay observed over fifty years ago: "No single act of the President transcends in importance the appointment of his cabinet. The country forms its judgement of his underlying purposes and theories of government, it takes his measure and draws more conclusions from this single act than it does from his platform, his campaign pledges, his inaugural address or his first message to Congress. It represents in a vivid way the President's concept of the essential, vital and controlling organization of the executive government." See "The New Cabinet and Its Problems," *Review of Reviews*, April 1921, p. 382.

3. Richard F. Fenno, Jr., *The President's Cabinet* (Cambridge, Mass.: Harvard University Press, 1963), p. 17.

4. The centrality of purpose to the understanding of organizations is well established in the public administration literature. For example, Amitai Etzioni, in *Modern Organizations* (Englewood Cliffs: Prentice Hall, 1964), stated that purpose is "a source of legitimacy which justifies activities." Peter Blau in *Bureaucracy in Modern Society* (New York: Random House, 1956) defined bureaucracy essentially in terms of achievement of purpose. For the use of organizational purpose as a key element in distinguishing among types of organizations see Margaret Jane Wyszomirski, "Toward a Typology of Organizations: Public, Private, and Actuative," paper presented at the Annual Meeting of the American Political Science Association, New Orleans, Louisiana, August 29–September 1, 1985.

5. This bears a resemblance to Richard Neustadt's perspective that presidential power is essentially persuasive in nature and that the ability to persuade requires "bargaining advantages." In that sense, "political capital" accrued through personnel recruitment can be regarded as one source of "bargaining advantage." However my approach differs in emphasis from Neustadt in the sense that he regarded the department heads primarily as officers the president must bargain with (thus expending some of his political capital negotiating with them). In contrast, I emphasize the utility of cabinet members in providing the president with assets that can enhance (or diminish) his ability to "bargain"

with others. On Neustadt's approach see *Presidential Power* (New York: John Wiley and Sons, 1980 edition), especially pp. 26–33.

Paul Light employed the idea of "political capital" as being "directly linked to the congressional parties" (p. 26). As Light used the concept, it referred to party support in Congress, an element that may, in turn, be affected by presidential public opinion ratings, electoral margin, and professional reputation. See *The President's Agenda* (Baltimore: Johns Hopkins University Press, 1983), especially pp. 25–33.

6. The idea of preventive assistance is Fenno's; see *The President's Cabinet*, pp. 208 and 220.

7. Thomas E. Cronin, *The State of the Presidency* (Boston: Little, Brown, 1975), pp. 188–201.

8. For a fuller discussion of these three types of cabinet departments, see Kevin Mulcahy and Margaret Jane Wyszomirski, *White House Government* (Monterey, Calif.: Brooks/Cole Publishing Co., forthcoming).

9. The establishment of the Department of Health, Education, and Welfare in 1953 would appear to be something of a digression from this position of crisis management. In fact, many of the social welfare programs and agencies that were incorporated into HEW were originally started as New Deal emergency relief agencies. Hence the elevation to departmental status represents a belated recognition of the issue area's political importance.

10. Fenno regarded "availability" as an important factor in restructuring "the channels of access to the positions of power which the secretaryships represent." See the discussion in *The President's Cabinet*, pp. 67–77.

11. On McKay's campaign and its significance as a referendum on the Eisenhower administration's natural resource policies, see *New York Times Magazine*, October 14, 1956, p. 13; for similar comments during the primary see *New York Times*, March 10, 1956.

12. For a discussion of the negative impact upon the recruitment of presidential personnel played by economic factors—including both disclosure and compensation—see John W. Macy, Bruce Adams, and J. Jackson Walter, *America's Unelected Government* (Cambridge, Mass.: Ballinger Publishing Co., 1983), pp. 73–74 and 80–82.

13. This is in contrast to some earlier cabinet members, for example, in the Roosevelt administration, who virtually beggared themselves to remain in public service. Although economic constraints were becoming evident during the Eisenhower years, nevertheless a number of prominent businessmen managed to remain in the cabinet for longer than two years (for example, both Charles Wilson and George Humphrey served for four years as secretary of defense and treasury, respectively.)

14. See Edward Weisband and Thomas M. Franck, *Resignation in Protest* (New York: Penguin Books, 1975).

15. A recent and notable exception to the "rule" was the highly publicized resignation of President Carter's secretary of state Cyrus Vance.

16. See for example comments on cabinet changes in *Newsweek*, July 30, 1979. These firings were costly to the president not only directly in terms of

the direct political capital lost but also indirectly. President Carter's political reputation suffered because it looked as if he was "promoting his problems and firing his solutions" (p. 23).

17. For a discussion of presidential personnel recruitment processes from Truman through Carter, see G. Calvin MacKenzie, *The Politics of Presidential Appointments* (New York: The Free Press, 1981), especially pp. 11–78. On the Reagan transition, see Laurin L. Henry, "The Transition: From Nomination to Inauguration" in Paul T. David and David H. Emerson, eds., *The Presidential Election and Transition, 1980–1981* (Carbondale, Ill.: Southern Illinois University Press, 1983), pp. 195–218, especially pp. 200–207. For a detailed comparison of the cabinet recruitment efforts of Franklin Delano Roosevelt and Reagan, see Margaret J. Wyszomirski, "Roosevelt and Reagan: Cabinet Recruitment and Performance," paper presented at the Annual Meeting of the American Political Science Association, Washington, D.C., September 1984. For a comparison of the staffing of FDR and Kennedy see Richard E. Neustadt, "Approaches to Staffing the Presidency: Notes on Franklin Delano Roosevelt and John F. Kennedy," *American Political Science Review* 52, no. 4 (December 1963), pp. 855–862.

18. On the Nixon quest for executive control, see Richard Nathan, *The Administrative Presidency* (New York: John Wiley and Sons, 1975).

19. David S. Broder, "No 'New Generation of Leaders,'" *Washington Post*, December 24, 1976.

20. The Executive Office of the President included E. Pendleton James of the Office of Presidential Personnel; Martin Anderson, who evaluated those who would be involved in domestic affairs; and Richard Allen, who reviewed those considered for foreign policy positions; Lyn Nofziger, who reviewed the political and ideological record of potential nominees; Fred Fielding, who as White House counsel conducted legal and ethical checks; and Congressional Affairs Director Max Freidersdorf, who tested congressional opinion toward possible candidates.

21. *New York Times,* Sect. 4, December 7, 1980.

22. *New York Times,* December 12, 1980.

23. *New York Times,* November 8, 1980.

24. *Washington Post,* December 4, 1980.

25. See Chester A. Newland, "The Reagan Presidency: Limited Government and Political Administration," *Public Administration Review* 43, no. 1 (January/February 1983).

26. For example, see Lloyd N. Cutler, "To Form a Government," *Foreign Affairs,* Fall 1980, pp. 126–143.

27. See, for example, James L. Sundquist, "The Crisis of Competence in Our National Government," *Political Science Quarterly* 95, no. 2 (Summer 1980), pp. 183–208.

28. Edward Pendleton Herring, *Presidential Leadership* (New York: Farrar and Rinehart, 1940), p. 92.

29. Elizabeth Dole is married to Senator Robert Dole, a moderate Republican who chairs the important Finance Committee, and she was an often-

mentioned presidential hopeful. Margaret Heckler, a moderate Republican from Massachusetts, was defeated for reelection to the House in 1982, when redistricting pitted her against a Democratic congressional colleague who turned the election into a referendum on President Reagan's economic and military policies. As a member of Congress, Heckler had advocated women's rights and worked for the passage of legislation that addressed women's issues. Although these actions brought her the endorsements of many women's groups, Heckler was never a leader of politically organized women. Furthermore, as an opponent of abortion, she forfeited the support of the National Women's Political Caucus.

30. Kreps also had the "best" credentials of any of the female cabinet members as an expert in women's issues because she wrote a book on women's employment, entitled *Sex in the Marketplace*.

31. Cutler, "To Form a Government."

3
SELECTING CHIEF EXECUTIVES IN NORWAY AND THE UNITED STATES

Donald R. Matthews

Presidential government is a U.S. invention that—unlike jazz, blue jeans, and fast food—has not been widely emulated. As a result there are large differences between the office of chief executive in the United States and that of most other democratic countries. This distinction between the executives in presidential and in parliamentary forms of government has inhibited cross-national comparisons and led to a literature that stresses the uniqueness of the U.S. chief executive. In the United States, at least prior to Watergate, this exceptionalist view was exuberant and self-congratulatory.[1] The uniqueness of the American presidency has been accepted by most non-American scholars with rather different emotions.[2]

But if one penetrates beneath the institutional and legal forms to more basic processes and their consequences, one may find top-level executive politics much the same in all contemporary democracies. An effort to explore this hypothesis, no matter how partial, may help isolate what is truly unique about the American presidency from those attributes it shares with other chief executives. This in turn may contribute to a better understanding of executive politics in general.

In this chapter I shall compare only one aspect of chief executives—their selection—in Norway and the United States from the end of World War II. The differences between these two political systems are so substantial that a comparison of them seems almost bizarre. Norway is no larger in population than a medium-sized U.S. state—slightly more than four million people—and enjoys a startling degree of social, economic, and cultural homogeneity by U.S. standards. It is a unitary

state (rather than a federal one), a constitutional monarchy (rather than a republic), and a multiparty parliamentary system (rather than a two-party, presidential system). U.S. presidents are chosen in popular elections; Norwegian prime ministers (*statsminister*) are generated in Parliament (Storting), where they must attract majority support for (or more accurately avoid defeat of) a proposed cabinet and policy program. The national political executive in Norway is a collectivity in which the prime minister is the central and most powerful figure. The U.S. president is far more the "superstar,"[3] surrounded by a vast retinue but without real peers. Despite such basic differences, there are significant commonalities in the selection of chief executives in Norway and the United States. These take on added significance because of the unlikely comparison from which they emerge.

TENURE AND TURNOVER

From the reestablishment of normal politics in 1945 until 1985, Norway had thirteen governments headed by nine different persons (see Table 3.1). During the same period the United States had a like number of administrations—thirteen—headed by eight different presidents (See Table 3.2).

The similarity of these numbers is not just the result of the fact that both countries hold national elections at four-year intervals. Of the thirteen Norwegian governments, only three were organized immediately after national elections. The Labor government headed by Trygve Bratteli resigned and was replaced by the Lars Korvald coalition, after the proposed entry into the European Economic Community (EEC) was defeated in an advisory referendum. All other changes in government were triggered by party decisions (five times) or defeats in Parliament (two cases). Thus governments come and go in Norway at different points in the electoral cycle and for a variety of reasons. In the United States, access to the presidency is more firmly and directly tied to electoral outcomes. In the ordinary case, one becomes president of the United States by leading a successful national election campaign; "electability" is a necessary condition to becoming president. It is not a necessary condition for Norway's chief executive.

Although this is an important difference, we should be careful not to exaggerate it. First, "accidental presidents" are inescapable in the U.S. system, and three of the eight presidents between 1945 and 1985 fall in that category. Truman and Johnson became president after the deaths of Roosevelt and Kennedy, and Ford, after the resignation of Nixon. Truman and Johnson were nominated as vice presidential candidates largely for electoral reasons—it was believed that both would

Table 3.1
Norwegian Governments, 1945-1985

	Type of Government	Formation: No. Months After Election	Duration in Months
Gerhardson II[a] (11/45-11/51)	Labor majority	0	72
Torp (11/51-1/55)	Labor majority	24	38
Gerhardson III (1/55-8/63)	Labor majority before 1961; Labor minority after 1961	15	103
Lyng (8/63-9/63)	Minority coalition of Conservatives, Christians, Center party, Liberals	23	1
Gerhardson IV (9/63-10/65)	Labor minority	24	25
Borten (10/65-3/71)	Majority coalition of Conservatives, Center party, Christians, Liberals	0	64
Bratteli I (3/71-10/72)	Labor minority	18	19
Korvald (10/72-10/73)	Minority coalition of Christians, Liberals, Center party	36	12
Bratteli II (10/73-1/76)	Labor minority	0	26
Nordli (1/76-2/81)	Labor minority	26	72
Brundtland (1/81-10/81)	Labor minority	40	8
Willoch I (9/81-6/83)	Minority Conservative	0	20
Willoch II (6/83-10/85)	Majority coalition of Conservatives, Center party, Christians	20	28

[a] Einar Gerhardson served for several months as prime minister of a transitional government of national unity before the 1945 elections. Hence the first postwar government is the second Gerhardson government.

Table 3.2
U.S. Presidential Administrations Since 1945

	Party	Duration in Months
Truman I (4/45-1/49)	Democratic	40
Truman II (1/49-1/53)	Democratic	48
Eisenhower I (1/53-1/57)	Republican	48
Eisenhower II (1/57-1/61)	Republican	48
Kennedy (1/61-11/63)	Democratic	39
Johnson I (11/63-1/65)	Democratic	9
Johnson II (1/65-1/69)	Democratic	48
Nixon I (1/69-1/73)	Republican	48
Nixon II (1/73-8/74)	Republican	20
Ford (8/74-1/77)	Republican	28
Carter (1/77-1/81)	Democratic	48
Reagan I (1/81-1/85)	Republican	48
Reagan II (1/85-)	Republican	48

strengthen the party's ticket with groups and in states where the presidential candidate was not strong—but neither possessed the broad electoral appeal of Roosevelt or Kennedy at the time those two became president. Ford was chosen to succeed Nixon because Ford was acceptable to the House of Representatives, not because he looked like a winner in a presidential election. Thus accidental presidents usually have less impressive electoral credentials than those elected in their own right.

Second, although Norwegian prime ministers are not usually picked at election time, anticipated election results are a major cause of changes in Norwegian governments. Local elections, held at the midpoint of the four-year national electoral cycle, always have been studied with care in Norway for signs of shifts in electoral sentiments. The development of respected public opinion polling organizations in recent decades has made electoral predictions scientific; the results of political polls are widely circulated. When a governing party's prospects do not look good it frequently makes changes. Thus in January 1955, Oscar Torp was replaced as *statsminister* by the more popular and dynamic Einar Gerhardson because of the Labor party's disappointing showing in the 1953 elections. Trygve Bratteli was replaced by Oddvar Nordli in 1976 in the hope that a new and younger prime minister might breathe new life into the party before the elections of 1978. Six years later Gro Harlem Brundtland was chosen party leader because she was

the only Labor party politician who might lead the party to victory in 1981 (and who had the polling evidence to support that claim). Mass popularity and electioneering skill is becoming more important in the selection of prime ministers in Norway, at least within the Labor party.

The length of tenure of chief executives seems to be declining in both countries. Ronald Reagan was the first president to serve two full terms since Dwight Eisenhower. Only two of the eight governments during the period under discussion in Norway have lasted more than four years. It seems quite unlikely that any Norwegian politician currently in view will come close to Einar Gerhardson's twenty-year domination of national politics.

The heightened pace of executive turnover in both countries would seem to have multiple causes. The number and complexity of problems on the public agenda seem to be growing in all advanced, industrial states. Television, in its relentless search for novelty, tends to shorten the life span of both issues and political careers. The normal post–World War II majority party in both countries—Labor and the Democrats—have experienced substantial erosion in their electoral bases while no other party has succeeded in attracting a solid majority of electoral support. The result of these and perhaps other factors has been a string of one-term presidents in the United States and an increasing number of minority governments in Norway. Majority governments in Norway, be they one-party or multiparty coalitions, last twice as long as one-party minority governments and six to eight times longer than coalition minority governments (See Figure 3.1).

A recent trend in the United States has been a growing chasm between the "majority" needed to win the presidency, and the "majority" needed to govern. U.S. presidents, no matter how popular at their election, may or may not be able to govern once in the White House. Because prime ministers are chosen according to their demonstrated political power in Parliament, lack of ability to govern would not seem to be a potential difficulty in Norway. But it is becoming so. The last single-party majority government in Norway ended its reign in 1961. All governments since then have been either coalitions or minorities or both. A Norwegian prime minister's capacity to govern is less problematic than a U.S. president's, but it is far more uncertain than it used to be.

CHIEF EXECUTIVE NOMINATIONS

Students of U.S. politics agree that the most critical stage in the selection of presidents is the party nomination. Once the two major parties have chosen their candidates, the realistic contenders for the presidency have

been reduced to two. The processes by which the Democrats and Republicans do this winnowing have changed drastically since 1968, and a large literature has appeared describing, explaining, criticizing, and defending these changes.[4]

The closest equivalent to presidential nominees in Norway are the leaders of the five political parties that have participated in post–World War II governments: the Labor party (Det Norske arbeiderspartiet), Liberals (Venstre), Center party (Senterpartiet), Christian People's party (Kristelig folkeparti), and Conservatives (Høyre). The smaller parties on the fringes of the Norwegian political spectrum attract more than their share of attention; perhaps at times they may even be important. But it was unthinkable, in the period studied here, for a member of one of them to become prime minister. Norway's five mainstream parties thus share a monopoly of access to the prime minister's office as imposing as the Democrats' and Republicans' control over the White House.

Formally, the leadership of the national political parties in Norway is shared by the leaders of the parties in the Storting and the leaders of the parties' electioneering organizations. Fairly often, these two positions are held by the same person (see Table 3.3). When the positions are held by different persons, the relative power and prominence of the two leaders may be unclear, although the parliamentary leader is usually the more likely future prime minister. In the United States, presidential nominees are the undisputed leaders of their parties throughout the election campaign. But if they lose the election, their position as acknowledged leader of the national party is lost, too. In Norway, one can be a party leader (and hence a potential prime minister) for many years, even surviving several party defeats at the polls.

How do the forty-seven mainline party leaders in Norway from 1945 to 1985 compare to the fourteen presidential candidates nominated by the Democrats and Republicans during the same time interval?

VARIETIES OF POLITICAL EXPERIENCE

Both political systems select highly experienced public officials as potential chief executives. The average U.S. presidential nominee had held public office for fourteen years before his first nomination; the average party leader in Norway had been in public office for sixteen years prior to assuming a national leadership position for the first time (see Table 3.4). Thus while the selection process in the United States is more open to outside candidates with little or no previous experience, such candidates have seldom won nominations. Even President Reagan, often

	Storting Majority	Storting Minority
Single-party Governments	Gerhardson II Torp Gerhardson III (until 1961) (Mean duration = 65 months)	Gerhardson III (after 1961) Gerhardson IV Bratteli I Bratteli II Nordli Brundtland Willoch I (Mean duration = 27 months)
Multiparty Coalition Governments	Borten Willoch II (Mean duration = 46 months)	Lyng Korvald (Mean duration = 7 1/2 months)

FIGURE 3.1 Types of Norwegian Governments, 1945-1985

Table 3.3
Positions Held by Leaders of Major Political Parties in Norway, 1945-1985

	No. of Leaders Who Held			
	Parliamentary Leadership and Party Chair Position	Parliamentary Leadership Only	Party Chair Only	Total
Labor	3	4	1	8
Liberal	3	2	5	10
Center	3	5	3	11
Christian People's	5	3	2	10
Conservative	4	2	2	8
Total	18	16	13	47

Sources: K. Heider (ed.), *Norske politiske facta 1884-1982* (Oslo, Universitetsforlaget, 1983); O. Torp (ed.), *Stortinget i navn og tall, 1981-1985* (Universitetsforlaget, 1982); *Hvem er Hvem?* (Oslo, Kunnskapsforlaget, various years).

Table 3.4
Number of Years in Elective Offices Prior to Becoming Norwegian Party Leader or U.S. Presidential Candidate

	Norwegian Party Leaders (%)	U.S. Presidential Nominees (%)
0-4	13	14
5-9	15	7
10-14	19	29
15-19	11	14
20-24	23	22
25-29	11	14
30-34	6	0
35-39	2	0
	100%	100%

Sources: For Norwegian leaders, Norsk Samfunnsvitenskapelig Datatjeneste, *Politikerarkvivet 1814-1976* (Bergen, NSD, 1976); K. Heider (ed.), *Norske politiske facta 1884-1982* (Oslo, Universitetsforlaget, 1983); O. Torp (ed.), *Stortinget i navn og tall 1981-1985* (Oslo, Universitetsforlaget, 1982); *Hvem er Hvem?* (Oslo, Kunnskapsforlaget, various years). Data on U.S. presidential nominees from J.N. Kane, *Facts about the Presidents*, 4th ed., (New York, Wilson, 1981); *Who's Who in America* (Wilmette, Ill., Marquis, various years); *Current Biography* (New York, H.W. Wilson, various years).

considered a rank amateur, had served as governor of the most populous state in the union for eight years before achieving a presidential nomination. Dwight Eisenhower, whose first elective office was the presidency, was highly experienced in international-politico-military affairs. It may be that less experience is demanded in both countries today (see Table 3.5 for that trend in Norway) but meteoric rises to power have been rare in both countries so far.

Whereas Norwegian party leaders and U.S. presidential candidates have approximately the same amount of prior political experience, the *nature* of that experience differs in important ways. The Americans have had a far wider range of office-holding experience than the Norwegians. A complex federal system affords a larger array of public offices than a small, unitary state; there is no equivalent in Norway to the fifty U.S. state governments with their thousands of elective offices. Nor does the Norwegian system include the large numbers of elective judges, prosecutors, attorneys general, and other law enforcement offices that are such important stepping-stones in the early political careers of lawyer-politicians in the United States.[5]

Although the U.S. presidential nominees have had a wider range of experience than their Norwegian counterparts, their experience seems less clearly linked to the responsibilities of future chief executives than does the experience of Norwegian party leaders. Most presidents since 1945 have gotten to the White House via the Vice-presidency, either through the death or resignation of the incumbent (Truman, Johnson, Ford) or by subsequent nomination for the presidency (Nixon) (see Figure 3.2). Since the choice of vice presidents was tied to the presidential vote after the contested election of 1800, the vice presidency has had little attraction for leading presidential contenders. This seems to have changed somewhat in recent decades, but the office remains largely ceremonial.[6]

Table 3.5
Number of Years in Elective Public Office Before Becoming Party Leader in Norway, by Decade

	Years in Public Office Prior to Becoming Party Leader	Number of People
1940s	18.7	12
1950s	19.4	7
1960s	16.8	9
1970s	13.3	13
1980-1985	14.5	6

Sources: For Norwegian leaders, Norsk Samfunnsvitenskapelig Datatjeneste, *Politikerarkvivet 1814-1976* (Bergen, NSD, 1976); K. Heider (ed.), *Norske politiske facta 1884-1982* (Oslo, Universitetsforlaget, 1983); O. Torp (ed.), *Stortinget i navn og tall 1981-1985* (Oslo, Universitetsforlaget, 1982); *Hvem er Hvem?* (Oslo, Kunnskapsforlaget, various years).

The vice presidency might be made into a learning experience for future presidents, if presidents wanted to do so. But few presidents have the time or inclination to train a successor who was chosen to please a different party faction or different political orientation than his own. Thus Truman quashed the presidential aspirations of his vice president, Alben Barkley, and supported Adlai Stevenson. Eisenhower was cool to the presidential hopes of Vice President Nixon. Kennedy and his vice president, Lyndon Johnson, were longtime competitors with very different electoral bases and political styles. President Johnson humiliated Vice President Humphrey before supporting him for the presidential nomination at the last moment in 1968. Nixon stood

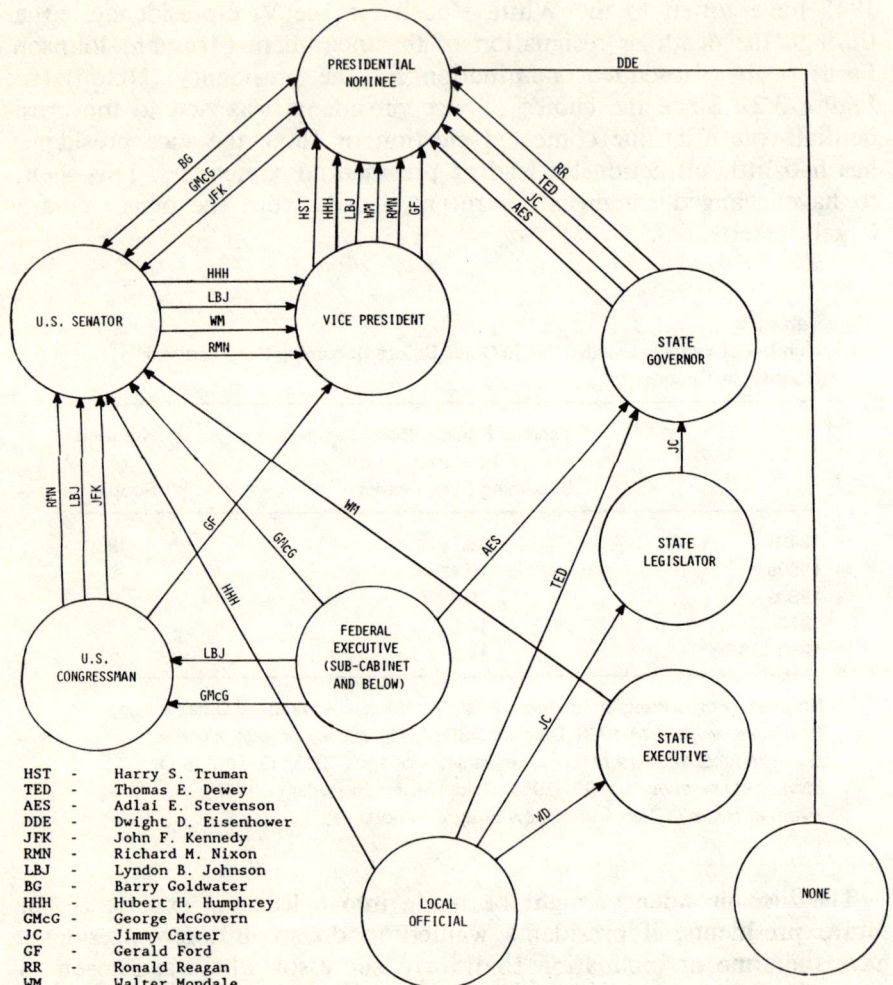

FIGURE 3.2
Office-holding Careers of Presidential Nominees in the United States, 1945-1985

silently aside as his first vice president, Spiro Agnew, was forced to resign, and his second vice president was defeated in a reelection bid. The last thing Mondale wanted in 1984 was to be associated with the unpopular Carter administration, in which he had served as vice president. Vice President George Bush was Reagan's most outspoken critic in the competition for the Republican nomination in 1980. Although Bush has seen the light and no longer calls President Reagan's program voodoo economics, he may have lost some plausibility in the process of conversion. Inescapable political realities seem to dictate that the vice presidency provides visibility but little power or experience at the job of chief executive.

More often than not, U.S. vice presidents have been U.S. senators first (Johnson, Humphrey, Nixon, Mondale). Three of the presidential nominees were nominated for the presidency directly from the Senate (Kennedy, Barry Goldwater, George McGovern). Next to the vice presidency, the Senate now seems the most advantageous location from which to launch an assault on the presidency.

The Senate emerged as a promising base from which to seek the presidency in the 1950s, along with the importance of television. Senators Estes Kefauver and Joseph McCarthy demonstrated how easily a national reputation could be acquired by skillful manipulation of this new medium. But there are other advantages to being a senator. Senate terms are long, and because they are not coterminous with presidential terms, two-thirds of the senators have an opportunity to run for president without giving up their Senate seats—a so-called free shot. There is little party discipline and no effective control over debate in the Senate, parliamentary quirks that afford the ambitious almost endless opportunities for self-promotion, a temptation encouraged by the presence of a large and prestigious Washington press corps, looking for news. Most public business in Congress is conducted on Tuesdays, Wednesdays, and Thursdays, leaving four days a week that can be devoted to campaigning elsewhere. Even midweek absenteeism is much less noticeable among one hundred senators than absence from other offices of comparable stature. The Senate's special constitutional responsibilities regarding treaties give members some claim to familiarity with foreign and defense policies, a desirable attribute of potential presidents. But as training for presidential responsibilities, service in the Senate is less than satisfactory. The views from either end of Pennsylvania Avenue are just too different.

State governors, of whom four became presidential nominees between 1945 and 1985 (Thomas Dewey, Stevenson, Carter, Reagan), do obtain experience at managing large-scale governments, some of which are bigger than many nation-states, including Norway. But there are im-

portant limitations to the office for presidential contenders. The issues and problems with which governors deal are unglamorous and do not include foreign and defense matters. The national news media are concentrated in New York, Los Angeles, and Washington, making it difficult to obtain national visibility from most statehouses.

Finally, a governor with a hankering for the White House is constrained by the fact that he or she needs to be on the job—or at least appear to be. Dewey and Stevenson were nominated for the presidency while still active governors, but Carter and Reagan had been out of the governor's office and running for the presidential nomination for six and two years, respectively, before they were nominated. The presidential nominating process has become so long and demanding since the 1950s that governors are put at a competitive disadvantage to vice presidents and senators. Perhaps that is not much of a loss, for the state governorships do not appear to provide significantly more relevant experience for future national executives than the vice presidency or the Senate. The truth of the matter seems to be that there is no job, or series of jobs, that adequately prepares a person to be president of the United States. In this sense, the presidency *is* a unique office.

In Norway, as in the United States, there is only one chief executive at a time. But Norwegian politicians who become potential prime ministers seem better equipped by experience than their U.S. counterparts. Over 20 percent of them (over *60 percent* of Labor party leaders) have served in a government before becoming a national party leader (see Table 3.6). Moreover, Norwegian cabinets tend to be real policy-making entities, at least compared to cabinets in many other countries, including the United States.[7]

About half the members of a Norwegian government are drawn from the Storting, and the remainder, from the higher reaches of private associations and the civil service. To fill all governmental portfolios from the Storting would seriously deplete the party's strength in the parliament because members of the cabinet must relinquish their seats in the Storting to an alternate (*varamenn*) as long as they serve in the government. (Upon leaving the cabinet, the former member of the Storting reclaims the seat and the *varamenn* goes home.) This system encourages lateral mobility between national executive and national legislature and the development of a small set of generalist politicians at home in both milieus. The U.S. system, with its separation of powers and legislative seniority system, largely eliminates lateral mobility. Legislators and executives usually follow separate career tracks.

The Storting is clearly a more important means of upward mobility for leaders of the nonsocialist parties than for the Labor party: Almost all leaders of bourgeois parties have served in the Storting prior to

becoming a leader, whereas only about half of the postwar Labor leadership has (see Table 3.6). How useful Storting experience is for a potential prime minister may change over time. In the current political era in Norway with its weak majority or minority governments and new issues that cross established party and ideological lines, the Storting committees and party caucuses are a major arena in which bargains are struck and policy decisions are made. In other times, with strong governments and conflicts over policy following established lines of cleavage, the Storting may do little but debate—and accept—government initiatives.

Table 3.6
Public Offices Held by Norwegian Party Leaders Prior to Achieving Leadership Position, 1945-1985 (percent)

	Labor (N=8)	Liberals (N=10)	Center (N=11)	Christian (N=10)	Conservative (N=8)	All (N=47)
Cabinet member	62.5	0	45	0	12.5	23
Storting member	50	70	91	100	100	80
Local council member	62.5	90	91	90	75	83

Sources: For Norwegian leaders, Norsk Samfunnsvitenskapelig Datatjeneste, *Politikerarkvivet 1814-1976* (Bergen, NSD, 1976); K. Heider (ed.), *Norske politiske facta 1884-1982* (Oslo, Universitetsforlaget, 1983); O. Torp (ed.), *Stortinget i navn oq tall 1981-1985* (Oslo, Universitetsforlaget, 1982); *Hvem er Hvem?* (Oslo, Kunnskapsforlaget, various years).

Being an elective politician in Norway differs from being an elective politician in the United States in still other ways. Executive positions in Norway are filled by appointment, not direct election, leaving only legislative bodies at the municipal (*kummune*), county (*fylke*), and national levels as popularly elected offices. Seats in these legislatures are filled by a proportional representation list system of elections. Politicians run for office, not as individuals, but as members of a slate of candidates put forward by a party; the chances of election to office in Norway depend as much on the candidate's rank on the party list as on how well the party performs in the campaign. How candidates are selected and arranged into lists by local party elites has been little studied,[8] but the process probably makes the people who control party nominations (and renominations) the equivalent of what Richard Fenno

has called in the U.S. context the "primary constituency."⁹ Certainly it is not surprising that the Norwegian party leaders studied here have been continuously active in the internal affairs of their party, both nationally and locally, whereas the U.S. presidential candidates have not. Indeed, there was considerable doubt about whether General Eisenhower belonged to the Democratic or the Republican party until shortly before the latter nominated him as its standard-bearer in 1952.

SOCIAL ORIGINS AND POLITICAL CHANGE

A cursory look at the personal characteristics of U.S. presidential candidates and Norwegian party leaders results in few surprises. Both groups consist overwhelmingly of middle-aged, middle-class males. The U.S. leaders are more likely to be lawyers, and the Norwegians, more likely to have been civil servants or functionaries in the political parties, unions, and trade associations (see Table 3.7). Both groups, however, have much higher occupational status than the people they seek to lead. This seems to be a near-universal fact of political life.[10]

But this overall picture obscures some important differences between Labor party leaders and the leaders of the other Norwegian parties. Traditionally, the Labor party has relied almost exclusively on leaders with working class *origins* (see Table 3.8). The only clear exception during the forty years in this study has been Gro Harlem Brundtland, whose father was a physician (and a nationally prominent Labor party politician). The post–World War II Labor party "establishment" has been made up of working-class men who worked their way into white-collar respectability and political prominence through the various arms of the labor movement—the unions, party, newspapers, cooperatives. Their formal education was minimal. Brundtland is the first "academic" (that is, college-educated person) to rise to the top of the party.

This type of political career has been nearly impossible in the United States, given the lack of a labor or socialist party and the relative weakness of unions. But the U.S. educational system has provided more opportunities for upward mobility through higher education than have existed in most European nations, including Norway.

All this is changing. The labor movement in Norway and its political arm are not so strong or cohesive as they used to be—in part they are victims of their own success. Higher education has been opened to all on the basis of demonstrated merit. "Nowadays," one old-time Labor party leader complained to me, "the smart and ambitious working class kid goes to the University, studies computer science, and then goes to work for one of the oil companies. The Labor movement loses him along the way."

Table 3.7
Occupation of U.S. Presidential Nominees and Norwegian Party Leaders, 1945-1985 (percent)

	U.S. Presidential Nominees (N=14)	All Norwegian Party Leaders (N=47)	Labor Party Leaders Only (N=8)
Public servant	14	30	12.5
Professional	72	36	25
Businessman	14	8	0
Party/interest group official	0	11	50
Farmer, fisherman, woodsman	0	15	12.5
Manual worker	0	0	0

Sources: For Norwegian leaders, Norsk Samfunnsvitenskapelig Datatjeneste, *Politikerarkvivet 1814-1976* (Bergen, NSD, 1976); K. Heider (ed.), *Norske politiske facta 1884-1982* (Oslo, Universitetsforlaget, 1983); O. Torp (ed.), *Stortinget i navn oq tall 1981-1985* (Oslo, Universitetsforlaget, 1982); *Hvem er Hvem?* (Oslo, Kunnskapsforlaget, various years). Data on U.S. presidential nominees from J.N. Kane, *Facts about the Presidents*, 4th ed., (New York, Wilson, 1981); *Who's Who in America* (Wilmette, Ill., Marquis, various years); *Current Biography* (New York, H.W. Wilson, various years).

Table 3.8
Father's Occupation of U.S. Presidential Nominees and Norwegian Party Leaders, 1945-1985 (percent)

	U.S. Presidential Nominees (N=14)	All Norwegian Party Leaders (N=47)	Labor Party Leaders Only (N=8)
Public servant	0	24	0
Professional	21.5	19	12.5
Businessman	57	11	0
Official in party, union or trade association	0	0	0
Farmer, fisherman or woodsman	21.5	30	12.5
Manual worker	0	15	75

Sources: For Norwegian leaders, Norsk Samfunnsvitenskapelig Datatjeneste, *Politikerarkvivet 1814-1976* (Bergen, NSD, 1976); K. Heider (ed.), *Norske politiske facta 1884-1982* (Oslo, Universitetsforlaget, 1983); O. Torp (ed.), *Stortinget i navn oq tall 1981-1985* (Oslo, Universitetsforlaget, 1982); *Hvem er Hvem?* (Oslo, Kunnskapsforlaget, various years). Data on U.S. presidential nominees from J.N. Kane, *Facts about the Presidents*, 4th ed., (New York, Wilson, 1981); *Who's Who in America* (Wilmette, Ill., Marquis, various years); *Current Biography* (New York, H.W. Wilson, various years).

Those college-educated Laborites who do stay with the movement differ in style from their elders. The younger leaders of the Labor party are interested in new and symbolic issues—women's rights, the environment, nuclear disarmament, and the like—while the old-timers' "bottom line" remains the paycheck. The Old Guard prides itself on being team players and problem solvers, on being the hard-nosed vanguard of a "revolution in slow motion."[11] The new generation of leaders is more verbal, ideological, radical, impatient. These leaders have a flair for the dramatic gesture, a familiarity with the politics of publicity and protest. The future of the Labor party depends, in good part, on how it handles this generational conflict.

The Democratic party in the United States has faced a similar conflict since the 1960s. Young anti–Vietnam War protestors, militant nonwhites, and feminists all have demanded a larger role in the party and more sympathetic presidential candidates than the leftover leaders of the New Deal/Fair Deal days. The party's first response was negative and defensive, leading to violence at the 1968 national convention. In the wake of this debacle, the Democratic party sought to reform its own rules to ensure that young people, nonwhites, and women would receive their fair share of the action. Quotas were established. Procedural safeguards put in place. These sometimes draconian measures had their intended effects—but at a very heavy price of largely unintended side effects: a drastically altered presidential nominating system that has tended to produce losing Democratic presidential candidates.[12]

SELECTION PROCESSES AND THEIR CONSEQUENCES

The processes by which politicians become prime ministers and presidents have important consequences on what future chief executives learn about politics and their place in it, on the skills they bring to office, and on their capacity to govern. Most observers probably would also agree that these selection processes are changing—certainly in the United States and probably in most other industrial democracies as well. The behavioral and systemic consequences of these changes deserve attention, no matter how speculative the conclusions that can be drawn about them at this time.

I find the typology presented in Figure 3.3 to be of help in making cross-national and cross-time comparisons of leadership selection processes. Four "ideal types" (in the Weberian sense) of leadership selection processes are proposed, each with a distinct set of relationships between established leaders, contestants for leadership positions, and the party membership at large. Some additional attributes and consequences of

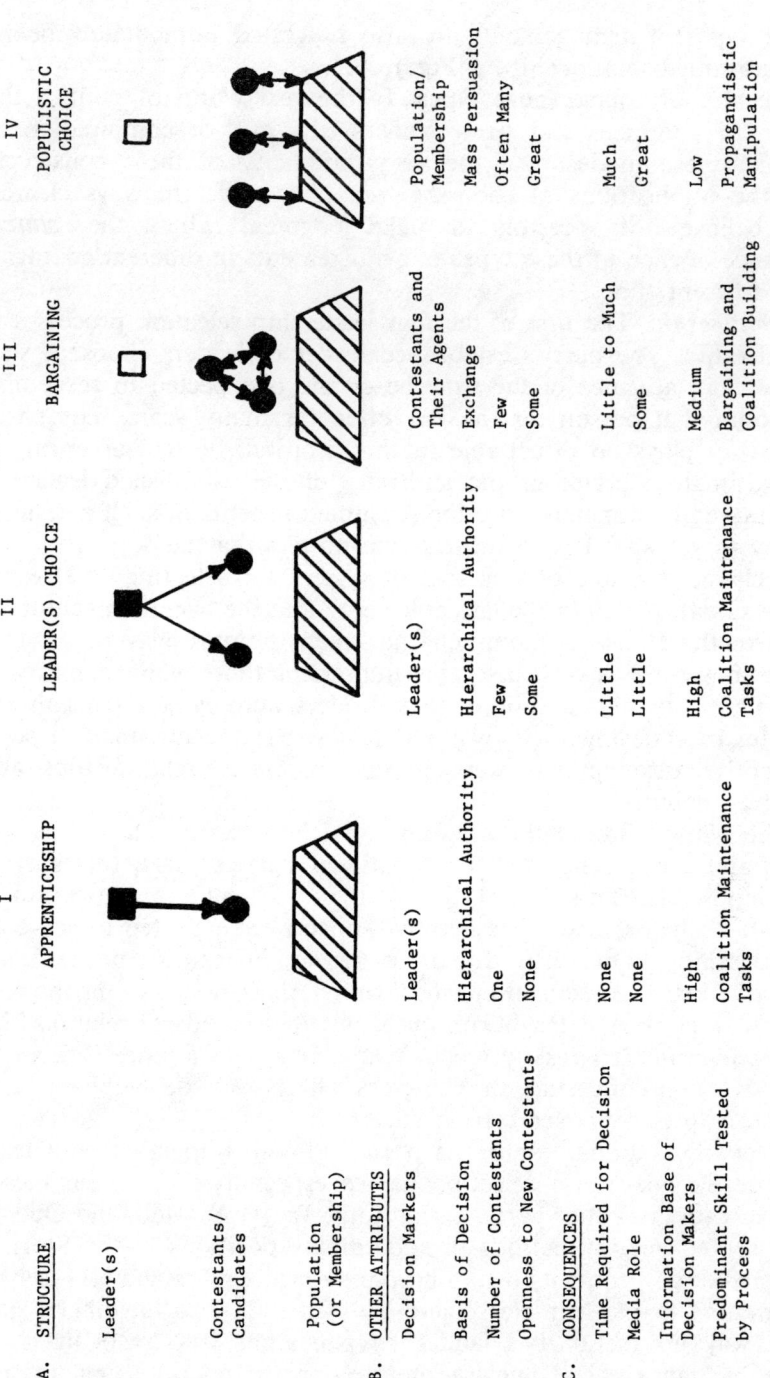

FIGURE 3.3
Leadership Selection Processes

the four types of arrangements are also suggested immediately below the diagrammed relationship in Figure 3.3.

These are, of course, pure types: In the real world of politics the selection of nominees and party leaders is a mix or combination of several of these modes. But the very simplicity of these constructs makes the implications of choosing leaders in different ways clearer. And I believe it is possible to make judgments about the *relative* importance of each of these types of arrangements in different countries and at different times.

Apprenticeship. The first of the four leadership selection processes is apprenticeship. The party's established leader or leaders choose a successor well in advance of the time he or she is expected to serve and then groom that person for the job, often for many years. The party membership plays no direct role in this decision, beyond accepting it as a legitimate exercise of the authority of the established leader(s). Continuity and competence are the presumed benefits of such a system. The way to get ahead is to impress the powers that be.

The classic example of this sort of system for selecting chief executives is Great Britain in the late nineteenth and the twentieth centuries. Service in the House of Commons has been the only way to the top, and one moved upward by favorably impressing those who were already there. Prime ministers and other party leaders were by no means always successful in choosing their own successors, but the dominant aspects of executive development were master-apprentice relationships and sponsored mobility.

In the United States, the separation of the executive from the legislature and the absence of strong national parties make this sort of thing impossible. This is not to say that political apprenticeship is unknown—senators and representatives once were expected to serve an apprenticeship.[13] One also thinks of the graduates of Speaker Sam Rayburn's Board of Education who learned their politics (and how to hold their bourbon) at Rayburn's knee. But these kinds of relationships have declined in Congress in recent years in favor of a more Hobbesian style. And apprenticeship in Congress affects the development and selection of presidents scarcely at all.

In Norway, apprenticeship has been far more important as a leadership development and selection device especially, but by no means exclusively, in the Labor party. Oscar Torp, Trygve Bratteli, and Oddvar Nordli served lengthy periods in subordinate positions in the Storting and in Labor governments before becoming prime ministers themselves. Conservative Prime Minister Kaare Willoch is said to have been sped on his way up the party's ladder by patriarchs who recognized his urbane brilliance early. Such apprentice-master relationships are not

always admired in Norway. Political observers sometimes refer to men being groomed for higher offices as "broilers," a comparison to the very small and stringy chickens for sale in Norwegian food stores.

Leaders' Choice. The second pure form of leadership selection process is quite similar to the first. In a situation of leaders' choice, the established leadership decides the successor, again with no direct role for the membership beyond acceptance, but only after an open and sometimes lengthy competition for approval has been waged by two or more contestants for the office. This process may provide a better reading on how effectively future leaders are likely to perform in competitive situations—in the parliament or on the stump—than an apprenticeship system does. Indeed the established leader's presumed ability to judge competence on the basis of competitive performance is the key to success of this system. The U.S. experience suggests that if enough members of the party rank and file lose confidence in its established leadership, the leadership is likely to abandon this approach.

Leaders' choice was the dominant decisional process of the U.S. national political parties from the midnineteenth century until 1968. The party's national nominating conventions were under the control of established party leaders—national, state, and local—and *not* the candidates for the presidential nomination or the party's rank and file.[14] Although competition within the party's leadership cadre often was intense, the leaders shared a desire to win elections—not just the presidency and not just the next election. This tended to mute the win-at-any-cost orientation of individual candidates and their organizations. Leaders' choice remains the dominant leadership selection procedure in Norway but has been vastly weakened in the United States by a number of factors: the erosion of the parties, the emergence of TV, shifts in the policy agenda, the reduction of uncertainty by political polling, misguided efforts to reform the parties and election financing, among others.

Bargaining. The third leadership selection process, bargaining, and the fourth differ sharply from the first two. Party leaders are no longer in control; either candidates and their organizations or the party rank and file end up making decisions. The clearest examples of bargaining as a leadership selection process can be found in the process of forming coalition governments. This process has occurred four times in Norway between World War II and 1985, resulting in the short-lived John Lyng government in 1963, the Per Borten government from 1965 to 1971, the Korvald government which served for a year after the defeat of EEC, and the Willoch II government formed in 1983 and still in power as this chapter is being written.

The government formation process in each of these cases was profoundly affected by the partisan division of the Storting seats at the past election. This, along with the circumstances that led to the need for a new government, determined who the potential coalition partners were.[15] Then the division of Storting seats among the parties of the potential coalition provides *both* an approximate measure of "power" and a benchmark allocation formula: the division of government positions to the parties at the same ratio as seats were distributed among the parties in the Storting.[16]

The hardest stage in forming a Norwegian coalition government is almost always the selection of prime minister. A variety of claims can be and have been advanced by the parties in negotiations, for example:

- My party played the central role in the creation of the vacancy. (This was the most important argument in favor of John Lyng as prime minister in 1963).
- My party is the biggest in the proto-coalition. (This argument allowed Kaare Willoch to control the formation of his second government. The nearly equal size of the parties made the formation of the Borten government particularly difficult in 1965.)
- My party provided the winning increment of votes/seats since the last election.
- My party is ideologically central within the proto-coalition. (An argument used by the Center party and Christian People's party against the Conservatives in 1965.)
- My party has the best qualified leader. (Argument used occasionally by all parties.)

When these various claims to the prime minister's office fail to lead to agreement between the parties, then, as one participant put it, "the package is broadened." The allocation of ministries in the government to the parties in proportion to their seats in the Storting results in fractional seats, which must somehow be rounded up or down to the nearest whole number. And the ministries are of unequal value to the different parties. If this does not provide enough to bargain about, side payments of offices in the Storting and policy commitments can be made as well. Thus the 1965 logjam was broken when the Conservatives agreed to forgo their claim to the prime minister position if they could have foreign affairs. The Christians made the same deal for their favorite ministry, church and education. When the Liberal and Center parties refused to forgo their chance at the prime ministership and were unable to agree on a prime minister, they were able to agree on a tie-breaking procedure—a preference vote by the Christian and Conservative Stort-

ing members. Per Borten defeated Bent Røiseland in that vote and became prime minister.

Allocating the ministries not included in the prime minister bargain is relatively easy. Usually this involves only minor deviations from the benchmark allocation formula provided by the outcome of the past Storting election. In 1965, for example, the Liberals were given Finance because every other party in the coalition had received a high priority post. Once all these decisions are made, the parties proceed to appoint people to their positions. The prime minister may or may not have some say in this matter. Per Borten learned of the membership in "his" government by reading about it in the newspapers. Kaare Willoch insisted upon having some say.

Bargaining and exchange processes occur *within* political parties, too, if the established leadership is too weak or unwilling to make a decision. A case in point was the decision made by the Labor Party Convention in 1976. The party was faced with two strong contenders for the party chairmanship—Oddvar Nordli, a popular Storting member and a middle-of-the-roader who had been pro-EEC, and Reiulf Steen, the leader of the Left, the young, and those who had opposed entering the Common Market. The solution was to make Steen chairman of the party and Nordli, prime minister—a departure from previous Labor party practice of awarding both posts to the same person. Of course, the putting together of presidential/vice presidential tickets in the United States usually involves similar bargaining between candidates and their organizations.

Bargaining provides a way of achieving agreement in the absence of authoritative leaders. In a situation where all participants do not want exactly the same thing with equal intensity, all contestants and their organizations can "win" something. Whether the resulting bargain is equally satisfactory to the party rank and file is another matter.

Populistic Choice. The fourth type of leadership process is populistic choice. Here decisions about leaders and candidates are made by the rank and file. The arguments in favor of this approach boil down to the view that it is "democratic" and/or that all other methods have failed.

Since 1968, especially in the Democratic party, a series of new rules and several statutes have changed the rules of presidential nominations in the United States. Most convention delegates today are chosen and bound by direct primaries. Party leaders have lost control over the nominating process. "Both parties have become little more than passive arenas within which the real political actors—groups committed to particular candidates and particular issue positions—contend for the nominations," Austin Ranney wrote. "The prizes are the two party

labels, but the parties no longer control who bears them."[17] Efforts by Mondale supporters to reverse this trend in 1984 were indifferently effective.

Nothing this drastic is about to happen in Norway any time soon. And yet there have been discernable movements in the direction of populistic choice. The meteoric rise to power of Gro Harlem Brundtland is the main case in point. In fall 1974, at the age of thirty-five, Brundtland was named minister of the environment by Trygve Bratteli. A physician with a degree in public health from Harvard, Brundtland was unusually well qualified to take the lead on environmental issues and on another troublesome issue in Norwegian politics of that time: abortion. Although she had not held public office before, her father had been prominent in the Labor party and her mother, a party activist. She was young, female, and from Oslo—all characteristics the government needed at that time. She was not identified with either side in the bitter fight over EEC, nor was she associated with Nordli or Steen. Thus, even though she was a newcomer to politics, she came with many conventional political assets.

What was not conventional—indeed was quite extraordinary—was that Brundtland was elected vice-chair of the Labor party nine months later. Recently Brundtland explained how. "The people liked me and how I behaved on TV . . . at first I didn't even know which camera was on. But I was a woman. I would not be pushed around and I said what I thought."[18] Brundtland became Norway's first TV politician.[19] Five years later she was Norway's first woman prime minister. The circumstances of her elevation were quite unlike those by which the Labor party had gone about making these decisions in the past.

The popularity of the Nordli government was sinking fast in spring 1981.[20] Secret discussions about making a change were held within the national leadership of the party. Rolf Hanson, highly experienced, highly capable, highly uncharismatic, was the clear front-runner among the party leadership. And then the Labor press bureau (which provides national news for the Labor newspapers) broke a leaked story about Nordli's declining health and likely departure from the prime minister's post. A whirlwind grass roots campaign for Brundtland was begun out in the constituencies. The Labor press bureau—attacked by Nordli and others as irresponsible—canvassed the members of the party committee that would make the decision and on a Sunday reported that Brundtland was ahead. On Monday, NRK-TV, the state-owned TV channel (there is only one) predicted her victory. The next day she was elected. The similarities to the hard-ball, media-oriented politics of the United States did not go unnoticed. The election campaign that occurred the following year became "The Gro and Kaare Show" because of its focus on the

leaders of the two largest parties. Willoch won. But it would be a mistake to expect Norwegian politics to return to the status quo ante. The things that made Brundtland's sensational rise possible—the emergence of TV as the dominant medium of communication, public opinion polling, the emergence of new, symbolic, and cross-cutting issues, the pressures from women and the young to play a more important role in the nation's politics, the emergence of an aggressive newspaper press emulating the *Washington Post,* seem here to stay. In the United States, the same kind of changes contributed to the quiet revolution that transformed presidential nominations from the choice of leaders to popularity contests. It remains to be seen how successfully the Norwegian parties and political institutions can resist the populistic thrust of these same social and political trends.

NOTES

I have accumulated an embarrassing number of debts while working on the subject of this chapter. The largest of these are to my academic, journalistic, and political friends in Norway. They are too numerous to name here, but I've learned most of what I know about Norwegian politics from them. Financial support from the John Simon Guggenheim Memorial Foundation, the University of Bergen, the University of Oslo, the Norwegian Marshall Fund, and the Norwegian Information Service was also essential. *Takk skal du ha.*

This chapter is a slightly revised version of a paper presented at the International Political Science Association meetings, Paris, France, July 1985.

1. The high-water mark of writing in this genre was Clinton Rossiter's *The American Presidency* (New York: Harcourt Brace, 1956).
2. See, for example, James Bryce, *The American Commonwealth* (London: Macmillan, 1888); Harold J. Laski, *The American Presidency* (New York: Harper, 1940).
3. The comparison and the label are from Johan P. Olsen, *Organized Democracy: Political Institutions in a Welfare State—the Case of Norway* (Oslo: Universitetsforlaget, 1983), pp. 81ff.
4. To begin, see Austin Ranney, *Curing the Mischiefs of Faction: Party Reform in America* (Berkeley: University of California Press, 1974); William Crotty, *Party Reform* (New York: Longman, 1983); Nelson W. Polsby, *Consequences of Party Reform* (Oxford: Oxford University Press, 1983).
5. See Joseph Schlesinger, "Lawyers and American Politics: A Clarified View," *Midwest Journal of Political Science* (1957) 1:26–39; Heinz Eulau and John D. Sprague, *Lawyers in Politics: A Study in Professional Convergence* (Indianapolis: Bobbs-Merrill, 1964); Mogens Pederson, "Lawyers in Politics: The Danish Folketing and United States Legislatures," in Samuel Patterson and John C. Wahlke (eds.), *Comparative Legislative Behavior* (New York, Wiley, 1972), pp. 25–63.

6. Paul C. Light, *Vice-Presidential Power* (Baltimore: Johns Hopkins Press, 1984).

7. Compare Olsen, op. cit., Ch. 3, and Richard Fenno, Jr., *The President's Cabinet* (Cambridge, Mass.: Harvard University Press, 1959).

8. H. Valen, "The Recruitment of Parliamentary Nominees in Norway," *Scandinavian Political Studies* (1966), 1:121–166.

9. Richard Fenno, Jr., *Home Style* (Boston: Little, Brown, 1978).

10. See for example Donald R. Matthews, "Legislative Recruitment and Legislative Careers," *Legislative Studies Quarterly* (1984) 9:547–585, and the literature cited therein.

11. The phrase is Olsen's, op. cit., Ch. 9.

12. See the literature cited in Note 4.

13. See Donald R. Matthews, *U.S. Senators and Their World* (Chapel Hill: University of North Carolina Press, 1960), Ch. 5.

14. See Paul T. David, Ralph M. Goldman, and Richard C. Bain, *The Politics of National Party Conventions* (Washington, D.C.: Brookings Institution, 1960); William Keech and Donald Matthews, *The Party's Choice* (Washington, D.C.: Brookings Institution, 1976); Nelson W. Polsby and Aaron B. Wildavsky, *Presidential Elections,* 5th ed. (New York, Scribners, 1980).

15. At least until 1985, potential coalitions crossing the socialist-bourgeois dividing line have not been considered.

16. This section is based upon interviews with participants conducted in 1981.

17. Austin Ranney, "Candidate Selection," Ch. 5 in David Butler, Howard Penniman, and A. Ranney (eds.), *Democracy at the Polls* (Washington, D.C.: American Enterprise Institute, 1981), p. 96. For a historical account of these developments see Byron E. Shafer, *Quiet Revolution: The Struggle for the Democratic Party and the Shaping of Post-Reform Politics* (New York, Russell Sage, 1983).

18. Personal interview, June 14, 1984.

19. It should be understood that Brundtland would have been an outstanding political leader without TV.

20. This section is based upon personal interviews conducted in spring 1981 with several participants in these events.

4
HOW TO BECOME A CABINET MINISTER IN ITALY: UNWRITTEN RULES OF THE POLITICAL GAME

Mattei Dogan

According to the ancient Roman jurists, if you take as a rule the most frequent cases, without worrying about possible exceptions, you adopt the principle of *plerumque fit*. It is in this sense that I am proposing here to codify Italian political rules that are not formally expressed, that were never written down, but that are well known by the entire Italian governing class, even by its less refined and less ambitious minority. They constitute the watermark of Italian history since World War II.

These rules institutionalize the recruitment process for positions of executive power. They have the advantage of rationalizing the means of access to governing positions and of avoiding congestion in the crossroads of political careers as if through a series of signals and traffic regulations. Thus political competition, which is extremely individualistic in Rome, has been ordered as in a chess game.

The Italian political system was dominated by the Christian Democratic party from the first elections after World War II until August 1983, when a Socialist leader, Bettino Craxi, was appointed prime minister, and a new historical phase began, after a very long crisis that had lasted ninety-eight days, from April 28, 1983 (fall of the fifth Amintore Fanfani cabinet) to August 4, 1983.[1]

My analysis focuses exclusively on the party that has dominated Italian political life, the Christian Democratic party (DC), from whose ranks all prime ministers were recruited during this period (except for the first, Parri, and the next to last, Spadolini) as well as most of the cabinet ministers and under secretaries of state.

Between the fall of fascism and August 1983, forty-seven governments followed one another, four before the end of the war. Among the forty-three postwar governments, from Parri to Craxi, fourteen were composed of just Christian Democrats, and twenty-nine were coalition governments.[2] This is the highest level of governmental instability among democracies since World War II. (See Table 4.1.)

It is important to stress that the Christian Democratic party has governed alone for relatively little time, a fact too often forgotten, even in Roman political circles. Of the fourteen single-party (*monocolori*) governments, only five remained in power more than one year (Zoli, Segni II, Fanfani III, Fanfani IV, Andreotti III). All others were "semestrial," "for the summer," on a "temporary armistice" basis, or stillborn. Criticisms of the Christian Democratic party neglect the fact that governmental responsibilities were shared by several parties most of the time.

These rules were progressively generated by the hegemonic party in a relatively short period of time[3] and were formally established toward the end of the Alcide De Gasperi reign, in light of the experiences during the years 1953 and 1954: Two Christian Democratic governments were stillborn, for they did not obtain a vote of confidence in Parliament (De Gasperi VIII, Fanfani I), another was formed but finally not appointed (Attilio Piccioni), and a fourth was invested but survived only five months (Pella).

The various governmental experiences have given birth to a very rich vocabulary currently used by the mass media: monocolor government, monochromatic, bicolor, tripartite,[4] quadripartite, pentacolor, center-left, organic center, convergence, parallel convergence, limited spectrum, enlarged spectrum, total spectrum, minority government benefiting from the nondefiance of some parties, and so on.

It would consequently be naive to try to analyze such a complex phenomenon by mathematical models, no matter how sophisticated they may be. In Machiavelli's country, political leadership is made up of a thousand nuances, and any attempt at quantification would soon become simplistic and naive. Even an application of "coalition theory" would be deceptive.

How can one elucidate this apparent paradox of ministerial instability despite the fact that one party remained in power uninterruptedly? One of the explanations of this fact is that the Christian Democratic party, although dominant, did not hold an absolute majority of parliamentary seats in the Chamber of Deputies, not even between 1948 and 1953.[5] It therefore had to ally itself with other parties, most of them small, and the disagreements between them were a source of ministerial instability.

The other explanation of this apparent contradiction between immovability and instability comes from the factional nature of the Christian Democratic party. A coalition government does not only rest on a big party flanked by two or three other small parties but also on several factions of the major and central party. If one or two of these factions want a change in policy, they can endanger the life of the government. Because the political game often takes on a Byzantine character, many governments have been overturned by an initiative coming from within the dominant party. It is not possible to establish a direct relation between the activity of this or that faction and the fall of the government. There is always a conjunction of factors.

The rules of promotion are enumerated here according neither to their importance nor to any chronological sequence in the selection process, as they intervene simultaneously. The logic of their linkage is nevertheless clear. Undoubtedly, it is Rule 7 that is most dependent on the political game and that receives, in times of ministerial crisis, most attention. I was able to codify these unwritten rules through interviews with politicians, high civil servants and astute observers. My interlocutors, including ex-ministers and potential future ministers, recognized them as true, even if they mentioned exceptions here and there. Departures from these rules are possible, but only for well-founded reasons.

THE SUMMIT OF THE CHRISTIAN-DEMOCRATIC PYRAMID

From 1945 to 1983, 663 persons, 423 of whom were Christian Democrats, occupied executive positions.[6] Seen from afar, these 423 personalities situated at the summit of the dominant party's pyramid share many characteristics.[7] In reality, however, it is a very diverse ruling group. To fully comprehend it, one must observe it from several angles and consider the varying weights of the different ministries and political generations.

One can distinguish four levels among Christian Democratic ministerial personnel:

1. The leaders of the party and of the factions, constituting what could be called the governmental nucleus—namely, the prime ministers and the most important ministers, those who belonged to eight governments or more (see Table 4.2). This nucleus included 37 personalities.[8]
2. The ministers who belonged to a maximum of seven governments and a minimum of three; they formed, around the nucleus, what could be called the governmental circle. It included 47 ministers.

Table 4.1
Italian Cabinets During Christian-Democratic Hegemony (June 1945–August 1983)

Prime Minister	Political Composition	Preceding Crisis (Days)	Duration (Days)	Apparent Reason for Fall
Parri 21 June 1945 24 Nov. 1945	DC-PSI-PCI-PLI PRI-PD	9	156	Liberal ministers disagree over policy and resign.
De Gasperi 1 10 Dec. 1945 28 June 1946	DC-PSIUP-PCI-PDA	16	200	Election of De Nicola as President of the Republic
De Gasperi 2 25 July 1946 20 Jan. 1947	DC-PSIUP-PCI-PRI	27	179	Schism between Socialists and Social Democrats.
De Gasperi 3 25 Feb. 1947 13 May 1947	DC-PSI-PCI	36	81	De Gasperi excludes Socialists and Communists from government.
De Gasperi 4 21 June 1947 13 May 1948	DC-PLI-PRI-"Experts"	18	349	Legislative elections and election of Einaudi as President of the Republic.
De Gasperi 5 2 July 1948 12 Jan. 1950	DC-PSLI-PLI	50	559	Disagreement over agrarian reform.
De Gasperi 6 1 Mar. 1950 17 July 1951	DC-PSLI-PRI (PLI support)	24	503	Two factions (Dossetti and Fanfani) criticize Finance Minister Pella.

Cabinet	Coalition			Reason
De Gasperi 7 10 Aug. 1951 29 June 1953	DC-PRI	25	688	Legislative elections.
De Gasperi 8 28 July 1953 28 July 1953	DC (PLI support)	29	—	Rejection of new Cabinet by Chamber of Deputies (282-263).
Pella 24 Aug. 1953 12 Jan. 1954	DC (PLI, PRI, PNM support)	18	92	Disagreement within DC over new Minister of Agriculture.
Fanfani 1 30 Jan. 1954 30 Jan. 1954	DC (PRI, PLI support)	25	—	Rejection of new Cabinet by Chamber of Deputies (303-260).
Scelba 10 Mar. 1954 22 June 1955	DC-PSDI-PLI (PRI support)	39	469	Some DC factions critical of Prime Minister.
Segni 1 22 July 1955 6 May 1957	DC-PSDI-PLI	30	654	Disagreement within coalition. Saragat resigns.
Zoli 8 June 1957 19 June 1958	DC (MSI, PNM support)	34	375	Legislative elections. (Resignation June 1957 rejected by President of the Republic).
Fanfani 2 19 July 1958 26 Jan. 1959	DC-PSDI	30	191	Chamber rejects decrees on trade due to defection of the PSDI's left wing.

(continued)

Table 4.1 (continued)
Italian Cabinets During Christian-Democratic Hegemony (June 1945–August 1983)

Prime Minister	Political Composition	Preceding Crisis (Days)	Duration (Days)	Apparent Reason for Fall
Segni 2 7 Mar. 1959 25 Feb. 1960	DC (PLI, MSI, PNM support)	39	355	Liberals withdraw their support of the minority government.
Tambroni 29 Apr. 1960 19 July 1960	DC (MSI support)	65	81	Antifascist demonstrations.
Fanfani 3 5 Aug. 1960 2 Feb. 1962	DC (PSI, PSDI, PRI, PLI, PNM support)	17	546	DC Naples Congress gives Fanfani green light for *centro-sinistra* coalition.
Fanfani 4 15 Mar. 1962 16 May 1963	DC-PSDI-PRI (PSI support)	41	427	Legislative elections.
Leone 1 11 July 1963 5 Nov. 1963	DC (PSI, PSDI, PRI PDIUM support)	56	116	"Bridge" government. Resignation of Cabinet to open road to *centro-sinistra* coalition.
Moro 1 21 Dec. 1963 26 June 1964	DC-PSI-PSDI-PRI	46	188	Chamber of Deputies rejects law on private schools.
Moro 2 6 Aug. 1964 21 Jan. 1966	DC-PSI-PSDI-PRI	41	531	Chamber of Deputies rejects law on nursery schools.

Moro 3 15 Mar. 1966 5 June 1968	DC-PSI-PSDI-PRI	53	816	Legislative elections.
Leone 2 17 July 1968 19 Nov. 1968	DC (PSI, PRI support)	42	124	Resignation to facilitate reconstruction of tripartite coalition.
Rumor 1 23 Dec. 1968 5 July 1969	DC-PSI-PRI-PSU	34	194	Socialist schism.
Rumor 2 12 Aug. 1969 7 Feb. 1970	DC (PRI support)	38	179	Resignation to facilitate formation of quadripartite coalition.
Rumor 3 17 Apr. 1970 6 July 1970	DC-PSI-PSDI-PRI	69	80	Resignation under threat of general strike.
Colombo 13 Aug. 1970 15 Jan. 1972	DC-PSI-PSDI-PRI	38	501	Resignation of Prime Minister after conference of coalition leaders.
Andreotti 1 26 Feb. 1972 26 Feb. 1972	DC (PLI support)	42	—	Minority government resigns to precipitate elections.
Andreotti 2 13 July 1972 13 June 1973	DC-PSDI-PLI (PRI support)	137	492	DC Congress reconfirms *centro-sinistra* coalition.

(continued)

Table 4.1 (continued)
Italian Cabinets During Christian-Democratic Hegemony (June 1945–August 1983)

Prime Minister	Political Composition	Preceding Crisis (Days)	Duration (Days)	Apparent Reason for Fall
Rumor 4 20 July 1973 2 Mar. 1974	DC-PSI-PSDI-PRI	34	225	PRI leader La Malfa resigns after conflict with PSI.
Rumor 5 27 Mar. 1974 3 Nov. 1974	DC-PSI-PSDI-PRI	25	221	Socialist leader Tanassi proposes end of *centro-sinistra* experiment.
Moro 4 7 Dec. 1974 7 Jan. 1976	DC-PRI (PSI, PLI PSDI support)	34	398	PSI withdraws support because of disagreement on economic policy.
Moro 5 12 Dec. 1976 30 Apr. 1976	DC (PSDI support)	38	105	Vote of no confidence.
Andreotti 3 11 Aug. 1976 16 Jan. 1978	DC (PCI-PSI-PSDI-PRI-PLI support)	103	519	Disagreement within DC over role of PCI. (Government of no "no-confidence.")
Andreotti 4 16 Mar. 1978 31 Jan. 1979	DC (PCI-PSI-PSDI-PRI support)	59	321	Communists return to opposition, breaking "national solidarity" against terrorism.
Andreotti 5 31 Mar. 1979 31 Mar. 1979	DC-PRI-PSDI	59	—	Vote of no confidence (by one vote).

Government	Dates	Composition	Duration	Duration of crisis	Reason
Cossiga 1	12 Aug. 1979 / 19 Mar. 1980	DC-PSDI-PLI (PSI support)	134	223	PSI and PRI end their absention in Parliament.
Cossiga 2	20 Apr. 1980 / 27 Sep. 1980	DC-PSI-PSDI-PRI	32	160	Decree rejected by Parliament (by one vote).
Forlani	29 Oct. 1980 / 26 May 1981	DC-PSI-PSDI-PRI	63	159	Government falls after scandal involving Justice Minister Sarti.
Spadolini 1	11 July 1981 / 7 Aug. 1982	DC-PSI-PSDI-PRI-PLI	66	393	Socialist ministers resign.
Spadolini 2	4 Sep. 1982 / 13 Nov. 1982	DC-PSI-PSDI-PRI-PLI	30	63	Disagreement among ministers in charge of financial affairs.
Fanfani 5	16 Dec. 1982 / 29 Apr. 1983	DC-PSI-PSDI-PLI	33	134	Withdrawal of socialist support.

DC	–	Christian Democratic Party	PSI	–	Socialist Party	PLI	–	Liberal Party	PCI	–	Communist Party
PRI	–	Republican Party	PSU	–	United Socialist Party	MSI	–	Neo-fascist Party	PDIUM	–	Monarchist Party
PDA	–	Democratic Action Party	PSDI	–	Social Democratic Party						

Duration of the crisis is the period between the resignation of the previous government and the day the new government received a vote of confidence in the second Chamber.

Duration is the period between receiving the vote of confidence and the day of resignation.

Support is either abstention or the giving of a vote of confidence without participation in the government.

The dates given are the date on which a vote of confidence was received in the second Chamber and the date of resignation.

3. The ministers who belonged to only one or two governments, making up an enlarged circle of power and including 53 individuals.
4. The under secretaries of state, who never reached the level of full ministership. They are twice as numerous as the full ministers: 286 versus 137. Obviously, these 286 under secretaries of state are of unequal importance, some having been much more well known than others. It would be possible to distinguish several types.

These figures, simple but essential, reflect the situation at a certain moment, as of August 1983, but it is evident that the career of some of these politicians is not finished. Over the years, a few young under secretaries of state will be promoted, some ministers will continue their careers, and newcomers will appear on the front stage. Nevertheless, the political careers of most of these 423 ministers and under secretaries of state have ended, for many, a long time ago. If the rules of the political game continue as before, in ten years tallies of ministers and under secretaries of state will indicate a distribution in four categories similar to the one I am presenting here.

One may observe three generations within the Christian Democratic political class. The first generation includes men born before 1910. Although this criterion is too rigid to be entirely satisfactory, it nevertheless has the merit of being precise. Of the 423 ministers and under secretaries of state, 161 were born before 1910. Many of the Christian Democratic leaders belong to this first generation: 21 out of 37 ministers of the governmental nucleus, 16 of the 47 ministers of the governmental circle, and 29 of the 53 ministers of the enlarged governmental circle. In total, 66 of the 137 full ministers of the period considered.

This first generation is illustrated by men of the stature of De Gasperi, Gronchi, Segni, Pella, Zoli, Tambroni, Vanoni, Togni, Gonella, A. Gava, Medici, Piccioni, Pastore, as well as many leaders of other parties, particularly Palmiro Togliatti, Pietro Nenni, Giuseppe Saragat, Einaudi, Sandro Pertini, and Parri. Twenty or thirty years before his accession to power, each one knew all the others and was known by all of them. The implication of this fact for the process of political co-optation is considerable. There is no spontaneous generation of leadership, even at the juncture of two historical periods. In effect, most of these men were elders of the Popular party. Others, without being ex-*popolari,* came from the network of Azione Cattolica. The group of 66 ministers born before 1910, who were no longer young at the breakdown of the fascist regime, include 48 whose biographies are marked by three characteristics: affiliation to the Popular party, activity

Table 4.2
Christian Democratic Party Ministers and Under Secretaries of State,
June 1945-August 1983

	Born Before 1910	2nd and 3rd Generations[a]	Total
Governmental nucleus			
Prime Minister	9	5	14
Minister 8 times or more	12	11	23
Governmental circle			
Minister 5, 6, 7, times	8	18	26
Minister 3 or 4 times	8	13	21
Extended circle			
Minister 1 or 2 times	<u>29</u>	<u>24</u>	<u>53</u>
Total ministers	66	71	137
Around the circle			
Under secretary of state 8 to 13 times	7	6	13
Under secretary of state 5, 6, 7 times	17	36	53
Under secretary of state 3, 4 times	22	48	70
Under secretary of state 1, 2 times	<u>49</u>	<u>101</u>	<u>150</u>
Total under secretaries of state	95	191	286
Overall total	161	262	423

[a] The distinction among generations is explained later in this chapter

in Azione Cattolica, and participation in the Resistance movement. This observation is also valid for 76 of the 95 under secretaries of state of the first generation.

It is not easy to give a definition of what should be considered participation in the Resistance, as the individual situations were extremely diverse. Some concrete examples will nevertheless suffice to

indicate the criteria that have been used. Those considered as Resistants include: Gonella, arrested in 1939 and paroled to a secluded residence; Gatto, arrested in Venice in 1943; Marcora, commander of a group of partisans in Valdossola; Piccioni, involved in clandestine struggles in Tuscany in 1943; Scaglia, provincial commissioner of the Committee of Liberation; Spataro, member of the national Committee of Liberation; Taviani, one of the leaders of the insurrection in Genoa; Zaccagnini, member of the Garibaldi Brigade in Ravenna. Those not considered as effectively engaged in the Resistance include: Cappa, elected deputy in 1919, 1921, and 1923, who withdrew from politics and resumed his career as a lawyer; Lucifredi, a lieutenant interned in a camp in Germany; Bettiol, whose clandestine action was limited to journalism. In any case, participation in the Resistance did not have the same significance in the south as in the north, in Salerno as in Bologna. The southern politicians did not have the opportunity to participate in the armed Resistance. Politically, the Resistance movement began, not in 1943, but in 1922.

One might be surprised not to see among the cabinet ministers some important Christian Democratic politicians: Dossetti, leader of a well-known faction; La Pira, under secretary of state in only one government soon after the end of the war; Enrico Mattei, famous manager of an enormous complex of nationalized enterprises; Giuseppe Cappi, national secretary of the Christian Democratic party in 1949, and later president of the Constitutional Court; Lazzati, to become rector of the Catholic University of Milan; Bonomi, president of the powerful organization of Coltivatori Diretti. The reason that most of these personalities did not become ministers can be found in the nature of the positions they attained outside of government. Dossetti and La Pira, however, simply lost the battle.

The second generation of ministers was born after 1910, raised in the Movement of Catholic Graduates and in the Federazione Universitari Cattolici Italiani (FUCI), and includes leaders such as Aldo Moro, Rumor, Taviani, Gui, Piccoli, and Fanfani (although born in 1908, Fanfani belongs sociologically to this second generation). These men erupted on the political arena at the Christian Democratic congress in Venice in 1949. The FUCI was more active than the Movement of Catholic Graduates. Many prominent Christian Democratic leaders knew each other as students. The FUCI was a greenhouse of political leaders.[9]

The third generation was raised in the "palace court" of the Christian Democratic party already in power, first in the youth movement, and then in the party apparatus. They are professional politicians in the sense that they never had any regular jobs other than political ones,

and they climbed the ladder by co-optation and patronage, in the noble sense of the word (in the sense of selection). This generation is illustrated by men of such calibre as Colombo, Andreotti, Forlani, Cossiga, Donat-Cattin, Gullotti, Sullo, Marcora, Luigi Granelli, De Mita, Adolfo Sarti, Malfatti, Ciccardini, Bodrato, Arnaud. Andreotti was sponsored by De Gasperi, Cossiga by Segni, Forlani by Fanfani, Ciriaco De Mita by Mattei, and so on. Many of the men of the third generation prepared themselves for their political career on the editorial boards of newspapers and weekly journals.

The second and third generations intertwine in their political careers. It is nevertheless clear that the roots of the second generation are embedded in the Catholic organizations, with a high proportion also involved in the Resistance movement, while most of the third generation began directly in the local, provincial, and regional organizations of the Christian Democratic party.

The various rules of promotion do not have the same significance for each of these three generations. Moreover, age is a nonnegligible variable in the selection of under secretaries of state and of cabinet ministers. The former have tended to be younger than the latter, except in the first ten years after the war. The ambition of a man in his early forties is usually for an undersecretariat of state. A politician in his sixties tends to be either appointed minister or not at all.

This analysis focuses on the first appointment as under secretary of state or as full minister. But the selection process continues for reappointments. For many politicians, the first appointment is also the last one. The "skimming" of the "super elite" is analyzed in Chapter 10.

I have counted only the governments during the period from June 1945 to August 1983 (Parri to Craxi), without taking into consideration the participation of a few in previous governments. For instance, De Gasperi was minister in the two Bonomi governments and in the Parri government. Only the latter was counted.

Rule 1: *The members of the government are recruited among parliamentarians.*

The aspirant to a ministerial position is a deputy or a senator. In effect, one can count only a handful of ministers who did not have a parliamentary mandate at the moment of their appointment (or who were not members of the Constituent Assembly). These few were experts or high civil servants, whose situation was then "regularized" in the sense that their election was arranged at the first opportunity. Among these exceptions, we could mention Corbellini, a railroad technician, appointed minister in 1947 because of his competence in the domain

of public transportation; Bonifacio, member of the Constitutional Court, appointed minister of justice; Stammati, former general director of the treasury and general accountant of the state, appointed minister of finance; Ossola, former governor of the Bank of Italy, appointed minister of foreign trade. Corbellini, Bonifacio, and Stammati were elected parliamentarians after their appointment as cabinet ministers.

It should be noted that this rule is practiced in most of the Western democracies. The exceptions are France and the United States, which have presidential systems, as well as the Netherlands and Norway, which have established an incompatibility between parliamentary mandates and ministerial positions. The mass media have given these experts a great deal of attention. Why? Should one see here the symptom of a certain discrediting of many professional politicians in public opinion? These experts are not apolitical. They have a double quality: They are considered competent in a particular domain, such as finance, but even if they do follow in the wake of a party, they are not members of the party's political apparatus.

About one quarter of the ministers and under secretaries of state were senators at the moment of their appointment. Nevertheless, among the ministers belonging to what I call the governmental nucleus, the deputies are in a majority of 85 percent. This is because most of the politicians who have dominated Italian political life during three decades were already in place at the beginning of the republic. They were elected to the Constituent Assembly in 1946, which is equivalent to the Chamber of Deputies, and they were reelected regularly.

Later, a certain number of leaders opted for the Senate because they preferred safer senatorial constituencies. The number of senators among Christian Democratic ministers has stabilized at between 25 percent and 30 percent since 1970.

This disproportion should be interpreted in light of the fact that there are twice as many deputies as senators (630 versus 315). For instance, in the 1953–1958 legislature, there were 263 Christian Democratic deputies and 114 Christian Democratic senators (70 percent and 30 percent of the party's parliamentarians, respectively); in the legislature of 1958–1963, 273 Christian Democratic deputies and 123 Christian Democratic senators (69 percent and 31 percent). It is from this original disproportion that the disproportion at the ministerial level results.

If the constitution had not provided that the government should obtain the confidence of both assemblies, and if, as in many countries, the confidence of the Chamber of Deputies had sufficed, the number of senators among ministers would have been considerably smaller, and

perhaps one of the causes of ministerial instability would have disappeared.

Ministers are selected among parliamentarians, but parliamentarians are themselves socially preselected a long time before their involvement in politics. Because intellectuals predominate among parliamentarians, it is unavoidable that they also predominate among ministers. Therefore, I observe among ministers a high number of lawyers, journalists, professors, high school teachers, and, particularly, professional politicians. The number of ministers of modest social background (working class, small peasantry, or lower-level white collar workers) is minimal. The few exceptions are those who made a career in unions before "jumping" to a political hierarchy.

Whereas the Christian Democratic party obtained nearly two-thirds of its votes from the female electorate,[10] between June 1945 and August 1983 only 8 women represented this party in the government and only 1 as a full minister, the other 7 having been only under secretaries of state at different moments. (However, a woman has repeatedly been elected president of the chamber.) This limited female representation in the government is the inevitable reflection of the low proportion of women among deputies (only 3 or 4 percent) and even lower proportion among senators. Rule 1 applies to women as much as to men. Why, then, so few women among parliamentarians? The responsibility belongs to women voters who gave preferential votes to men.[11]

Military men were excluded from political positions. They were not permitted to be candidates at legislative elections without having previously resigned from the army. In the young republic the political class manifested a kind of mistrust toward generals. Only in 1945–1946 were three military men appointed to ministerial positions: Admiral De Courten, twice minister of the navy; General Chatrian, under secretary of state for national defense (he later became a Christian Democratic deputy); and General Pellegrino, under secretary of state for the air force.

Rule 2: *One does not accede to government during one's first tenure.*

One must have been reelected in order to be eligible to reach the governmental level. What are the reasons for the adoption of such a rule? Because of the preferential vote system practiced in legislative elections, the number of defeated parliamentarians, and consequently of new deputies, is relatively high: on the average more than one quarter of the total membership of the Chamber of Deputies. If the choice of ministers is limited to reelected deputies, if the "greenhouse" is restricted, so much the better for those who are already there, the

reelected. The rule of the waiting term before promotion to government protects the elders against the competition and the impatience of the new parliamentarians. Furthermore, to the degree that the stature and prestige of the ministers reinforces their local electoral position by the practice of preferential voting and clientelism, this rule allows the former ministers to deprive the new deputies of a precious trump card for their reelection. Those not reelected leave room for new deputies, who will not immediately compete with their seniors.

However, Amintore Fanfani sought to change this rule at the national council of the Christian Democratic party in 1974, and he criticized "the practice of the parliamentary caucuses which do not accept the appointment of newly elected parliamentarians to government."[12]

This rule has allowed several exceptions, particularly during the first years after the war. These cases had to do with men who played an important political role before 1922 and in the opposition against the fascist regime and who found themselves together once again in the Constituent Assembly. I count 32 personalities, most of them well-known Resistants who came to power before 1948. But these 32 personalities are not the only ones who escaped the rule of the waiting term. There are 23 others who became ministers before the end of their first term: They represent less than 5 percent of the total number of ministers and under secretaries of state. Two-thirds of them were promoted to the ministerial level before 1954, that is, at a moment close to the foundation of the republic. After that, the exceptions to this rule became extremely rare, as in the case of Ferrari Aggradi, who made himself noticed by a report on the economic situation to the Christian Democratic congress in 1952, and who was appointed under secretary of state soon thereafter, even though he was then only a newly elected deputy.

This practice can be observed in other countries, too. In Britain, the chances of being appointed to a government position during the first mandate are minimal, except in certain historical circumstances such as when the Labour party arrived in power for the first time or when it returned to power after a long absence. (See Chapter 5.)

Rule 3: *One does not become a minister without having previously been undersecretary of state.*

One is first appointed under secretary of state and only later appointed full minister. Until October 1980, the Christian Democratic caucus in the Chamber of Deputies, according to the caucus's internal procedures, drew up a list of deputies by secret ballot, among whom the prime minister and the leaders of the party chose—after the ap-

pointment of ministers—the under secretaries of state. The list sometimes included twice as many names as positions to be filled. The prime minister and the party leadership could choose from among those elected by the group, but not among others. Through this ballot, the new and therefore "ineligible" deputies (according to Rule 2) played a role in the selection among the elders. This election by the group was not entirely satisfactory, for in October 1980 just before the constitution of the Forlani government, the group decided by a large majority to change this norm and to delegate to a committee of the parliamentary group the privilege of drawing up the list of "promotable" deputies. The committee drew up this list by taking into consideration the activity of parliamentarians in their party, their seniority in Parliament, the length of positions held elsewhere, and for some, their specialization.

Theoretically, it is the Council of Ministers that chooses and appoints under secretaries of state. In reality the council contents itself with confirming a list already established by the leaders of the parties of the governmental coalition. The proof of this is the fact—simple but enlightening—that the council makes this decision during a very brief session. For instance, the Council of Ministers headed by Forlani that met on October 20, 1980, did not take more than fifty minutes to appoint 57 under secretaries of state.

Some figures should be kept in mind. The total number of under secretaries of state for the period is 372, of whom only 86, or 23 percent, were later promoted ministers (at least until August 1983).[13] Among the 286 under secretaries of state who never reached the rank of full minister, 94 belonged to only one government, 56 to two governments, 43 to three governments, 27 to four governments, and 66 to five governments or more. A few of these under secretaries have been promoted to ministerships since August 1983, and others will be so promoted in coming years, but it is already evident that for most of them the undersecretariat of state was not a step but a summit.

From a different point of view, among the 137 full ministers, 86 started as under secretaries of state, and 49 were directly appointed full ministers. Yet, among these 49 ministers, 31 belonged to the first generation, and most of them were prominent in political life before 1922 or in the Resistance. Furthermore, they acceded to power before 1954, that is, in a period when this rule was still in its gestation.

The deviation from the rule for the remaining 18 men who were born after 1910 and who skipped the level of under secretary of state, could be explained by various intricacies. First, a position at the summit of the party may substitute for the position of under secretary of state. Piccoli became cabinet minister directly because he was then national

secretary of the Christian Democratic party. Forlani, Gullotti, and Bodrato were vice national secretaries of the party before their appointment as cabinet ministers. Regional or local notoriety may intervene in the same direction: Ripamonti, a Milanese personality, acceded directly to the rank of full minister; likewise, Restivo, president of the Sicilian regional council, and A. Gava, president of the regional assembly of Campania. The vice presidents of the Senate and of the Chamber of Deputies naturally skipped the level of under secretary of state. These titles imply a de facto predominant position within the Christian Democratic party. For instance, G. Bartolomei, president of the Christian Democratic group in the Senate during three legislatures, became minister directly. Among the 18 men of the new generation who have benefited from this exception are also included: Marcora, Rognoni, Signorello, Codacci, Pisanelli, Andreatta, Corbellini, Dal Falco, Lombardini, Scaglia, and Tesini.

The presidency of a standing parliamentary committee is not necessarily considered a position equivalent to that of under secretary of state. In a "classical" type of parliamentary system where Parliament is the regime's center of gravity, such as in France during the Third and Fourth republics, it is normal that political promotion be channeled in great part through the parliamentary committees. But in the Italian *partitocrazia,* where the most important decisions are made by the leaders of the parties, political careers are forged outside Parliament in the party organizations and factions. It is not astonishing, therefore, to find that in Italy, in contrast to other countries, the position of parliamentary committee president is not a springboard. In effect, there are very few politicians whose promotion to ministerial rank could be explained mainly by their active role in a parliamentary committee. Among these rare examples could be mentioned Angelini, president of the Transportation Committee; Monaldi, a doctor directly appointed minister of health; Azara, a jurist appointed minister of justice; Trabucchi, an industrialist appointed minister of finance; Medici, a specialist in agricultural affairs, appointed minister of agriculture.

The number of under secretaries of state progressively increased from 1946 to 1980. But the number of Christian Democratic cabinet ministers and of under secretaries of state varied according to "political space" resulting from the number of parties in the governmental coalition. Most of the monocolor governments included more newcomers than the previous or following governments. In the 1970s, there were twice as many under secretaries of state as ministers. In the monocolor governments, composed exclusively of Christian Democrats, 1 of every 3 deputies with five years seniority or more could receive a ministerial armchair or just a ministerial stool. (In the House of Commons, too,

a large number of members of Parliament [MPs] of the majority party are junior ministers.) Because other deputies and senators simultaneously hold important positions in the party hierarchy, it could be said that a large minority of Christian Democratic deputies and senators were variously rewarded.

A great number of under secretaries of state were appointed for the first or only time on the occasion of a monocolor government. Thus the second Rumor government (monocolor) in August 1969, which succeeded the first Rumor government (coalition), included 30 under secretaries of state who did not belong to the previous government (only 4 outgoing ministers were not reconfirmed).

Satisfying the greatest possible number of deputies is a necessity for the survival of the government in a parliamentary system that practices the secret ballot and thus permits all maneuvers. Several governments have felt stabbed in the back by "snipers" belonging to the governmental majority itself. Although a formal vote of confidence in government is nominal and consequently disciplined, the adoption of laws and the ratification of decrees are done by secret vote. The government can be put without warning in minority by the vote of snipers who hope to obtain a ministerial position thanks to a crisis and a change of government. The ambition of those who are or believe themselves to be potential ministers is a source of ministerial instability, as it was in France during the Third and Fourth republics.[14]

It should be noted that the undersecretariat of state as a necessary stage on the road to full ministership applies only to the dominant Christian Democrat party. This rule does not apply to the other parties, which participate in coalition governments after long periods in opposition and which receive, in these coalition governments, only a small number of ministerial posts; too many of their leaders have aged while in opposition.

What power do these under secretaries of state hold? Most of them have been ephemeral politicians at the governmental level, even if they are famous personalities in their provinces, where they may "reign as lords" for twenty to thirty years. Others were not ephemeral, belonging to three or more governments, but they remained outside the ruling group. The power of under secretaries of state depends largely on the delegation of functions that they receive from the full ministers; the amount of delegation varies enormously according to personalities and circumstances. There are no formal rules. In the coalition governments the under secretaries of state usually belong to a different party than the one represented by the respective ministers; sometimes the under secretaries play the curious role of political "spy."

Rule 4: *The position of under secretary of state is limited to five years.*

No one can remain under secretary of state more than five years. If the promotion to full ministership does not take place during this period, the holder is excluded from potential governmental circles. No one can indefinitely remain under secretary of state: promotion or exclusion! This is a custom that one finds in other countries too, particularly in Britain. It can also be found in certain public administrations that limit the time a person can occupy a certain position.

This rule of five years seniority poses a maximum, but not a minimum, limit. It is not necessary to be under secretary of state for five years in order to be appointed minister. The rule is interpreted with some flexibility. It is not applied in case of the reappointment of almost all outgoing ministers, for in such a case it is supposed that there is no available post of full minister. It is, however, rare that one returns to government as an under secretary of state after a long interruption.

What is the significance of this rule? Should it be interpreted in terms of experience or competence, as in Britain, where the junior minister must show that he or she has the quality of a statesman? Is it justified by the periodic need to make room for new faces? What if this rule were adopted not only to ensure a circulation, but also in a Machiavellian spirit, to eliminate a certain number of middle-of-the-road competitors? The rule facilitates the promotion of new aspirants to the rank of under secretary of state, but at the same time it protects the great leaders against the impatience of ambitious politicians who, having already unsheathed their swords as under secretaries of state, believe, rightly or wrongly, that their turn has come. Significant from this point of view is the unusual proposition formulated by a large number of Christian Democratic deputies in February 1976, at the formation of the fifth Moro government. They asked the designated prime minister not to choose as ministers personalities who already had held ministerial responsibilities for more than eight years (since their first appointment). This proposition focused on the desired exclusion from government of great leaders as Rumor, Colombo, Donat-Cattin, Andreotti, Fanfani, and a few others. It seems that this action was initiated by some under secretaries of state aspiring to become full ministers. They in turn would thus have liberated places for new under secretaries of state, and this explains why the proposition, judged unreasonable at the highest level, nevertheless found a favorable response among many junior parliamentarians. This incident reflects the latent competition between generations among Christian Democrats. If

Vilfredo Pareto were alive today, would he still say that the circulation of elites is "viscous"?

Once again, Christian Democratic deputies and senators met the Prime Minister–designate Andreotti, in March 1978, to discuss the problems concerning the designation of ministers in the fourth Andreotti cabinet. The deputies approved, among others, the following three recommendations: First, they proposed the incompatibility of positions in the government and positions in the party hierarchy; second, they reaffirmed the existing rule that the under secretaries of state should be chosen from among a list elected by the Christian Democratic party caucus; third, they reconfirmed the "rule of five years." The senators made similar recommendations.

Certain parliamentarians remained under secretaries of state for a long time, apparently breaking the "rule." Should this longevity be interpreted as a success or as a half-failure? It is good to remain under secretary of state, but it is even better to be promoted minister. A few concrete examples will provide us with some elements of a reply.

A. Salizzoni, who was under secretary of state thirteen times, in reality occupied a better strategic position than that of many ministers responsible for important administrations. He was, as under secretary of state to the presidency of the Council of Ministers, in effect one of the most intimate collaborators of the prime minister during five cabinets. The function of under secretary of state in the Ministry of Foreign Affairs or of the Interior, which he exercised at other moments, could be considered in certain circumstances more important than the function of full minister of tourism or of the post.

G. Bisori was under secretary of state in eleven governments between 1953 and 1963 almost without interruption, but always in the Ministry of the Interior, where he undoubtedly acquired high competence in a domain considered essential.

Maria Badaloni was appointed under secretary of state nine times, but always to the Ministry of Public Education. It was necessary to have a woman appear among the male ministers, even if she was only offered, albeit in a gallant manner, a ministerial "stool."

Why has a person who has already been appointed under secretary of state nine times never been promoted? It might be because of the difficulty of finding, in a coalition government, a position as full minister for someone who was not a leader of a faction (*capo corrente*). In any event, among the nonpromoted under secretaries of state who maintained their position for a long period, one could find deputies or senators specialized in a particular sector.

Another unwritten rule of the political game should be mentioned here, even if it is not directly related to the selection of ministers. A

Christian Democrat who has served four parliamentary terms, or twenty years, and who has not been promoted under secretary of state, "should," according to young militants, abstain from running for a fifth mandate. The other parties, particularly the Communist party, have also limited the length of the parliamentary careers of their members, except for the leaders; if Robert Michels were still alive, he could test his "iron law of oligarchy" once more.

In December 1982, in the new cabinet directed by Fanfani, four under secretaries of state who had seniority of more than five years and who belonged to the outgoing government were not reappointed, making room for new faces.

Rule 5: *All regions are represented in the government.*

The principle of regional representation is respected in various countries: Germany, Belgium (where it overlaps with linguistic representation), and others. But in Italy, this geographical prescription sometimes takes on the aspect of distribution among "baronages." In effect, because the Italian electoral system is based on proportional representation, large constituencies, and preferential voting, each great leader is well protected in his own constituency against the direct competition of other great leaders: Andreotti in Latium, Rumor in Veneto, Segni in Sardinia, Colombo in Basilicata, Taviani in Liguria, Tambroni in Marche, Gioia in western Sicily and Gullotti on its eastern side. Wise precaution: Male lions should not trespass on the territory of other male lions.

The regional leaders are at the same time leaders of factions at the national level. When a government is formed, the regional mix and the factional dosage (to be discussed later) are inseparable. To give a ministerial portfolio to a faction means to bring the "baron" of a particular region into government, and vice versa. Thus, among the ministers of faction A, one almost always finds a representative of Veneto, and of faction B, a representative of Sicily. To represent every region in each successive government would imply a monopoly of certain regional leaders. Fanfani was well aware of this. Recognizing "that the change was not always accomplished on the basis of wise criteria," he also admitted the incompatibility between a rigorous regional representation and personal competence: "Other obstacles came from the presumption that the candidates for various posts should have true territorial origins in order to respond to the expectations of regions, provinces and cities. These obstacles had so much impact on selection based on merit and competence that it restricted the range of choice."[15]

In practice, geographical representation is easily attained, as even an under secretary of state is sufficient to represent a region in the government. If it were otherwise, the Christian Democratic leader of each important region would be permanently present in the government. An analysis of the relation, for all regions, between the number of Christian Democratic electors and of the ministers, during the three decades from 1949 to 1978, shows that the relation has some significance, though far from a perfect one: Lombardia, Emilia, and Tuscany have proportionally fewer ministers than voters, the opposite being true for Campania, Calabria, and Basilicata.[16] This rule, too, tends to favor the men from the governmental nucleus and serves to justify the exclusion, after a certain time, of many under secretaries of state.

Rule 6: *Competence is acquired through experience.*

The belief that competence is acquired through experience clarifies the criteria for the selection of ministers as well as the subtlety of the political game in Rome. It could be argued that a person who is able to reach the highest levels within the party is a competent politician, in the most general sense of the word. But one could ask whether someone who shows himself to be astute in the partisan network, and who has succeeded in obtaining preferential votes by imaginative propaganda and a personal network, also necessarily possesses the qualities required of a statesman. Does a person who has spent twenty years in partisan politics and in the labyrinth of factions, without giving priority to parliamentary debates or activity in specialized committees, have the same profile as his French counterpart, who has acquired experience in the parliament and the administration rather than in the party? In the selection of ministers, representativeness certainly is sometimes as important as competence, but competence cannot be weighed by milligrams, whereas representation is very visible. Undoubtedly, it is an amalgamation that nourishes in practice the best selection process.

What is at issue here is the deliberate and systematic priority given to partisan criteria, often to the detriment of competence. Many Italian politicians have told me that "expertise is not essential for promotion to government."

The proof that competence is not the main criterion in the selection of ministers can be found in the chronology of government formation. The number of ministers to be attributed to each party and each faction is determined first. Only then are the departments distributed. The factions do not necessarily have competent representatives for the domains that are allotted them. The distribution of departments between parties and factions and the designation of parliamentarians by

the factions are two independent processes, usually occurring at different moments.

It is too easily admitted in the Roman political milieu that competence is acquired through practice, that it results from experience, that the intelligent politician should and can adapt himself rapidly to the governmental functions assigned him. How can this be possible if the minister in question does not remain in his position more than a few months, if he moves from agriculture to transport, from education to social security? No doubt the minister does not need to be a specialist. Yet he must still familiarize himself with the problems of the ministerial department with which he is charged.

The limited role played by the parliamentary committees in the selection process has already been stressed: Committee chairs do not constitute a springboard for ministerial appointment, as these chairmanships are usually reserved for ex-ministers, instead of being a channel of access to government. That means that the succession of stages is reversed. There are some exceptions: Pandolfi, Bressani, Cossiga, and others made themselves known in parliamentary committees. If the channel of committees is not an efficient one, it is because another channel, the faction, which will now be examined, plays a determining role.

Rule 7: *The composition of the government reflects the proportional strength of factions within the party.*

The national council of the Christian Democratic party is elected at the party congresses. It includes representatives from the groups in the Chamber of Deputies and in the Senate, as well as from the various satellite organizations. The election of the council is carried out according to lists that represent factions. The delegates have a number of mandates determined by the number of adherents and voters in their constituencies. The members of the national council are elected by proportional representation. So, in 1973, the Iniziativa Popolare faction (Rumor, Piccoli, Taviani) represented 35 percent of the national council; the Nuove Cronache faction (Fanfani, Forlani), 20 percent; Impegno Democratico (Andreotti, Colombo), 15 percent; Base, 9 percent; Forze Nuove, 8 percent; others, 10 percent.

The idea that the Christian Democratic representation in government should be proportional to the composition by factions of the national council became accepted soon after the retirement of De Gasperi. The proportional calculation has been ingeniously worked out. It is considered that a full ministerial portfolio is equivalent to three undersecretariats of state.[17] The value attributed to the presidency of the Council

of Ministers is very significant: it is worth only two ministries. The number of points thus calculated is distributed among the factions according to their strengths in the national council of the party. For example, if the government is composed of 20 ministers, representing 60 points, and 50 secretaries of state, counting for 50 points, we reach the total, including the prime minister, who "weighs" 6 points, of 116 points to be proportionally distributed. In practice, the allocation is not so simple, as witnessed by the length of negotiations at the moment of a new government's formation.

All factions of the party are normally represented in government. Nevertheless, in a few circumstances, one or two factions have refused to occupy the ministerial positions to which they had the right. For instance, one leftist faction did not participate in the Tambroni government, which was oriented toward the right. Similarly, the Democratic Left (Marcora, Granelli, De Mita) refused to participate in the monocolor Rumor government. Sometimes the collaboration of certain factions is obtained for "the management of current affairs." In this case, it is considered that participation is ideologically neutral.

In the coalition governments, the number of ministries and under secretaries of state going to the Christian Democrats is reduced, and consequently the application of proportionality is only approximate. In the late 1970s, it became difficult to apply a rigorous proportionality.

Some journalists, however, attach excessive importance to the so-called Cencelli manual, to which the Christian Democrats themselves almost never refer. This "manual" consists of several pages concerning the proportional calculations for the distribution of ministerial portfolios and undersecretariats among parties and factions. I verified how this principle of proportionality was applied in reality, but I did not find any rigorous correspondence between the spectrum of factions and the distribution of portfolios and semiportfolios, not even for the monocolor governments. It would be an insult to the intelligence of political leaders to believe that the distribution of ministerial departments could be made with a slide rule. Mentioning decimals in analyzing a sophisticated and complex political game is to caricature a principle that is legitimate in one sense and that has been practiced not only in the consociational democracies (the Netherlands, Belgium, Austria, Switzerland)[18] but also in many political regimes that have adopted proportional representation. In Italy, proportionality cannot be rigorous: first, because the ministerial departments are not all of equal importance;[19] next, because the co-optation of an expert, even "outside the quota," or of a personal friend of the prime minister, may render the calculus of proportionality obsolete. Furthermore, because the factions are unstable, a reference to the previous elections of the national

council can rapidly become invalid. But, above all, there are important positions within the party, as well as some positions in the parliamentary assemblies such as committee chairs, that can be offered as compensation to factions and personalities that are insufficiently rewarded. The criteria of equivalence are subtle and conform to democratic principles.

It would be useful to quote here one of the typical comments from the newspapers during ministerial crises. This comment implicitly confirms that, for the best-informed journalists, a rigorous proportionality in the distribution of ministerial positions is out of the question. It also shows, by its hermetic vocabulary, the distance that separates the political class from popular masses. It is highly probable that more than 90 percent of Italian citizens remained completely cool toward the competition between the factions. Here is the text, concise though it may be:

> For the Christian Democratic party, eight ministerial positions will go to the majority and six to the minority. Among the eight of the majority, three should be *dorotei;* one would go to the Fanfaniani who would also have the presidency of the Council; one to the friends of Colombo; one to the group of Rumor; and one to the Forze Nuove faction. Out of the six of the minority, four would go to the Zaccagnini reserve and two to the Andreottiani.[20]

The historian of the year 2000 will have to be a Rhadamanthus to orient himself in this labyrinth of factions.

Rule 8: *The ministerial positions are distributed to the factions, which in turn propose their representatives to government.*

Contrary to constitutional provisions, it is not the prime minister who chooses the ministers. The main preoccupation of the leader in charge of building a governmental coalition is "the dosage." He does not have the power to select the members of his government, for the parties do this according to the proposals of factions, which designate their own representatives. In fact, the government is a committee of delegates of factions. Consequently, the government is undermined from inside. Most often it falls from internal dislocation and not from the pressure of the opposition. The contrast between the solidarity of the British cabinet and the heterogeneity of the Italian government reflects the difference between the two political regimes.

The leaders who propose the representatives of their faction to government do not often forget to designate themselves. The entire system is based on this possible fusion of roles: The person who

designates can also be the designated person. A minister, B. D'Arezzo, asked if "a member of the delegation in charge of preparing, along with the prime minister designate, the list of ministers, could himself be appointed minister. It is as though he was choosing himself."[21]

There is no formal incompatibility between the ministerial functions and those of the party leadership. Most of the time one leads to the other. National secretaries of the Christian Democratic party have become prime ministers: De Gasperi, Fanfani, Rumor, Moro, Forlani. Most vice national secretaries of the party became ministers: Scelba, Piccioni, Taviani, Tupini, del Bo, Spataro, Gullotti, Ruffini, Antoniozzi, Donat-Cattin, De Gaspari, and others. About 90 percent of those members of the national council of the Christian Democratic party who were also deputies or senators in 1962 (at the time of the party congress in Naples) later became ministers. The existence of a permanent nucleus of influential leaders, on one side, and of a large number of ephemeral politicians, who only pass through, on the other, can be explained by this practice of self-designation.[22]

Among other things, the Craxi government innovated with respect to one crucial strategy in order to favor greater governmental stability. He included in his cabinet the national secretaries of four out of the five parties constituting his parliamentary majority: himself (Italian Socialist party—PSI), Giovanni Spadolini (Italian Republican party—PRI), Nicolazzi (Italian Social Democratic party—PSDI), and Biondi (Italian Liberal party—PLI). He embarked on his ship of state the most influential leaders.

One becomes minister because of being the chief of a faction. The chronology of the positions leaves no doubt about this. How the selection is done within the faction is a problem I cannot deal with here, for it would necessitate going into too many details.

This model has been in operation since 1954. After De Gasperi's resignation, his successor, Pella, in 1953, himself selected the ministers and under secretaries of state for a monocolor government; but this manifestation of independence was "penalized," and his government fell after five months. A new attempt in this same spirit, by Fanfani, resulted in failure ten days later. Scelba, who followed Fanfani, learned the lesson and constituted a government of "delegates and representatives" from various factions in his party (with which two small parties were associated: Social Democratic and Liberal). For a quarter century, the prime minister exercised only a very limited influence in the choice of ministers. This influence was also discreet because it could only be manifested during a meeting with the general secretary of the party and presidents of the groups in the Chamber and Senate. This "te-

trarchy," as it is called, could communicate beyond the "conclave" only with the chiefs of the factions—a detail full of significance.[23]

In 1979, Cossiga innovated when he formed his first cabinet after a series of seasonal governments and various ministerial crises: He asked the parties composing the majority, his own included, to indicate several names, among whom he could choose. From the Liberal party, for instance, he requested three times more names than there were positions to be filled.[24] This new strategy could in part be explained by the lesson that the new prime minister drew from the unfortunate experience of Pandolfi, who had been designated a few days earlier by President Pertini to build a coalition government. After laborious negotiations and multiple modifications of the list of ministers, Pandolfi presented himself to the Quirinale. During his audience with the president of republic, Pandolfi was called to the telephone by the leaders of the Socialist party, who told him that they did not like his "final list." Pandolfi was thus obliged to renounce his mission because the ministerial composition displeased the Socialists. "This is the first government of the Republic to fall by telephone," remarked a man in good strategic position, Luigi Granelli. At the time of the constitution of his second government in April 1980, Cossiga had to bow to the rules of the game and to accept the designation formulated by the parties.

A new infringement on the norm occurred with the formation of the Forlani cabinet, in October 1980, the gestation of which I observed in vitro. The national secretaries of the four parties forming the coalition (Piccoli, Craxi, Longo, and Spadolini), met at the Chigi Palace with the prime minister–designate. A list of new ministers was prepared, including 14 from the Left (Socialists, Social Democrats, and Republicans) and 14 Christian Democrats. Between 1 A.M. and 11 A.M., when Forlani arrived at the Quirinale Palace to present the list of ministers to President Pertini, 6 out of the 14 Christian Democrat nominees were replaced by others, because of pressures exercised by various leaders and also because of the unusual refusal by the president of the republic to change the 3 ministers directly responsible for the struggle against terrorism (interior, defense, justice), of whom only 1 was on the initial list. The prime minister–designate therefore had to accept the request of the president of the republic as well as the demands of the leadership of his own party in conformity with the practice of the past quarter century.

The representatives of the other three parties had been designated by their own parties before the meeting of the national secretaries. One could have read the following in the official newspaper of the Social Democratic party: "This morning the groups in the Chamber and Senate

together with the executive committee are meeting in order to designate the colleagues (comrades) who will be destined to assume ministerial responsibilities, either as ministers or under secretaries of state."[25] At the same moment many newspapers informed their readers of the meetings of the leaders of the two other parties for the same purpose: the designation of the representatives of the party to the government. As a good observer wrote, "the power to select the minister belongs to the parliamentary groups, and through them, to the parties and factions constituting the majority."[26]

It is certain that, with few exceptions, a career within the party precedes a career in the government. For example, nearly all members of the DC executive committee in 1949 were later called to governmental functions. This was likewise true for nearly all parliamentary members of the national council elected at the same moment (with the exceptions of Dossetti, La Pira, Cappi, Lazzati, and two union leaders). This also applies, as mentioned, to the parliamentary members of the national council elected in 1962.

On the contrary, very few provincial secretaries in office in 1952 were called to government during the following thirty years: 10 out of 93. The ambitious young people of today should learn the lesson: It is better, should they aspire to become ministers, not to focus on the position of provincial secretary. Not all provincial roads lead to Rome! Once these ambitious ones have arrived in Rome, having become deputies or senators, they would do better—as Machiavelli would have said—to devote the best of their time and energy to the party and its factions, not to the parliamentary committees, as a ministerial career depends essentially on the possibility of crossing the lofty footbridge that links the party to the government. To reach the leadership level of the party, there is only one road, and that is to adhere to a faction! To refuse such an engagement is to go down a dead-end road. One cannot pursue a career apart from factions.[27]

Rule 9: *Factions have no right to veto the representatives of other factions.*

Loyalty to party and faction has priority over the collective responsibility of the government. In case of conflict, it is to the party and to the faction that ministers and under secretaries of state show their loyalty. This is easy to understand because appointments depend first on the faction, second on the party, and only third on other considerations. The selection of the representatives of factions to government is an internal affair, which does not concern other factions. If someone is not elected by his own faction, he could not hope to be nominated by the chief of another. The only solution would be to switch factions.

Double allegiance is not possible nor are intrigues with neighboring factions. The chief of a faction cannot request the inclusion or the exclusion of representatives of other factions. It is forbidden to hunt on the lands of other factions; poaching is prohibited. Without such a division of territory, the coherence of the cabinet, with rivals sitting side by side, would be even weaker.

It should be noted in this regard that there is less democracy within the factions than in the party itself, which is a federation of factions. The faction is based on loyalty, lineage, and friendship, not on elections and ideology. It is a grouping for personal promotion and protection. As in other one-dominant-party systems, such as Japan, India, or Mexico, the faction has a clientelistic chain, which descends through many intermediary steps from the barons to the most peripheral electors.

This interdiction of veto did not exist during the breaking-in phase of the political system. De Gasperi opposed the appointment of Dossetti (who retired to a monastery) and of Gronchi, who finally opted for the presidency of the Chamber; this latter position showed itself to be an excellent springboard for the presidency of the republic. But the right to veto has sometimes been used in the formation of coalition governments. As a condition of their participation (or of their support without participation), some parties demanded the exclusion of this or that individual belonging to the Christian Democratic party.

One of the few clearly documented cases was the veto formulated by the leader of the PSDI, Saragat, against the appointment as cabinet ministers of 3 representatives of the Christian Democratic party in 1953. President of the Republic Einaudi charged Attilio Piccioni with forming a new cabinet. After eight days of consultations with benefit of Christian Democratic support, Piccioni officially accepted the leadership of the new cabinet. The Christian Democratic newspaper, *Il Popolo,* announced that the list of ministers was ready and that the former prime minister De Gasperi had accepted the position of minister of foreign affairs. But the following day Piccioni renounced the formation of a government. What had happened? The national secretary of the Christian Democrats, Gonelli, explained, "Saragat, at the view of the list of ministers proposed by Piccioni, declared that two ministers designate, Spataro and Togni, should be excluded, and that the appointment of Bettiol as minister of education was an error."[28] No parliamentary majority being possible without the support of the PSDI, Piccioni had the choice between accepting Saragat's conditions or renouncing the mission.

One again finds this rule, even if in diluted forms, in other countries because wherever the government is a coalition, the representatives of

the parties are divided between loyalty to the chief of the government and loyalty to their party. What was peculiar to Italy was the excessive importance of factions, which can be explained by the existence of a predominant party.

Rule 10: *The prime minister is an arbiter, not a selector.*

Is the prime minister the final selector of ministers? There is in the letter of the constitution a juridical fiction to that effect that is doubtless prudent and wise but that does not stand up to any analysis. Even the presidents of the United States and of the French Fifth Republic, even the British prime minister and the German chancellor, do not choose all ministers themselves. That is a well-established fact.

The selection is a complex process wherein the delegates of parties, fed by their national secretaries, propose or impose their representatives upon the prime minister–designate. Only since 1977 has the prime minister–designate asked, on several occasions, the parties of the coalition for a bouquet of names. He then had the option of choosing among the names proposed by the parties themselves.

At the moment of the formation of his first government, Spadolini expressed his good intentions: "The parties will give me several names from which I will choose, as Article 92 of the Constitution indicates. Naturally, the concern for political equilibrium will lead me to choices which I hope could be inspired by criteria of experience and confidence."[29] This statement provoked the following comment from an acute observer:

> The appointment of ministers is the most insidious obstacle for Spadolini. The few names that the parties will propose could become ambushes for the prime minister–designate, into whose hands will fall not the mission to freely choose the ministers, but rather to eliminate persons that the leaders of the parties are unable to exclude. This is an extremely delicate operation. Spadolini would like to include in the government an expert on economic problems: Visentini or Baffi to the Treasury. This will complicate the distribution of positions.[30]

Finally, "the good intentions of Spadolini vanished—it is useless to deny it—in the face of the implacable logic of parties,"[31] because "the problem is to build a political government composed of parties and not a utopian government without an anchor."[32]

The prime minister has sometimes been able to choose 1, 2, or even 3 ministers, and then he has given priority either to personal friends[33] or to experts, particularly in financial and economic matters. It is generally agreed that the prime minister has the right to choose his

principal collaborator in the government freely, that is, the under secretary of state to the presidency of the council, who, in spite of his title, plays in reality a more important political role than do most of the full ministers. For instance, Taviani, as direct collaborator of De Gasperi in 1951–1953, was undoubtedly more influential than many ministers, in spite of the fact that he was only under secretary of state. It is significant from this point of view that a former full minister F. Campagna accepted, for reasons of political equilibrium, the position of under secretary of state to the presidency of the council in 1981.

What is the position of the prime minister in case of conflict? Is he the chief of the majority faction or the arbiter of rivalries manifested within the government? How can he reconcile this double role? Or if he does not play the role of arbiter, who does? The frequent meetings of the executive committee of the party seem to indicate that there is a collective arbitration because the structure of power is collegial.

The distribution of portfolios among factions, accompanied by the designation of ministers by the factions themselves, might in a sense be considered a violation of the constitution, which grants to the prime minister the right to choose the ministers and propose them to the president of the republic. In fact, however, there is no violation because the government, no matter how it is made up, finally receives the vote of confidence in Parliament. But obviously, what interests us here is the real process and not the legalistic aspect. To these ten unwritten rules could be added a last one which is only partially written in the constitution.

Rule 11: *The president of the republic does not choose ministers and rarely chooses prime ministers.*

The role of the president of the republic in the selection of the prime minister is unavoidably limited. There is no doubt that the successive presidents have managed to facilitate the career of a few parliamentarians. For instance, Gronchi imposed Tambroni, Saragat recommended Colombo, Segni obtained the appointment of Carlo Russo, and Pertini supported Spadolini. But all analysts of the Italian system agree that the president's role is normally honorific, except in the choice of the prime minister himself in the event that the leadership of the dominant party fails to propose a name. The merry-go-round of party chiefs and of personalities from the entire range going to the Quirinale during ministerial crises is an illustration of this discreet power of negotiation, which the president can exercise in going beyond the inanimate paragraphs of the constitution.

The first politician chosen by the president of the republic outside the Christian Democratic party as a possible prime minister was Sandro Pertini, in November 1968, after the fall of the Leone cabinet. This attempt, under Saragat's presidency, failed. More than ten years later in February 1979, Pertini, who meanwhile had become president in July 1978, asked Ugo La Malfa, leader of the small Republican party, to explore the possibility of building a new cabinet. After nine days of meetings and consultations La Malfa was obliged to renounce his mission. The appointment as prime minister of someone who did not belong to the Christian Democrats still appeared premature. One month later in March 1979, Pertini took an initiative that astonished the Roman political circles. He wanted to appoint a "troika": Andreotti as prime minister with La Malfa and Saragat (former president) as vice prime ministers, in the absence of any proposal of the prime minister-designate.[34] He convened the three personalities at the Quirinale and stressed the political character of his initiative. This new attempt to increase the role of the president failed also. In June 1981, Pertini finally succeeded to "impose" his preferred candidate, the Republican leader Spadolini.

Has the president of the republic the latitude of imposing or excluding this or that personality from the list that the prime minister-designate proposes to him? Has he the right to veto someone? This issue has been discussed largely over the years. It was debated in the mass media in March 1980, at the moment of the formation of Cossiga's second cabinet. The president recommended that the prime minister-designate choose his ministers without consideration for the alchemy of factions, and the president reserved for himself the "right-duty" to examine the list of ministers-designate and to choose them according to their personal merit. The newspapers mentioned a letter sent by Pertini to Cossiga in which Pertini requested that the new ministers be "honest persons." He wrote that he had the legitimate right to accept or reject the persons proposed as ministers. It seems that this letter was read to the national secretaries of the DC, PSI, and PRI, included in the new majority.[35]

If taken literally, this assertion of the right of the chief of state would have had considerable constitutional implications. The ruling elite reacted wisely, by deliberate silence, as if it were not an issue of high priority, and therefore the presidential request fell by the wayside. The result was derisory: the cancellation of one name (Lattanzio) from the list of ministers-designate, replaced at the last moment at Pertini's formal request.

The constitutional theory and praxis remained unchanged. The president, not being politically responsible, cannot be involved in the highly

political process of the selection of ministers. The president does not have the right to choose or reject ministers, who are themselves politically responsible in Parliament, and who, being delegated by their party and factions, are not even chosen in complete freedom by the prime minister. Nevertheless, there is no doubt that the president can exercise an efficient, albeit discreet, influence. The personality of the president is, from this point of view, essential. The psychological distance between Gronchi or Pertini on one side, and Segni or Leone on the other, is enormous.

There is an important difference between the selection of the prime minister and of the president of the republic. The first is chosen by his peers. Few leaders are involved in the consultation process at the headquarters of the coalition parties and at the Quirinale. Among the 20 or 30 personalities invited for consultation to the Quirinale, some are "protocol visitors," such as the representative of the Communist party or a former president of the republic. Few can give the president useful advice. On the contrary, the electoral college, which chooses the president of the republic, has consisted of 1,000 politicians since 1971 (only 937 in 1964, 842 in 1962, 833 in 1955). The vote is secret, permitting subtle strategies. In 1971, Fanfani missed being elected by only about 40 votes. To elect Saragat in 1964, twenty-one rounds were needed; for Leone in 1971, twenty-three; Pertini was elected in the sixteenth round. But only one round was sufficient to elect the Christian Democrat Cossiga in 1981 with a majority of 76.8 percent. "A beautiful day for the Republic," exclaimed the socialist prime minister, Craxi.

One is tempted to believe the fairy tale narrated by well-informed observers of the Roman political arena, but who were not able to furnish a written documentation to the historian. The tale is about a secret agreement between Cossiga and Craxi, according to which the first helped the second become prime minister in August 1983, and the latter helped the former to become president of the republic in June 1985. Political wisdom in the best tradition of consociational democracy! A "historic compromise," but between the Christian Democrats and the PSI! Pending confessions and memoirs, one can note that only the Christian Democratic party had proposed a candidate for the presidency, the other parties not having suggested any alternative. Prior to the vote in Parliament, the Christian Democratic party convened its deputies, senators, and regional delegates, and by secret vote they nominated Cossiga. "We have worked for such a result," declared the vice national secretary of the PSI, Claudio Martelli, a friend of Craxi.

For a long time the four most important political positions, the presidency of the republic, of the Council of Ministers, of the Chamber,

and of the Senate, were occupied by Christian Democrats. When Craxi became prime minister, the president of the republic was a Socialist; the president of the chamber, a Communist; and only the president of the Senate, a Christian Democrat. If there were a Socialist in the Chigi Palace there should be a Christian Democrat in the Quirinale in exchange, at least on the first occasion.

Napoleon, before appointing someone to an important military or administrative position, used to ask: "Are you a lucky man?" He believed in chance, which is an irritating concept for historians. Nevertheless, to become president of the republic or prime minister one needs, obviously, favorable winds. It is possible to codify the rules of the game in the selection of cabinet ministers without reference to good fortune, but for presidents and prime ministers hazard may play a crucial role. One example: if Pertini had succeeded in becoming prime minister in 1968, perhaps he would not have been elected president of the republic ten years later at the age of eighty-two because a prime minister easily engenders unfriendliness with some rivals—particularly a man like Pertini. If Aldo Moro had not been assassinated two months before Pertini's election as president, he would have been a serious competitor to Pertini—or later to Cossiga.

CONCLUSION

What about the role played by the people in this selection process by the Christian Democratic ruling elite? Only a minority of the Italian electorate voted for that party: From 48.5 percent in 1948 to 38 percent in 1983. The Christian Democrats have nevertheless been the major party. Very heterogenous, it represented all social strata, even if in a distorted way. Situated at the center right of the political spectrum, the DC was unavoidable for the crystallization of any parliamentary majority. Within this majority it appeared always as the dominant party. By the preferential vote a minority of Christian Democratic voters—one in every four or five—participated in the first stage of the selection process: They chose the deputies and the senators among many candidates in the party list, intermittently every five years, in a truly democratic game. Thereafter, the selection process was transferred to the pyramid of the party, mostly to its summit, and to the Parliament.

What image does the Christian Democratic leadership—selected according to the rules here analyzed—reflect in the mirror of public opinion? In a survey taken in April 1986, concerning the honesty and competence of the politicians in power (*uomini di governo*), 52.6 percent of the sample formulated a negative judgment. An equal majority

expressed distrust of the administration of the state.[36] Already in 1965 a majority (53 percent) thought that politicians (of all parties) tend to give greater priority to the interests of their party and themselves than to the general needs of the country. A feeling of resignation appeared in the belief of half of the sample that "it is better to have a mediocre parliament than none at all" (only 9 percent expressed the opposite opinion and 45 percent abstained from replying).[37]

Such a severe judgment apparently contrasts with the results of surveys about the popularity of the prime ministers, such as one in which only a small minority formulated negative judgments about the prime ministers from De Gasperi to Craxi (see Table 4.3). The high proportion of those who did not express an opinion does not invalidate the results, in the same way as a low electoral turnout does not invalidate the elections. The proportion of favorable opinion is relatively high. It seems that the Italians condemn the "system" more than its leaders, as did the French people toward the end of the Fourth Republic.

The Italians appear less satisfied than their European neighbors with the way in which the democratic regime functions; in fact, it is in Italy that the proportion of dissatisfied people is the highest in Europe (see Table 4.4). The European community has periodically asked such questions of national samples in ten or twelve countries in the 1970s and 1980s, and regularly Italy has appeared as the country with the lowest legitimacy of the regime.

How should one interpret this fact? If one looks to the economic performance of the regime, and if one compares Italy with Britain, which has long been considered a model of democracy, one has to admit that in terms of economic growth Italy has performed much better than Britain during the period from 1950 to 1980. In spite of ministerial instability and other weaknesses of the system, Italy has experienced an economic miracle. In spite of the beauty of the model of democracy, Britain has, during the same third of the century, declined economically in comparison with the performance of other democracies, for a variety of reasons that do not need to be specified here. Only West Germany, Japan, and Austria have progressed economically more than Italy. If the choice were between a regime with high political performance accompanied by an economic relative regression and a regime with economic prosperity engendering political dissatisfaction, many would choose the latter. It is not clear how much of the merits and the faults of each regime can be attributed to the political leadership, and how much to the society itself, more or less independent of the state apparatus.

Table 4.3
Public Opinion Survey About Prime Ministers in the Italian Republic, 1947-1984[a]

		Statements:					
		I[b]	II[c]	III[d]	IV[e]	V[f]	VI[g]
De Gasperi	Sept. 1947	10	30	21	16	12	11
De Gasperi	Feb. 1952	8	30	21	14	13	14
Pella	Nov. 1954	16	30	10	5	7	32
Pella	Apr. 1956	17	24	8	4	6	41
Scelba	Nov. 1964	9	27	16	8	12	28
Scelba	Nov. 1965	5	16	11	13	18	37
Segni	Nov. 1965	6	22	17	5	7	43
Segni	Mar. 1956	11	31	21	8	8	21
Zoli	Jan. 1958	8	22	20	9	7	34
Fanfani	Oct. 1960	12	30	15	6	9	28
Fanfani	Feb. 1961	10	30	16	5	7	32
Fanfani	Dec. 1961	9	29	13	4	5	40
Fanfani	Jan. 1963	10	26	19	7	5	33
Moro	Mar. 1964	7	24	18	10	8	33
Moro	July 1964	7	19	14	11	13	36
Moro	Sept. 1965	6	20	17	7	7	43
Moro	Sept. 1967	11	30	20	7	6	26
Moro	Apr. 1968	9	31	29	10	8	13
Colombo	Apr. 1972	7	25	19	8	5	36
Andreotti	Dec. 1976	5	20	18	16	14	27
Andreotti	Dec. 1978	6	21	19	16	13	25
Cossiga	Oct. 1980	3	15	20	16	10	36
Forlani	Apr. 1981	4	16	21	14	9	36
Craxi	Apr. 1984	4	25	22	12	10	27

[a]The question was phrased: Which of the following statements expresses best your opinion about . . . president of the Council of Ministers?
[b]Statement I: Fully approve of his policy
[c]Statement II: Has done well in general
[d]Statement III: Has acted in a mediocre way but without too many errors
[e]Statement IV: Has committed too many errors that could be avoided
[f]Statement V: Completely disapprove of his policy
[g]Statement VI: Don't know

Source: *Bollettino della Doxa* 38, no. 11 and 12, June 1984.

Table 4.4
Public Opinion Surveys About the Functioning of the Democratic Regime, European Community Countries

	March/April 1985				Oct. 1985		April 1986
	Very Satisfied	Rather Satisfied	Rather Dissatisfied	Not At All Satisfied	Satisfied	Dissatisfied	Satisfied
Luxembourg	15	57	20	2	67	27	75
Germany	13	60	19	5	69	26	80
Denmark	19	49	21	7	72	21	74
Greece	19	40	20	13	51	42	56
Netherlands	7	49	29	9	58	37	61
Belgium	5	47	27	14	58	36	51
Britain	7	44	30	13	52	44	52
Spain	--	--	--	--	--	--	51
Ireland	8	41	28	17	51	39	49
France	5	39	35	13	39	51	52
Italy	2	23	45	27	28	69	30

Source: Eurobarometer, 1985 and 1986.

NOTES

Paolo Ungari, professor at the National School of Administration in Rome, gave me valuable suggestions and generously helped me with his critical comments. Carlo Dané, from the Research Office of the Christian Democratic party, read the manuscript, drew my attention to many important points, and corrected a number of errors. His help was essential in clarifying the rules. I express my gratitude to both of them and my admiration for their intimate knowledge of the Italian political class. Neither of them is responsible for the opinions presented here or for the insufficiencies that may exist in this analysis.

1. The Craxi government remained in power more than three and one half years. A miracle! But this length is not the only reason why a new historical phase began.

2. The fourth De Gasperi cabinet, in 1947, started as monocolor and included a few neutral "experts," but later became quadripartite. It is considered as the latter here.

3. The first De Gasperi government (December 1945 to July 1946) included representatives of seven parties, 3 from each party. The hegemony of the Christian Democratic party appeared later, particularly after the exclusion of the Communists from the cabinet in February 1947.

4. *Tripartite* and not *tricolor,* which is a word used by the nationalist Extreme Right. The antifascist attitude caused the disappearance from the political vocabulary of words used too much by the fascists, for instance, *nazione.* This word was replaced by *paese* or *territorio.* The Italian political class, better educated than most politicians of many other European countries, expresses itself with care.

5. Contrary to a tenacious error, committed even by some historians, the Christian Democratic party did not hold the majority of the seats in the Senate between 1948 and 1953. It held only 149 out of a total of 344, including 106 appointed senators, among whom only 18 were Christian Democrats. These senators by right were parliamentarians before 1922, most of them active Resistants against the fascist regime.

6. Among the 663 ministers and under secretaries of state, there are in addition to Christian Democrats, 89 members of the PSI, 53 PSDI, 34 PRI, 36 PLI, 15 PCI (Italian Communist party), 7 "experts," and 6 others.

7. The summit of the party does not include all the secretaries of state. A few of them had less political weight than some party officials who have never held a ministerial position. For instance, the vice national secretary of the party, Sandro Fontana, was not even a parliamentarian.

8. The vice prime ministers were usually important senior leaders. Most of them represented the other parties in the coalition governments, and few of them belonged to the Christian Democrats. They are considered here as cabinet ministers.

9. One example among dozens: Moro was president of the Federation of Catholic Students at a moment when Taviani and Andreotti were members of the executive board.

10. On the female preponderance in the Christian Democratic electorate, see M. Dogan, "Le donne italiane tra il cattolicesimo e il marximo," in A. Spreafico and J. La Palombara (eds.), *Elezioni e comportamento politico in Italia,* Milano, Comunita, 1963, pp. 475–494, and "Les conséquences politiques du vote féminin: comment les femmes ont porté les conservateurs au pouvoir," *International Political Science Journal,* 1985, no. 3, pp. 306–316.

11. The Italian electoral law, based on proportional representation, gives the voters the right to express a preferential vote for three candidates of the list chosen. The candidates on each list who have the highest number of preferential votes are elected. In most of the constituencies there was usually at least one woman among the candidates, but she did not obtain a sufficient number of preferential votes to be elected.

12. Cf. Democrazia Cristiana, *Atti del Consiglio Nazionale, 18–21 luglio 1974,* Roma, Edizioni Cinque Lune, 1974, pp. 69–70.

13. In Table 4.1, the 86 under secretaries of state who were promoted to be ministers are counted as ministers, even though some of them participated in four or five governments as under secretaries of state and only once as cabinet minister.

14. For this reason de Gaulle required the inclusion in the Fifth Republic constitution of the principle of incompatibility between ministerial position and parliamentary mandate: Deputies appointed ministers resign from Parliament.

15. Cf. Democrazia Cristiana, *op. cit.,* p. 70.

16. Cf. M. Calise et R. Mannheimer, "Misurare i governi: la distribuzione territoriale dei governanti italiani, 1948–1978," *Il Mulino,* 1981, no. 4, p. 579.

17. This equivalence is the most important point in the so-called Cencelli Manual. The paternity of this equation has been attributed by some to Adolfo

Sarti, minister in many governments. During an interview, he told me that the true author is his old secretary, Massimo Cencelli. What is significant is the almost spontaneous acceptance of this proposition by the Christian Democratic apparatus and by the faction chiefs.

18. In the consociational democracies proportionality is instead applied to linguistic and religious communities. For instance, in Belgium the Walloons and the Flemish have the right to an equal number of portfolios no matter what the political composition of the government.

19. Some ministers are obviously very important: treasury, budget, interior, justice; others are prestigious: foreign affairs and ministries without portfolios; others are more advantageous from the electoral and clientelistic point of view: post office, industry, nationalized enterprises. When a reform is planned, a department may temporarily become of strategic importance. There are also departments of routine management that were accepted instead of nothing, for these positions allowed for participation at the meetings of the Council of Ministers.

20. *L'Umanità,* October 14, 1980.

21. Statement by a former minister, B. D'Arezzo, to a journalist of the *Corriere della Serra,* October 29, 1980.

22. See Chapter 10 in this volume.

23. The "tetrarchy" does not meet at the central headquarters of the party but in a villa in the middle of a well-protected garden, where visitors are not accepted during the "conclave."

24. Interview of Salvatore Valitutti, Liberal minister in the Cossiga government.

25. *L'Umanità,* October 17, 1980.

26. G. F. Ciaurro, "Ministro," *Enciclopedia del diritto,* vol. 26, Milano, Guiffre, 1976.

27. Among the testimonies concerning the importance of factions one could mention that of the Christian Democratic Senator F. Martinazzoli, who denounced the "degeneration" of the factions, "instruments for the self-selection of the ruling groups," *L'Unità,* June 25, 1981.

28. Quoted in Attilio Piccioni, *Scritti e Discorsi 1944–1965,* edited by Carlo Dané, Roma, Edizione Cinque Lune, 1979, pp. 638–640.

29. From newspapers of June 24, 1981.

30. *L'Unità,* June 25, 1981.

31. *La Repubblica,* June 30, 1981.

32. *La Voce Repubblicana,* June 30, 1981.

33. It is well known that the appointment of C. Mazza was principally due to his friendship with President Leone. It would be possible to give several examples of under secretaries of state or ministers who owed their first appointment to the friendship of the president. But political patronage cannot be maintained if the beneficiary does not prove that he or she possesses the qualities required of a member of government.

34. Article by Bassanini, "L'Ultimo tentativo," *Il Messaggero,* March 12, 1979, and article by Tosi, "Il punto costituzionale," *La Nazione,* March 8, 1979.
35. *La Repubblica,* April 2, 1980.
36. *Bollettino della Doxa,* June 10, 1986.
37. *Bollettino della Doxa,* October 5, 1965.

5
JUNIOR MINISTERS AND MINISTERIAL CAREERS IN BRITAIN

Donald D. Searing

When Harold Macmillan suggested there were only four reasons to be in the House of Commons—to become prime minister, chancellor of the exchequer, foreign secretary, or home secretary—he was expressing the bias of ambitious aspirants whose "dreams of office and power" drift through the halls of parliamentary history. As recently as the eighteenth century, however, such ministerial aspirants were a small minority, for offices were few and much of political life was a matter of indifference to most members of Parliament (Namier 1968:7). When many more offices became available during the nineteenth century, the number of aspirants expanded to fill them and filled as well the six political novels of Anthony Trollope's Palliser series. Later, the rise of the administrative state created still more opportunities for office and introduced a professionalization that turned the eighteenth-century pattern on its head and reduced to a small minority the former majority of politically indifferent members. The outlooks of those members of Parliament who very much desire to become apprentices and officeholders were captured in the following remarks from an ambitious Labour member: "What is enjoyable about politics? Power and the exercise of power which I find absolutely delightful. If I thought for one moment I was going to spend forty years in the House of Commons and never exercise power again, I would find it an absolutely dreadful and appalling and arid prospect" (King 1974:114).

    This chapter examines apprenticeships for ministerial office in Great Britain and, in particular, the training of the junior minister, whose experience constitutes the most important of these apprenticeships. The complex career ladder extends, of course, all the way from the back

benches to the cabinet. On the back benches are those who take up the informal role of "ministerial aspirant" and spend their time seeking strategies by which they might rise to the next rung. The next established rung is assigned to the parliamentary private secretary, "the minister's eyes and ears" in the House of Commons, or, less sympathetically, "the minister's dogsbody." This position is well established but unofficial; it is, in effect, a preapprenticeship where incumbents serve their ministers as errand runners and serve themselves by increasing their prospects for attaining office. The first official rung on the ladder is that of the junior minister, the focus of my inquiry. The junior minister is definitely a member of the Government and is usually in very active training for higher things. Above the junior ministers we find ministers-not-in-the-cabinet and then, finally, cabinet ministers themselves. Thus, service as a junior minister is not the only apprenticeship for service at the top, but it is nevertheless regarded by ministers as the key apprenticeship in the career structure. It is the learning and testing ground where candidates are sorted out, half of them to return to the back benches, and half of them to journey on.

The data for this study are drawn from transcripts of interviews that I conducted in 1972 and 1973 with 521 British Members of Parliament. These interviews concerned career patterns and roles that crystallized after the war and that have proved relatively stable throughout the postwar period. The respondents also filled in printed forms and returned a mail-back questionnaire. A response rate of 83 percent applies to backbenchers, members of the Government, and Opposition spokespersons alike. A great deal of quantitative data has been generated from the written materials and from coding the transcripts. Much of this has been published elsewhere (e.g., Searing 1986, 1985, 1982, 1978). What I would like to do in the present chapter, however, is an analysis of a more qualitative kind that will rely mainly on the transcripts and seek to reconstruct the apprenticeship experience as it is seen by those involved in it. Thus, I shall focus mainly on the interviews with ministers and particularly on the interviews with junior ministers, whose apprenticeships will be the focus of my inquiry and whose words will be the building blocks of my analysis. During the period of the interviews, a total of thirty MPs served as junior ministers. Twenty-five of them were interviewed as part of our study.

SEEKING THE REAL APPRENTICES: PLACEMEN AND JOURNEYMEN

The role of the junior minister emerged in its modern form during the middle of the nineteenth century (Heasman 1960:16). Its predecessor, the "parliamentary secretary," was not separated from the permanent

secretary, and the parliamentary secretary was not, therefore, a candidate for promotion to minister. The change in the nature of the role began after Lord Liverpool appointed a reluctant Robert Peel to the post of parliamentary secretary on the grounds that it was good training for higher things. And soon people did begin to step up from these positions into the ministerial hierarchy, as permanent secretaries began to take over the parliamentary secretaries' nonministerial work.

This transfer of certain work from the parliamentary secretary to the permanent secretary had two consequences: One was that the parliamentary secretary was cut loose to develop a new and different character; the other was that the junior ministers no longer had very precise duties or automatic powers (Heasman 1960). Hence, their role emerged as a clearly differentiated but not clearly defined cluster of attributes, and this lack of clarity in established expectations for the apprenticeship has continued down to the present. The differentiation became formally recognized when parliamentary secretaries acquired their supplementary title, "junior ministers." The lack of clarity in established expectations for the apprenticeship turned on the distribution of their duties between Westminster and Whitehall (Parliament and the executive). Originally focusing on the ministries, junior ministers began to take up as their major function the representation in Parliament of their department's interests and perspectives (Milne 1950:437). Gradually, however, the role came full circle as the growth of governmental responsibilities created the need for further differentiation, particularly for an augmentation of the junior minister's responsibilities to include, once again, duties within the department.

Although the position of junior minister was not originally created as an apprenticeship for service as a minister, it evolved to serve this training function. Such training is not, however, the only function it serves, for some junior ministers are appointed more by way of reward than recruitment (Rose 1971:404). No one expects them to go on to higher posts. This is the institutional basis among junior ministers for two informal attitudinal roles: "placemen" and "journeymen." These two role types are widely recognized, although they are not well defined in the minds of MPs, nor are they well discussed in the interview transcripts. Still, the material is adequate for brief sketches of each. It is important to distinguish the placeman, who is not a true apprentice, from the journeyman, who is, for the placeman or his functional equivalent exists at every level of the career hierarchy.

Placemen

I shall begin therefore with the placemen, who, outside Westminster, are much less familiar than the journeymen. Placemen are junior

ministers who express uncertainty, pessimism, or defeatism about their prospects. They express uncertainty because where there is life there is hope: "I would have thought, um, well, you can—you can never tell, can you?" They express pessimism because they are usually realistic about their chances of achieving further positions—"I mean . . . not very high." They express defeatism because, in the end, "I quite accept my present place . . . and I accept that I would never be more than a junior minister." They accept the fact that they have climbed their own personal career ladder and have nowhere else to go but out.

Placemen are junior ministers because it has been decided to reward them for past services or to imprison them for recent transgressions. They are not high climbers. And they often have mixed feelings about their positions, feelings that surface in hints of insecurity. Thus, placemen can be a little pompous and a little touchy, especially when they are reminded that their posting resembles a sinecure. In the modern age of achievement, they occasionally feel embarrassed about that resemblance and a little concerned that they might be "found out." This was certainly the case for the junior minister who, throughout the interview, repeatedly described himself as "a long-standing and highly-respected Member of Parliament." It also rang true for the junior minister who was proud to be positioned on the deck of the ship of state "participating in what the Prime Minister said to me was a great embarking on a great adventure . . . to change . . . the course of life in this country."

In the same vein, it is not at all uncommon for placemen to sound more like members of Parliament than like junior ministers. Thus, one described himself as a "former M.P." because "that's what I did for so long before I became a junior minister." Another explained that although he "has now got some little chancellery fame in as much as I'm a junior minister," he drew his real satisfactions from his membership in the House of Commons and is always aware that that is where he will return. He can always be proud to be an MP, whereas "there is nothing so dead as the ex–junior minister of _____ ." Placemen sound as though they are outside the ministry looking in as privileged spectators. They feel like outsiders because for them the stress is more on "House work" than on "department work." They spend most of their time at the House and see as quite significant the label "parliamentary" in their title, "parliamentary under secretary of state." This is how they interpret their role. And this is how their minister sees it too: "The danger is you sometimes get some parliamentary secretaries who get so involved in their department, you know, and see themselves as, as a, a deputy managing director, that they forget their responsibilities to represent their department in the House." Most placemen find that they

Table 5.1
Junior Ministers: Attitudinal Roles by Age

	Age at Appointment			
	Under 40	40-44	45-50	Over 50
Placeman	0	0	7	5
Journeyman	5	5	3	0

are not particularly busy and so have a good deal of time to spend with their constituents too.

The placemen are not noticeably old, but they are not noticeably young either. The fact that they "would love to have been in government office by the age of about 30," but were not, is an important clue to their present situation. "When I first came in here seventeen years ago," one frank placeman explained, "I think there were more people like myself, a bit older . . . you know, Knights of the Shires, . . . or in the Labour Party half way up. . . . And whenever they were fifty, if they were fortunate, they would be elevated to a minor post in the Government." Placemen enter late and leave early. In and out in three years is a common pattern. They are the "people who should be given three years of fat ministerial life as reward for services rendered but whom one shouldn't keep longer than that" (Crossman, vol. 2, 1976:761).

One can see the numbers of junior ministers who assume the attitudinal roles of placemen and journeymen and the ages at which they were appointed to their posts on Table 5.1. The coding for these subtypes is based on their own assessments of their prospects for promotion and on their own descriptions of the character of their current duties. Still, because this coding is impressionistic and based on comparatively little information, the role types of placemen and journeymen will not be pursued systematically in my analysis. Nevertheless, their distribution is reported in Table 5.1 in order to provide rough estimates of their proportions among junior ministers and of the relationship between their statuses and the age variable that is said to be a marker for them. According to my reading of the transcripts, and much to my surprise, approximately half (twelve out of twenty-five) of the junior ministers see themselves as placemen. This high proportion of placemen is important not only because the two role types play the role of junior minister somewhat differently but also because it suggests that only slightly more than half the junior ministers, the journeymen, are serious competitors in the race to the top. Contrary to the as-

sumptions in many rational-choice models of political ambition, it may therefore be misleading to assume that everyone in the same formal position on a career ladder is reaching for the next rung.

Very similar subtypes are found among parliamentary private secretaries (PPSs), although at this stage a smaller proportion of the incumbents are sitting out the contest. Such considerations must count heavily in the interpretations of the proportions of MPs who rise from one rung of the leadership ladder to the next. In particular, the high rate of failure in rising from PPS to junior minister, and from junior minister to minister, may have less to do with failure than with the fact that two quite different types of MPs are recruited to each role: journeymen, who are expected to pass through if they pass muster, and placemen, who are expected to stay a while and then return from whence they came. It is clear from Table 5.1 that age has a great deal to do with whether a junior minister sees himself as a placeman or as a journeyman. All the MPs who were appointed to the post of junior minister after their fiftieth birthdays view themselves as placemen, whereas all those who were appointed before they turned forty-five have more ambitious career plans. The early arrivals are the journeymen, and they interpret their roles as apprenticeships for higher things.

Journeymen

The journeyman, the second type of junior minister, constructs his role interpretations around his desire to carry on with the climb: "I mean I just want to go on, I can't envisage giving up the climb you know." Journeymen are ambitious apprentices, and some of them are very ambitious apprentices indeed, such as the aggressive former businessman who claims an extraordinary capacity for making big decisions and fully expects to be able to do this sooner rather than later in Government. He also assumes, as do a number of his colleagues, that "anybody who you meet in this place who says he doesn't want to be Prime Minister is a liar. That's what we're here for." Journeymen believe that their aspirations are widely shared and that, in their case at least, the chances are good that such aspirations will be fulfilled. They are ready to "go wherever the Prime Minister sends me" and expect it to be upward. For them the major uncertainty is only the question of which "department of state would interest me . . . um, I would like to have a chance of serving in the Foreign Office."

Journeymen believe they are leaders. Several also share the belief of the one who said, "I've been trained since I left school, um, to . . . take responsibility, my whole training, my whole background has been

to take responsibility." They expect to lead, to lead in minor posts today, in major posts tomorrow. They see their role of junior minister as a time and place for learning, as an apprenticeship for bigger and better things. It is an opportunity to absorb the formal knowledge and also the tacit knowledge that is necessary to become a good minister—square one and also square two: "This (formal knowledge) is what I call the sort of square one stuff. Or, coming on to square two I think is learning how things happen, which is by no means the same way as occur in the books on constitutional procedure. In practice it's rather like if you're studying the management structure of a great organisation. There is the official chart of the hierarchy, but the . . . interesting things are the unofficial ones you know."

A busy, professional approach to the job is another characteristic that distinguishes journeymen from placemen. Rather than complain about the burdens on their social life, journeymen seem almost proud of the infrequency with which they go out to dinner or the theater or enjoy the sort of social life they had before they became junior ministers. They are also critical of their colleagues who complain so much about it: "You have to make some kind of sacrifice, and if you find you haven't been to a play for a year, or that you're losing out on the number of days you go to Wimbledon, that's just hard luck." Journeymen are likely to characterize themselves as professional politicians and to mean by that the same sort of thing that others mean by the terms "professional banker or professional industrialist." They feel they are members of a particular professional subculture, members who, when they meet professionals from other tribes, might find it "interesting to discuss things with them, but they don't see things my way and I don't see things their way."

Part of this professional interpretation of their apprenticeship is the stress they put on the departmental side of the job. Journeymen, like placemen, do their liaison work between the department and the House; and in this way they earn their keep as *parliamentary* under secretaries. But they also spend much more time than do placemen in the department itself, and they are much more likely to be delegated serious responsibility for a range of specific policy matters. One journeyman at the Home Office, for example, was delegated responsibility for examining individual cases involving paroles and life sentences. He was also typical in that he was comparatively young among junior ministers. High flyers tend to be fast flyers, quickly appointed and quick to rise: "In fact, immediately after the last general election I was appointed the most junior of all junior ministers."

ACTIVITY AT WESTMINSTER

Junior ministers spend a great deal of time at Westminster. "The adjective *parliamentary* in the title "is no accidental one . . . you are meant to be closely in touch with Members of Parliament in the House of Commons about the affairs of your department." In fact, until the postwar period, this was virtually the junior minister's only function—defending and explaining to Parliament the position of his department (Milne 1950:440–41). The task is indispensable and never more so than when the minister is in the House of Lords and therefore not available for cross-examination in the Commons. The point is to be, on behalf of the department, accessible to backbenchers, to spend time round the House, "in the Smoking Room or the Tea Room or having meals there so that other MPs can buttonhole him about their problems."

Compared to their ministers, junior ministers are expected to spend far more time in Parliament, as much time as is necessary "to get the feel of the place," to know what members are thinking, to try to assess beforehand how they are going to react. Most of them don't mind at all because this is their element: "The essence of this place is that it is a market. It's like the Stock Market or the cattle market or Christie's, where all the experts come to market ideas, to pick each other's brains, to argue and to swap information." As junior ministers, they serve their apprenticeship in this market, collecting information, selling ideas, and smelling the political atmosphere. "If you don't like being in the market," they say, "then there's no point in being here at all."

Liaison with Backbenchers

Junior ministers, who might rather deal with ministers and civil servants than with backbenchers, find themselves nevertheless in the House so much because their apprenticeship is structured more by assigned duties and responsibilities than by their own inclinations. They are in and out of the House of Commons the whole time because they are assigned the responsibility for liaison with backbenchers. Junior ministers have to be there so that backbenchers will have the opportunity to come and talk to them, to explain views, to tell them what they are feeling, and to listen to the department's case that the junior minister will set out in Parliament. "A prudent minister like Sir Keith Joseph must keep in very close touch with opinion in the House, and that is one of my principal tasks as his parliamentary secretary." Prudent ministers wish to be known as the sort who are open to receiving advice from backbenchers. "He must be in continual consultation with Members on both sides of the House concerning his poli-

cies." Prudent ministers therefore see that their junior ministers spend, like it or not, a great deal of time on liaison with backbenchers. Ministers cannot do it themselves. Nor can their civil servants. And yet they very much need to sound out what they "can get through and what [they] can't get through and how far [they] can go."

So they send their junior ministers to take the temperature, to chat around the corridors, and to pay particular attention to those backbenchers who have a continuing and knowledgeable interest in the affairs of their department. Experience in Opposition helps junior ministers do this effectively because it familiarizes them with the routines by which backbenchers seek to keep the Government on its toes and probe its weaknesses. Most junior ministers in the sample had this experience and regarded it as invaluable, "particularly, I think, where the majority is not a very large one, where you really have, for purposes of self-preservation, you really have got to keep in touch with what, particularly with what your own backbenchers are thinking." Junior ministers are on the front line.

The place where they can gather their information most expeditiously is at the relevant back-bench party committees. The secretary of state may meet privately and perhaps regularly with the officers of the back-bench committees that focus on his department's subjects. But the junior minister will be expected to attend the committees' meetings regularly and to appear before them formally. Usually it is a pleasant exchange for the junior minister, for he will be regarded as well informed and will be speaking from a position of modest authority. But on "what we might call the rather excitable issues of policy," it can become very trying indeed: "I had a very, very difficult time with them over the decision to bail out the Upper Clyde Shipbuilders, where the views of this Government or this department and the party committee were completely at loggerheads. I mean there was simply a hundred and eighty degree split, er, and in the end of course the views of the Government had to prevail, but, er, not until after there'd been a great deal of very vigorous and painful discussion."

The bulk of the work, however, involves an endless series of informal contacts with members of Parliament, who come up and ask questions, make points, raise constituency issues, inquire about a letter that has not been answered or whether there is going to be a follow-up. The aim is to deal satisfactorily with all these approaches but also, and perhaps more importantly, to do a little public relations, to give members "the feeling that they are important and an important part of the policy-making processes as they affect this department." If ministers fail to do this, their department may develop the image of being administered by cold, distant bureaucrats. This will be reflected, junior

ministers believe, first in the House and then in the press. Once the department and its ministers are viewed in this way, then even policies based on the best of intentions become easily misunderstood. Blunders in the department become magnified and add to its poor reputation. Moreover, the secretary of state may gradually become widely criticized in the House and in the press—and then the prime minister may feel compelled to transfer him or to give him the sack. In all this, the junior minister can do his bit to help prevent the department and the secretary of state from becoming unstuck by promoting the impression that his masters are ministers who care, ministers who respect the House.

The junior minister is sent to Westminster to keep in touch, to listen carefully, and to promote the right impression. But he is also sent to Westminster to persuade. For some this is "my, my main role obviously is to explain our foreign policy in the House of Commons, um, helping Sir Alec Douglas-Home." He does this by seeking to convince his parliamentary colleagues that the department's "line of action is good and valid and proper." Through debate and argument, he draws their attention to "aspects of the question which they haven't seen before or understood properly." All in all, it is a useful apprenticeship for the Westminster side of ministerial work. Junior ministers learn by doing. And if some of them will never themselves make use of this learning, the doing will at least have been useful to the department.

At the Despatch Box

One of the best opportunities that junior ministers have to distinguish themselves in the eyes of their party, and to build a sound reputation in the House, arises when they speak for their department at the despatch box. In the big debates, "the big shots are wheeled in, as it were, the secretaries of state come down." But for much of the routine debates, it is the junior ministers who are assigned to cope with the House and to try to convince or at least impress it at the despatch box. "You have at least two parties to convince" in your audience: "You have your own backbenchers who will include a number of positive enthusiasts about some particular course of action, and you have to convince them or appease them. Much more difficult, you have to convince and appease a probing Opposition which is out to find fault, out to cut down the impact you're making to a smaller size." And unless junior ministers can convince the House of Commons that their policies are right, they will not convince anybody: "You're not going to convince a lot of people outside if you have criticism right

across the spectrum in the House." Thus, junior ministers gradually become aware that "the reception that Parliament is likely to give a new series of measures from your department must become very much a factor in considering what these measures should be." This will prove to be one of the most significant lessons they learn during their apprenticeships.

When speaking at the despatch box, and elsewhere in the House too, junior ministers are generally regarded as spokespersons for their senior colleagues and for the department. MPs are aware that most of them do not have important, independent decision making functions in Whitehall (Heasman 1960:16). Allowances are often made, therefore, such that "it's assumed that he's, you know, you don't have to look for his weak spot." "But it doesn't automatically happen," and "if weaknesses are shown, the hounds may latch on to it." Junior ministers must learn the art of convincing or appeasing the House. The first requirement, they believe, is to "know your stuff, know what your subject is about, have read the brief and know at least as much about it as anybody who is likely to cross-examine you knows." It is not just eloquence, which is more important in Opposition than in Government. In Government, the focus is on substance. Eloquence is still important, "but these are the minister's own policies, he must be seen to understand them, he must have answers to the questions."

Junior ministers struggle to master their subjects and also to master themselves. It is essential they find a convincing way to express self-confidence, for only then, they believe, will their listeners have confidence in them: "Above all to try and give the impression that he is confident—even if he isn't—and that he knows what he is doing," said one of the least confident junior ministers, who was particularly sensitive about the subject. Yet, it is not easy even for this normally confident and articulate Etonian who readily admits that "one is a little nervous obviously if you're going to take a debate, if you are going to open and close it, or if you've got a particularly rough question to deal with." It isn't easy because, despite the fact that the House sometimes makes allowances, junior ministers feel that their careers are on the line every time they speak. It is their most public performance on Westminster's stages. They are carefully judged, and they constantly face the chance that if "he slips up and in a speech makes a rather silly remark . . . they'll give him stick." These apprentices have watched the House cut pompous and poorly informed ministers down to size, and they know that, as junior ministers, a reputation of being unable to answer the arguments with appropriate substance and style may label them incompetent and get them sacked.

Contact with leaders on the other side, which is an occasional part of the job, can be a new and interesting experience for junior ministers. They are occasionally instructed by their superiors to give information to leaders of the Opposition, which, it is hoped, will help make them more reasonable critics, "information, er, which helps to clarify a situation which is not clear to them without that information." They are also sent to exchange semiconfidential information with shadow ministers about matters such as dates of statements, and they usually find that "they regard it as confidential and don't broadcast it . . . and I've never been disappointed . . . (with the respective confidences) in these matters."

A Narrowing Experience

Junior ministers may make a few new contacts with leaders on the other side, but on the whole, service as a junior minister in the House of Commons is a narrowing experience. "The most narrowing period," observed a cabinet minister, "is when you're a junior minister, I found myself." Cabinet ministers can be concerned "about general policy . . . about government policy as a whole." Whips too, complained a former whip who felt constricted as a junior minister: "Whips know more about what is going on than most ministers except those in the Cabinet." Even backbenchers, and sometimes especially backbenchers, added the cabinet minister, can be "concerned right across the political spectrum . . . insofar as you have any influence you have it in spheres that you choose yourself." One can be part of policy debates over a wide front. "I mean my former colleagues in the whip's office," added the former whip, "now know a lot more about what's going on in the Government than I do, except of course for this department." The point is that junior ministers are fenced in within the fields of their assignments.

That fence is built by the doctrine of collective responsibility and by the fear that junior ministers' words on any political topic might be taken as the opinions of their superiors. Junior ministers are required therefore to be comparatively quiet and constrained—which is not easy for junior ministers like Norman St. John-Stevas who, as a backbencher, was characterized as "a bird of paradise in Trafalgar Square" and by the *Times* as "the Conservative Party's gift to the media." When he was elevated from the back benches to the Department of Education and Science, the *Times* (7 November 1972) lamented that "We can expect to hear from him in the Parliament, I suppose, once a month at Question Time and perhaps giving three speeches a year."

The role did not used to be such a narrowing experience. During the first part of the nineteenth century, junior ministers were not subject

to the norms of collective responsibility because it was believed that their positions held too little authority to warrant it—they were regarded as in no way responsible for government policy (Milne 1950:439–40). By 1869, however, Trollope's (1869:47) Phineas Finn was beginning to worry about the pressures that were spreading beyond deeds in the division (voting) lobbies ("Where he knew that it would be his duty as a subaltern to vote as he was directed") to words in the other lobbies:

> ... now that Phineas had consented to join the Government (as a Junior Minister). ... He could no longer be a free agent, or even a free thinker. He had been quite aware of this, and had taught himself to understand that Members of Parliament in the direct service of the Government were absolved from the necessity of free-thinking. Individual free-thinking was incompatible with the position of a member of the Government, and unless such abnegation were practiced, no Government would be possible.

Junior ministers are "junior" ministers. They are subordinates who, as formal members of the Government, have offices in Whitehall, but who, whether placemen or journeymen, carry their department's cans at the House, and who, at the House, may suffer the embarrassment of sharing an office with another junior minister, "which means that if for example I'd been seeing you over there today he would have to get out of the office, and he might have an appointment, and you know this is damned difficult." The fact that this junior minister shares an office at the House but has his own office in Whitehall suggests the direction in which the role's assigned duties are developing. "Parliamentary" under secretaries no longer focus so exclusively on Parliament. They are being increasingly relied upon, via delegation, to help their ministers run the departments.

ACTIVITY IN THE DEPARTMENT

Some junior ministers have genuine, assigned responsibilities for segments of "the policy-making aspect of the department where you can get hold of a field which is, let us say, underdeveloped or neglected, and impose a little bit of direction in getting that field worked up." There is no question at all that many more junior ministers are today heavily involved in policy work than ever was the case in the past. Whereas before it was unusual to have serious departmental responsibilities, now it is quite common. "I've had responsibilities now for the last two and a half years on European affairs and Asian affairs," explained a junior minister at the Foreign Office, "and I've been very

much involved in the evolvement of our European policy . . . and I've also been much involved in the development of our relations with China."

Learning from Ministers

Throughout the postwar period, junior ministers have increasingly been assigned administrative tasks in Whitehall in order to lighten the load on the ministers above them. This has been a simple case of responding to increasing complexity with increasing differentiation. The amount of work delegated, however, varies widely by department according to departmental traditions and to the desires of the secretary of state.

The service departments, the Foreign Office, and the Scottish Office have usually taken the lead. But in the Heath Government, the model for delegation came from the Department of the Environment, a megaministry under the direction of megamanager Peter Walker. Walker and his ministers (and this included junior ministers) ran the department as a team. They met together every morning to make collective decisions about the big issues of the day. These meetings made delegation less dangerous for Walker than it might otherwise have been, because they provided a daily opportunity for his ministers to assess his thinking and therefore to be guided by it. Because the team had been developed in Opposition, most of its members were friendly and experienced at working together. And this team produced some of the strongest junior ministers in the Government. Keith Speed, for example, was given unusual responsibility for new road plans. It was he who at the end of the day made the decision about whether or not such plans would go ahead. Junior ministers in the Walker team sounded more like ministers than like apprentices. And when they went to the House, it almost seemed as though they were there on their own behalf:

> Since I've been a Departmental Minister, I take the view very strongly . . . that it's critical that I'm across in that place as often as possible because I'm dealing with things that are very sensitive. . . . All these things are very much of constituency interest to MPs. It's not as if you're talking about the problems in Hong Kong. These are real domestic bread and butter things, and so I'm normally over there every evening from six o'clock onwards. I dine over there . . . and people come into my room, and they see you in the lobby and they say, 'Oh, what about _____.' If I get a feeling that we're getting a bit out of touch . . . it's, you know, up to me to try and take remedial action.

The Walker team was unusual, but only in the degree of relative autonomy given to its junior ministers. The delegation of specific areas

of responsibility was widespread: "You're getting the same now in the Department of Industry where you're seeing ministers and junior ministers—parliamentary-secretary level ministers—delegated, handed specific blocks of work." Another department with which the new delegation was frequently illustrated was Northern Ireland, in which the junior minister was "sort of Acting Minister of Commerce, of Finance, of Agriculture." For the majority of these cases, the institutional impetus was overload; and the motivation was the same one Richard Crossman expressed when, as minister of housing, he wished to increase his control over what he regarded as key areas of his ministry's work. To facilitate *control*, he explained, he decentralized several areas of responsibility to his junior ministers: "I have managed to devolve London housing entirely on Bob Mellish and planning appeals almost entirely on Jim MacColl (only a few important cases came up to me)" (Crossman 1975:312).

The really important cases still had to come up to him because, ultimately, ministers retain responsibility for the affairs of their departments and thus feel that, ultimately, they must retain control. Even the junior ministers in the Walker team were operating like civil servants—applying the ministers' mind rather than making wholly independent decisions. Delegation is not devolution. Junior ministers must refer important and sensitive matters to the chief. The importance that senior ministers place on retaining ultimate control is reflected in the fact that when they are away from London for a time, their responsibilities are usually not taken up by their junior ministers but instead are delegated to ministers in other departments.

Ministers become especially reluctant to delegate too much authority to their junior ministers when these juniors are not as ideologically compatible with them as they would like. They may also fear them as potential rivals (Heasman 1960:17). Thus, the more opportunity the junior minister has to shine in the department and at the despatch box, the more opportunity he has to shine more brightly than his superior—and the greater the danger that he might replace his superior or replace one of his superior's favored lieutenants. In the same vein, senior civil servants often try to discourage their secretary of state from delegating much responsibility to junior ministers, because they don't like taking orders from "small fry" and abhor wasted effort and confusion. The greater the delegation, the greater the effort required, for then they must get to know the mind of the junior minister, who may, in the end, be overruled by his ministerial master anyway. Thus, there is serious delegation, but extensive delegation is still unusual. More common is the junior minister who receives genuine responsibility for segments of the department's work, but who is very much aware

that he is not involved in any major issues of policy and that the bill he has been working on is not controversial: "To be absolutely realistic, one's influence on the center of things is not all that dramatic . . . one's influence is limited as a junior member."

In addition to helping administer specific areas of policy, junior ministers may also help their ministers more directly with tasks such as formulating answers to difficult parliamentary questions and speculating about supplementaries. In the best of apprenticeships, junior ministers work closely with their secretary of state. They learn from him and, if he is successful, tie their cart to his horse: "I feel my own prospects are bound up with what the P.M. decides to do about my secretary of state," worried a junior minister at Health and Social Security. "If he is displaced, sent elsewhere, the P.M. will probably break up the team, he may think the time has come for a clean sweep." It is not easy being an *under* secretary. You may lose your mentor; and you may also lose your patience from "being number four in a department when you have so often been on top in your business experiences. I've been a very active director of many companies and trade associations." Some subordinates do not at all enjoy the subordination.

Coping with Civil Servants

Junior ministers are sometimes uneasy about their relationships with the department's civil servants as well. When they were backbenchers, these junior ministers did "not come across civil servants, other than when you go and see a minister a civil servant will be in attendance; no, not much direct contact with civil servants." And thus they arrived with very little personal knowledge to demystify their impressions of these mysterious mandarins: "Well, when you become a minister, you've got to work with the civil service and it's, it's different from any other form of business organisation, quite obviously." What it resembles, however, is hard to say. The apparent uniqueness adds to the mystery and to the likelihood that the new junior minister may feel just a little overwhelmed by the civil servant's expertise:

> You are looked after by highly qualified professional men whose work is to concentrate on a narrow area and to be extremely well-informed and expert about it. . . . You're more dangerous as a Minister if you think you know as much about it as they do. But if you recognize your limitations and appreciate your role . . . Indeed, I would say it's a disadvantage for a Minister to be an expert in the field which he is helping to administer. He thinks he's up to date, in fact he's not. . . .

He thinks he knows as much as his professional advisors do, which is not true.

Placemen in particular can become intimidated. One of them, whose private secretary was nearly half his age, insisted that the latter be present throughout our interview and at the end of every response looked to him for approval. Another junior minister in much the same boat seemed very pleased indeed that his civil servants gave him his due. "The civil servants put all the options, they operate very well," he said. "I like working with them because there is good mutual respect . . . they recognize that you bring an expertise yourself." Yet another seemed more intimidated still, despite the fact that he had been appointed to a department in whose subject matter he had specialized on the back benches. Compared to the civil servants, however, he still felt like a generalist. And he coped with their "authority of expertise" by working hard "to maintain all the outside contacts which I built up whilst I was specializing on the backbenches—by no means all of which I'm prepared to, to reveal to my civil servants."

What makes it difficult to avoid feeling a little disadvantaged in these relationships is that one's standing as a junior minister appears to be below that of the department's senior civil servants. In the department, it is generally known that junior ministers have less income, less respect, and less influence than the senior civil servants who are serving them (Rose 1971:396). At best, their situations might be characterized as an ambiguous relationship in which they stand outside the normal chain of command (see Figure 5.1) (Milne 1950:444–45).

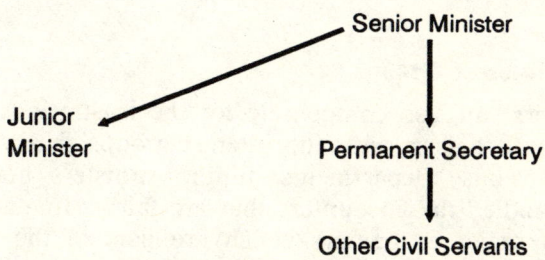

FIGURE 5.1 Chain of Command

This interpretation, which saves face for junior ministers and avoids irritating civil servants, clearly locates the junior minister under the senior minister for whom he works—but not over the civil servants whom he may have mistakenly assumed would be working under him. Civil servants prefer, "when they are able, to isolate and exclude junior

ministers as they like to do with PPSs." Ministers who are aware of this and dislike it believe that they must seek to ensure time and time again that their junior ministers are invited to meetings and are in line to receive documents. They must push against the system. When a new Government comes to power, the prime minister distributes information and instructions that sometimes include the following guideline: "The junior minister is not subject to the directions of the permanent secretary. But equally, the permanent secretary is not subject to the direction of the junior minister" (Linklater and Leigh, 1986:96). Thus, under the cover of a specious reciprocity, the wind is taken out of the sails of aggressive juniors.

Not surprisingly, there are many junior ministers whose ambitions and egos will not be trumped in this way. They may have to put up with not being able to give orders to the permanent secretary, but the interpretation that puts them wholly outside the chain of command and, hence, possibly unable to give orders to any civil servants at all is something that they will not put up with. The strongest ones, like those in the Walker team, certainly did win the authority to make decisions and to give orders to the civil servants who worked for them. And this pattern was becoming increasingly common: "I mean, after all, I'm a political animal, and sometimes civil servants get the thing wrong and, you know, I say, 'Look, we're to take a decision, this is a political decision, we're going to do this, to hell with the fact it may not be administratively the best decision.'" When it does not work, such junior ministers become irritated and begin to make sharp comments about civil servants being out of touch with the people and out of control.

Liaison with Interest Groups

Junior ministers can also compensate for the frustrations by diverting their attention to liaison with the interest groups that work with the department. In busy departments, junior ministers find themselves assigned to handle "the encounters that are fairly ritualised, they turn round certain major encounters which are part of the process. . . . They're always in the background, you're always seeing them." The process is one of consultation, whereby, on behalf of the secretary of state for health and social security, for example, the junior minister will be "in touch with the big professional bodies like the General Nursing Council, the BMA and so on . . . discussing the terms and conditions of service, the rates of pay and so on." Or on behalf of the secretary of state for agriculture, the junior minister "will be seeing trade organisations and farmers and things . . . there's a very strong

lobby in food and agriculture and they're always making their views known to you. . . . This is one of the jobs of a junior minister . . . we keep very much in touch." The junior minister at the Scottish Office keeps in touch with the Scottish Trades Union Congress (TUC) and chambers of commerce, whereas his colleague at the Home Office spends his time with representatives of the police association and prison staffs and so on.

Junior ministers meet such interest groups on a regular basis, "not just on specific topics, but quite regardless," as part of the department's contribution to functional representation, the semiconstitutional doctrine that suggests that interest groups likely to be affected by a policy should be consulted in its formulation. If ministers are going to construct a proper pensions policy, for instance, then there must be consultations with the pensions interests, with those who are involved in selling pension policies, with employers, with trade unions. In other words, "the whole of this policy has to be worked out with the closest possible links, you know most of them fairly informal, with people who are going to be on the receiving end." Junior ministers are assigned to maintain such links.

Occasionally they are also given a hot potato: "If there is a great period of interest or concern nationally about let us say, mental hospitals, then you will find yourself spending a lot more time with psychiatric people, mental nurses, the neurologists." But these delicate tasks are usually handled by ministers, leaving to junior ministers mainly the routine exchanges, one of the most common of which is "eating for the minister." Associations and interest groups concerned with the department's responsibilities regularly hold lunches and dinners and invite the minister to attend. Ministers cannot attend them all, and some ministers are inclined to attend very few. So they send their junior ministers in their place.

It is useful to the department. And it is another apprenticeship lesson, a lesson in the importance of functional representation, of good liaison with interest groups for the success of policies, ministers, and departments: "I've learned that one cannot get one's policies right unless one is in contact with them, unless they feel they have had a chance to have their say while policy is being formulated. . . . Before making up your mind you want to have a pretty clear indication as to the way in which the policy is eventually going to be received." In the process, some junior ministers notice that their perspectives are undergoing change. A former businessman, for example, finds himself disappointed that the businesspeople he encounters are not "sufficiently sophisticated to understand the problems which the politicians are actually grappling with." Businesspeople, and trade unionists too, want direct and easily

identifiable objects like a grant for a firm or keeping a factory open, "whereas the politician is not, he's trying to hold the line between all sorts of interests . . . he may be trying to stimulate investment or employment or something like this . . . a very complex relationship." As the big picture, the broad view, comes into focus, attitudes also begin to change about one's major counterplayers in corporatist politics—which are, for Conservatives, the leaders of the major trade unions: "I have become somewhat more friendly towards them since I have been a minister."

Even those junior ministers who spend most of their time at Westminster are still relatively more interested in Whitehall, in their relationships with ministers, civil servants, and interest groups. Their attention is drawn to Whitehall because they already know something about the House of Commons and feel that work in the department is both more interesting and, for the journeymen, more useful in preparing them for the role of the minister that they one day hope to play. Ministers, civil servants, and interest groups are the principal actors with whom they deal in their departmental work, but the variety of tasks to which they may be assigned in these relationships goes well beyond what I have identified thus far. Among the more important additional activities included in their roles are meeting with deputations and going on inspections and visits in the name of the minister. "For example, you know the Rank organisation who are making some of our motorways signs, well I went up recently to Leeds to look at the factory, to see what was going on. And obviously there, I mean I met everybody from the factory floor people up to the, you know the chairman of the appropriate company."

Junior ministers also enjoy getting involved in the production of White Papers for the department and in attending meetings of cabinet committees, where they are usually confined to the departmental briefing and to matters of direct interest to the department (Headey 1974:104–05). In addition, several are permitted to do a little public relations, mainly in the provinces where they may hold a little press conference about, for example, plans for hospitals or road plans that might be of local concern. Finally, there are some junior ministers who find their pleasure not in any one particular task but rather in the great variety of tasks that the role itself provides, "the enormous variety in the work . . . from say a cabinet committee to the chat we are having now, giving my Tory women tea when they come from their conference in a few moments' time, official functions again later on. The tremendous variety of the work is the one thing which I find attractive." And the one thing that he and every other junior minister finds fascinating is the opportunity to watch their ministers in action. For the journeyman,

this is his opportunity to learn about and to reflect upon the role for which he is being prepared and for which he is preparing himself. He uses analogies to help him organize and interpret what he sees:

> The analogy I find applicable is that of the farmer. A farmer is a professional man . . . a professional manager. A farmer doesn't have to be a chemist, he doesn't have to be an engineer, he doesn't have to be a horticulturalist, but he has to know enough about these subjects to draw in these specialists when he needs them. The Minister is in exactly this position. He's a manager, he has to be able to assemble the data he needs, he has to know enough about the subject to know what the ingredients are for a clear picture, he has to evaluate, to make judgements—he is a professional man in his own right, he's not a stumbling amateur.

A SERIES OF APPRENTICESHIPS

Although acting as junior minister is the principal apprenticeship for ministers, the junior minister role is itself built upon a foundation of prior apprenticeship experiences on the back benches and in work as parliamentary private secretaries, whips and Opposition spokespersons. This series of parliamentary apprenticeship experiences is important to set out, because "unlike what the American experience is . . . you have to be orientated to the House of Commons to be a successful minister in England." The orientation is mainly a matter of learning to cope with Parliament. But although this occupies so much of the time of junior ministers, their views about the apprenticeship process as a whole are only slightly more crystallized than are those of the backbenchers, PPSs, and whips from among whom they came. Virtually everyone is aware that this series constitutes the full apprenticeship. And yet it seems to be mainly the ministers who take the time to look back over the process as a whole and assess its experiences and lessons. It is therefore to the views of these ministers, mainly senior ministers, that I shall turn to put the apprenticeships of junior ministers into perspective. I shall begin with the experience of serving as a parliamentary private secretary.

First of all, the quality of the training that the PPS receives depends, senior ministers say, a good deal on the ministry, particularly when it comes to learning about Whitehall. Some departments, such as Health and Social Security or the Home Office, are less "closed" to the eyes and ears of PPSs than are other departments such as Defence where the confidentiality of the subject matter is such that everything seems secret. Still, the principal responsibility of the parliamentary private

secretary is at the House in liaison with backbenchers on behalf of the minister, "talking to backbenchers, explaining the minister's views to them . . . and equally reflecting their views back to him." This constitutes an apprenticeship for the parliamentary side of the role of the minister because through it the parliamentary private secretary begins to learn about the relationship "between minister and Parliament, minister and backbenchers. You begin to see . . . the craftsmanship, the art of it." This is the major focus of the role of the PPS and a preview of the work that may later be undertaken more formally and more often at the despatch box by the junior minister.

Whips are in an even better position than PPSs to learn about their parliamentary party and what it takes to be a success at Westminster. Service as a whip is not usually recognized as a rung on the career ladder, and yet it teaches everything about administration of the House, "about how to get legislation through and what is acceptable . . . how far you are going to have to have a struggle and just brazen it out." The role of the whip puts the apprentice in the engine room where he or she begins to learn about the pressures within the party and begins to see colleagues in a different and more interesting light than before. The apprentice begins to see the relationship between policies and types of personalities and begins to learn how to spot the snags: "All ministers would be helped by this period in the whips office, because then when you bring legislation forward you are watching for the sort of snags which as a whip you learn to watch for." It is the breadth of experience that several junior ministers have in mind when they say, "I learnt more in the eighteen months I was in the whips office about Parliament and politics as a whole than I'll ever learn as a junior minister here." Perhaps it is a better apprenticeship for some aspects of the House side of the work, but it is positively unhelpful, as can be the role of the PPS, in one very important aspect of this work. Both positions restrict participation in the House, which makes it difficult for apprentices to make a mark in the usual way and difficult as well to develop the skills of debate and argumentation that are being honed by ambitious backbenchers. When one becomes a PPS within months of getting in, and a whip directly afterward, one has little chance to engage in normal back-bench life.

From hindsight, ministers regard back-bench life as part of the series of apprenticeships—observation that might surprise some backbenchers: "There is a certain danger," ministers say, "in coming in and rocketing up to the top . . . without the hard grind which goes with being on the backbenches. The hard grind is valuable. It can be very depressing at times, but it can be a very valuable experience." It teaches about the nature of the beast, it gives a feel of Parliament, it gives an

understanding of the importance of the debating chamber; it gives a knowledge of the way backbench groups and influence come into being and operate. One learns how to handle the House by watching others succeed and fail in doing so, and, if one is lucky, one learns by more direct experiences such as attempting to pilot a private members bill through the House.

It is a matter of learning how "to cope with Parliament," to cope with the despatch box, to get through one's business and to get to the end of what one is saying without causing such an uproar that one does not get to the end of it. It is a matter of learning that the House of Commons is a very moody place—"if you just touch it wrong it hits back at you and makes you look rather a fool." It is a matter of learning dozens of little lessons about where one will have to give way and where not, about how the debate on the floor will probably not affect the vote at the end of it, but that the way it goes will affect the way the bill is handled at committee stage "by determining where the Government thinks it will and won't have to give way." It is a matter of learning which sort of members one can attack with impunity and which one cannot. And, here, as with most of the other lessons, one learns by observing the blunders of others or by trial and error oneself.

Ministers were asked explicitly in the interviews about the value of apprenticeships in back-bench committee work, the whips office, and in service as a PPS. What they were not asked about but what nevertheless cropped up in the discussions of apprentice experiences was the value of the opportunities available to a backbencher in Opposition. Ministers emphasized experience in Opposition because it had been important to them. The problem of backbenchers in Government is that they are often faced with faits accomplis, with decisions that have been taken by their Government. In Opposition, by contrast, backbenchers find it easier to be active participants rather than observers; they get to criticize new Government legislation, and they get to work on policy formulation on their own side.

As Opposition backbenchers, future junior ministers work under the guidance and under the eyes of their party's top leaders; they meet them, work with them, and learn from them:

> In Opposition you have the advantage of meeting all the top men of your party. When they're in Opposition they're looking round for young men to do their fetching and carrying for them, for they've been bereft of the civil service. So you have a chance of meeting the great men: Ted Heath, Reggie Maudling, Enoch Powell, Ian MacLeod. None of them would have known my name in a whole session of Parliament, in five years of Parliament, if they'd been in office and I'd just been a back-

bencher. But all thrown together in Opposition you get to know them within the first fortnight because you're doing jobs for them—and you can pick their brains and get the feel of the tactical side . . . you learn a lot that way.

Some of these backbenchers become junior members of the Opposition front-bench team. And there they learn by doing; they learn about Opposition by opposing. They will help organize part of the fight—and in the process of learning how legislation is best resisted, they will learn useful lessons about how legislation is best pushed through.

Ministers have experienced a wide variety of different apprenticeships before becoming junior ministers and therefore have a wide variety of views about which of these experiences are the most valuable. But though they may disagree about the value of different types of apprenticeships, there is virtually no disagreement at all with the claim that the absence of apprenticeships is a recipe for ministerial failure. That is why prime ministers have usually decided against "lateral entry," against appointing outsiders to top positions. They have been reluctant to do so partially because so many of their party's leading MPs expect office and feel they are first in line. But they have been reluctant to do so mainly because those who have served the appropriate apprenticeships, those who are best experienced in Parliament, are those who are best prepared to deal with Parliament on behalf of a department: "In our way of doing things, ministers have to be Members of the House of Commons. So they've got to know the House of Commons, they've got to know its ways, its customs, its procedures. And those ministers who tend to get promoted straight from outside . . . none of these people have been really very successful ministers. I think the reason for this is that they have not had a grounding in the House of Commons, they haven't understood the strange animal that the House of Commons is."

CONCLUSIONS

Very few junior ministers climb all the way to the cabinet, but virtually all cabinet ministers have served as junior ministers and have, in retrospect, regarded this experience as their most useful apprenticeship. Among junior ministers, the placemen are either appointed as a reward and never tapped to go on or, once in the role, realize that they have reached their ceilings. For them it is usually in and out in three years and not much of an apprenticeship. The journeymen, by contrast, see

themselves as future ministers and see their present role as their golden opportunity to learn the job and to prove their worth. Like the placemen, they spend a great deal of time in Parliament where they make themselves accessible to backbenchers and keep in touch with backbench opinion for the department. They test the waters at the despatch box and explore strategies by which they might best persuade the House about their case and their competence. They also chafe under the yoke of collective responsibility and try to get out and over to Whitehall as much as they can.

In Whitehall, they learn about the departmental side of the minister's responsibilities, the side about which they know the least and are the most curious. These days they are likely to be delegated at least a little administrative responsibility, and if they are fortunate enough to be attached to the right minister and department, they are likely to be delegated a considerable amount of administrative responsibility, albeit under a tight policy rein held by their superiors. They also develop strategies for coping with civil servants who may try to isolate and exclude them, and who will certainly try to overwhelm them with expertise. Beyond the mandarins lie the encounters with representatives of interest groups. Junior ministers eat with them, chat with them, and negotiate with them, for the junior ministers will need to be effective ambassadors and public relations officers for their departments should they fulfill their desires to rise further in the ministerial hierarchy.

I have said much about apprenticeships at the lower rungs of the ministerial career ladder but very little about the ladder itself. Yet this ladder provides the structure of opportunities that frame and condition all apprenticeship experiences. It also provides the frame for this study and is therefore an appropriate place to conclude this essay. The structure of opportunities for those who would be ministers in the British House of Commons is presented on Table 5.2.

The data in Table 5.2 are derived from Macdonald's (1987) study of ambition and careers in the House of Commons. For all 521 members of Parliament interviewed as part of the present study, Macdonald traced their career histories forward to 1986 and back to their first entry into the House. Her results suggest that the prospects for promotion to ministerial office are more than sufficient to entice the ambitious into apprenticeships and to keep alive their hopes. Among backbenchers, 30 percent go on to become junior ministers. Among junior ministers, 45 percent go on to become ministers, almost exactly the same proportion that Frankland (1977:139) found in his study of cohorts that first became candidates during the 1950s. And, finally, among ministers-not-in-the-cabinet, 52 percent proceed to the top rung

Table 5.2
Percent Promoted to Ministerial Positions

	Destination		
	Junior Minister	Minister	Cabinet Minister
Backbencher	30	11	4
Junior minister		45	3
Minister			52

Source: Stuart Elaine Macdonald, "Political Ambition in Britain: A Dynamic Analysis of Parliamentary Careers," Ph.D. Dissertation, University of Michigan, 1987.

to become cabinet ministers. Furthermore, there are no significant party differences in these data. The results are very similar for Conservative and Labour MPs.

It should be emphasized that the individual's promotion prospects increase with each further step he takes (Macdonald 1987). If one is fortunate enough to be among the 30 percent of backbenchers who rise to junior minister, then one's chances increase to 45 percent for the next step to minister. Similarly, the likelihood of attaining the next level, cabinet minister, increases again once one has reached the previous level, although the prospects for any given individual rising all the way from the back benches to the cabinet are still extremely slim. Most MPs are roughly aware of these promotion prospects. But what they usually underestimate is how much better the actual promotion prospects are than they seem—because at each rung below minister, a substantial portion of the field is simply not running in the race. Thus, at least half the backbenchers are excluded by virtue of age, education, tenure, and inclination. Likewise, approximately one-fourth of the parliamentary private secretaries (not included in Table 5.2) are older confidants and political batmen. And nearly half the junior ministers in the survey are placemen, who expect to stay in place, rather than journeymen, who expect to go on.

The race is not as competitive as it seems. But the climb has become highly structured as the ministerial career ladder has become institutionalized. Ambitious politicians must therefore increasingly temper their political ambition with the patience required for slow ascents. Only a minority of MPs share Harold Macmillan's reasons for being in the House of Commons. But to share his success, the members of this minority must be prepared to serve more systematic and lengthy apprenticeships than did their predecessors in previous generations.

REFERENCES

Burch, Martin, and Michael Moran, "The Changing British Political Elite, 1945–1983: MPs and Cabinet Ministers," *Parliamentary Affairs* 38, 1 (Winter 1985), 1–15.

Crossman, Richard, *The Diaries of a Cabinet Minister*. Vol. 1 (London: Hamish Hamilton and Jonathan Cape, 1975).

———, *The Diaries of a Cabinet Minister*. Vol. 2 (London: Hamish Hamilton and Jonathan Cape, 1976).

Frankland, E. Gene, "Parliamentary Career Achievement in Britain and West Germany: A Comparative Analysis," *Legislative Studies Quarterly* 2, 2 (May 1977), 137–54.

Headey, Bruce, *British Cabinet Ministers; The Roles of Politicians in Executive Office* (London: George Allen and Unwin, 1974).

Heasman, D. J., "Ministers' Apprentices," *The New Society* 16 July 1960, 16–17.

———, "The Ministerial Hierarchy," *Parliamentary Affairs* 15, 3 (Summer 1962), 307–30.

———, "Parliamentary Paths to High Office," *Parliamentary Affairs* 16, 3 (Summer 1963), 315–30.

King, Anthony, *British Members of Parliament: A Self-Portrait* (London: Macmillan, 1974).

———, "The Rise of the Career Politician in Britain and Its Consequences," *British Journal of Political Science* 11, 3 (July 1981), 249–85.

Linklater, Magnus, and David Leigh, *Not With Honour; The Inside Story of the Westland Scandal* (London: Sphere Books, 1986).

Macdonald, Stuart Elaine, "Political Ambition in Britain: A Dynamic Analysis of Parliamentary Careers." Ph.D. Dissertation. University of Michigan, 1987.

Milne, R. S., "The Junior Minister," *Journal of Politics* 12, 3 (August 1950), 437–49.

Namier, Sir Lewis, *The Structure of Politics at the Accession of George III* (London: Macmillan, 1968).

Rose, Richard, "The Making of Cabinet Ministers," *British Journal of Political Science* 1, 4 (October 1971), 393–414.

Searing, Donald D., "Measuring Politicians' Values: Administration and Assessment of a Ranking Technique in the British House of Commons," *American Political Science Review* 72, 1 (March 1978), 65–80.

———, "Rules of the Game in Britain: Can the Politicians Be Trusted?" *American Political Science Review* 76, 2 (June 1982), 239–58.

———, "The Role of the Good Constituency Member and the Practice of Representation in Great Britain," *Journal of Politics* 47, 2 (May 1985), 348–81.

———, "A Theory of Political Socialization: Institutional Support and Deradicalization in Britain," *British Journal of Political Science* 16, 3 (July 1986), 341–76.

Trollope, Anthony, *Phineas Finn* (London: Oxford University Press, 1973, first published, 1869).

6
THE MAKING OF A JAPANESE CABINET

Hiromitsu Kataoka

In Japan between 1946 and 1985, fourteen prime ministers chaired twenty-eight cabinets, with regular reshuffling in between. The average tenure of office of a prime minister was 2 years. A cabinet, new or reshuffled, stayed in office for an average of 9.5 months. Accordingly, the duration of a minister in office was very short, an average of 11.6 months. Many factors could explain this frequent making and remaking of the cabinet. The most probable one is intraparty strife among the factions of the Liberal Democratic party (LDP). The merger of the conservative parties into a continually ruling party promised at first a stabilization of the government. After Hayato Ikeda retired due to illness, Eisaku Sato set the record as prime minister of 7 years and 8 months, uninterruptedly. But the ruling party had already incorporated the factional structure. As soon as Sato retired, those leaders who had been kept waiting for a long time started a fierce race for the premiership, making a frequent shift of power inevitable. Sato's immediate successor, Kakuei Tanaka, held power for 886 days; Takeo Miki, for 747 days; Takeo Fukuda for 714 days; Masayoshi Ohira, for 554 days; and Zenko Suzuki, for 863 days. At the beginning of 1986 Prime Minister Yashuhiro Nakasone, the last of the long-waiting, had been in power more than three years. But he then was facing a cut-throat challenge from so-called new leaders. In Japan, the premiership has to be rotated.

In order to maximize their chances of survival, prime ministers make use of the ministerial posts as political resources to be distributed. They punctually reshuffle the cabinet at least yearly to name as many ministers as possible and to console the discontented members of the

party and factions. This practice began with Prime Minister Shigeru Yoshida, who replaced seventy-nine ministers in order to make up for the lack of a power base of his own. At the same time, he made a custom of picking distinguished scholars, business leaders, and civil servants from outside the Diet to important cabinet posts. As the value of a ministerial post has risen, it has become more and more difficult to give it to a non-Diet man or to any woman. Some recent, but rare, exceptions are Education Minister Michio Nagai in the Miki cabinet; Minister of State Nobuhiko Ushiba, in charge of foreign economics, in the Fukuda cabinet; and Foreign Minister Saburo Okita in the Ohira cabinet. The constitution requires only that a majority of the members of the cabinet be chosen from among Diet members. Nevertheless, the prime minister can no longer afford to give a ministerial post to a person outside the Diet.

Theoretically as well as constitutionally, prime ministers are free in choosing those colleagues with whom they share collective responsibility to the Diet and who serve at their pleasure. Nevertheless, they are under pressure to distribute ministerial posts to the factions according to their strength in the Diet—although a past contribution, or the promise of future support can count to some extent instead. It is more than as a matter of courtesy that they have to seek an opinion from the leaders of the factions on the specific persons to be chosen from among them. As a rule, the factions have prepared their own lists of prospective ministers. As a result of a wide distribution of ministerial posts, it is no wonder that there are so many members of the Diet who have been, at least once, a minister. At the end of 1985, 108 LDP members of the House of Representatives, 42.5 percent of the total, had served or were serving as ministers in some post or other. Thirty-one out of the 140 LDP members of the House of Councillors, 22.1 percent of the total, had had the same experience. In addition to these, 3 members of the New Liberal Club belonging to the lower house had thus far rotated one ministerial post among themselves. When Nakasone reshuffled his cabinet on December 28, 1985 the distribution of power among the factions was as follows: Tanaka's faction received six ministries; Suzuki's, four; Fukuda's, four; Nakasone's, three; Komoto's, two; and the New Liberal Club, one. Tanaka's, Suzuki's, and Fukuda's factions each included 1 member of the upper house; three of the twenty ministerial posts were thus reserved for its members. The distribution among the factions is difficult to change as long as the configuration of power remains the same.

In the distribution of posts, a prime minister cannot neglect the seniority rule. As indicated by Table 6.1, at the end of December 1985, every LDP member of the House of Representatives who had been

THE MAKING OF A JAPANESE CABINET

Table 6.1
Number of Ministerial Posts of LDP Members of the House of Representatives, By Number of Times Elected (December 28, 1985)

Times Elected	Number of Representatives	Number Named Minister	Number of Posts				
			1	2	3	4	5 or More
18	1	1 (100%)	0	0	0	0	1
17	0						
16	2	2 (100%)	0	1	1	0	0
15	3	3 (100%)	0	0	0	2	1
14	6	6 (100%)	0	1	1	3	1
13	6	6 (100%)	2	1	2	0	1
12	6	6 (100%)	1	3	1	1	0
11	3	3 (100%)	0	3	0	0	0
10	5	5 (100%)	1	2	1	1	0
9	13	13 (100%)	4	5	2	2	0
8	14	14 (100%)	10	3	0	1	0
7	18	16 (88.8%)	13	2	0	1	0
6	34	25 (73.5%)	24	0	1	0	0
5	24	6 (25.0%)	5	1	0	0	0
4	32	1 (3.1%)	0	0	0	1	0
3	38	2 (5.3%)	1	1	0	0	0
2	17	0	0	0	0	0	0
1	32	0	0	0	0	0	0
Total	254*	108 (42.5%)	61	23	9	11	4

*The total includes two dead persons.

returned eight times or more had been a minister at some time, without exception. Those persons who had occupied more than one post were concentrated among this group. More surprisingly, 88.8 percent of the seven times elected group, 73.5 percent of the six times elected group and 25 percent of the five times elected group had been made minister. This suggests that a novice to the cabinet is normally chosen from the sixth return group and occasionally from the fifth return group. It is rather unusual for a minister to be chosen from the rank of a lower return, although some are so chosen. Because the tenure of members of the House of Councillors is fixed for six years, they are chosen after their second or third return. In general, they serve a minister only once.

There is a widespread expectation among the rank-and-file LDP members of the Diet that they will be ministers someday. It is so deeply ingrained in the political culture that no prime ministers are bold enough to cut the vicious circle between the practice of rotation and this expectation, even though they know that it undermines their leadership. Of course, not all necessarily depends on the seniority rule alone. The seniority of a member of the Diet is the result as well as a cause of cabinet service. Members have a chance to prove their talents by serving in one or another position, thereby enhancing the probability of their reelection and promotion. Through a very tedious and difficult process of natural selection, there emerges a stratification of members. Prime ministers know from which strata across the factions they can recruit the kind of persons they need in the cabinet.

A so-called best member cabinet or all-star cabinet is beyond Japan's reach. Sometimes a prime minister tries to take every big leader into the cabinet. But a cabinet consisting of the big figures is prone to an early death, for political expediency forces its disintegration. As a rule, a cabinet is made of three different groups: a group of novices selected from the lists prepared by the factions, some of whom have already proved themselves to be capable politicians; a group of experienced and proficient politicians who have shuttled between various ministerial posts and positions as party officials; and a few confidants of the prime minister, one of whom might be a cabinet secretary. Prime ministers have a chance to show their political dexterity in the blending of the three different groups.

In his December 1985 cabinet reshuffle, Nakasone appointed twelve novices and eight experienced politicans, four of the latter, carryovers from the previous cabinet. Foreign Minister Abe and Finance Minister Takeshita set a record by holding the same posts four consecutive terms. These new leaders were retained in the cabinet so that they would not openly campaign against the incumbent prime minister. Through the making of a cabinet, the prime minister shows his determination to lead the nation; it also shows the kinds of social problems on which he puts the most emphasis.

OCCUPATIONAL BACKGROUND AND PREMINISTERIAL CAREERS OF MINISTERS

A distinction used to be made between party politicians and bureaucratic politicians. Of the fourteen prime ministers under the present constitution (until the end of 1985), eight were bureaucratic politicians. The archetype of a bureaucratic politician was Shigeru Yoshida, who became prime minister without having had any experience in party

Table 6.2
Occupational Backgrounds of Japanese Cabinet Ministers

	1970	1975	1980	1985
Party official	9(9.8%)	6(5.8%)	5(5.4%)	4(3.7%)
Local politician	11(12.0%)	20(19.4%)	22(24.9%)	26(24.1%)
Political staff	2(2.2%)	2(1.9%)	3(3.3%)	14(13.0%)
Organized group official	4(4.3%)	4(3.9%)	3(3.3%)	4(3.7%)
Civil servant	34(37.3%)	34(34.0%)	31(33.6%)	31(28.7%)
Journalist	8(8.8%)	9(8.7%)	8(8.7%)	10(9.3%)
Professional	5(5.5%)	8(7.8%)	4(4.3%)	7(6.5%)
Businessman	18(8.8%)	19(18.4%)	16(17.4%)	12(11.1%)
Total	91(100%)	103(100%)	92(100%)	108(100%)

politics. Because of his distrust of party politicians, and perhaps also because of a shortage of available talent in the aftermath of World War II, Yoshida appointed many civil servants to his cabinet, either directly, or after they had obtained a seat in the Diet. Of the members of his second cabinet, 45 percent were ex-civil servants. He nursed an entourage called the Yoshida School. His two most trusted disciples, Hayato Ikeda and Eisaku Sato, followed his example of recruiting civil servants, with peaks of 52.2 percent in the first Ikeda cabinet and 57.1 percent in the third Sato cabinet. Vestiges of this practice have remained (see Table 6.2). Party politician Kakuei Tanaka filled 48 percent of his second cabinet with ex-civil servants. However, the tide changed at about this time. Bureaucratic politician Takeo Fukuda's cabinet consisted of only 30.4 percent ex-civil servants.

The same was true of Nakasone's 1985 cabinet reshuffle. Nakasone was notorious for his bureaucratic arrogance—or, to use a more appropriate word, brightness—in spite of his very short tenure in the civil service. The second Nakasone cabinet, as reshuffled on December 28, 1985, included six ex-civil servants, six prefectural councilmen, three political staff persons, one journalist, and four others, including one business leader. The ex-civil servants were still numerous, but no longer a majority. If one adds the prefectural councilmen and the political staff persons into a single category of professional politicians, it would surpass the civil servants not only in number but also in the importance of ministries assigned them. Foreign Minister Abe was a journalist, and Finance Minister Takeshita was a local prefecture councilman. All ministerial posts crucial to the success of Nakasone's grand programs of social reform were entrusted to party politicians. For

example, the education minister, returned to his former office in order to tackle urgent educational reforms, was a former political staff person. The transportation minister was a prefectural councilman originally, but he had already established a reputation as capable of the difficult task of dividing and privatizing the ailing National Railways. The minister of trade and industry, who had to negotiate with foreign countries to alleviate friction over trade issues, was a tactical professional politician, a prefectural councilman previously. The director general of management and coordination, in charge of administrative reform in general, was classified as "other," but was a genuine professional politician who commuted between posts as minister and as party official. The secretary general of the cabinet, who acts as the prime minister's alter ego, and the director general of the defense agency were the only bureaucratic politicians in key posts.

The development of a category of professional politicians is clearer if we look at the overall picture over time. Among the LDP members of the House of Representatives, civil servants still constituted the largest single group in 1985. However, the size of this group had fallen from 37.7 percent in 1970 to 28.7 percent in 1984. This declining fortune was shared by the category of "others," among whom the most important used to be business leaders. By 1984, there were only a few business leaders in political circles. The group of officials of organized groups, journalists, and professionals (including lawyers) remained more or less constant. The group of local politicians included governors, subgovernors, mayors, town chiefs, and the numerous prefectural councilmen as well as other local councilmen. This group achieved an increase, from 12 percent in 1970, to 24 percent in 1985. New on the scene was the group of political staff persons, who had served the members of the Diet in several capacities in their youth. In 1970, they were of almost negligible importance, but in 1985 they were 13 percent of the total. Together with others in this new category, professional politicians amounted to 40 percent of the total, far exceeding the group of civil servants.

In the past, bureaucratic politicians were overrepresented in the cabinet. In 1985, their percentage in the cabinet and in the lower house converged, with some margin of overrepresentation remaining. A decline of the bureaucratic group reflects a professionalization of politics, by which I mean the naming of professional politicians to crucial cabinet and party posts on the one hand, and on the other, the fact that Diet members must pass through the crucible of successive elections before they are qualified to be ministers. Even a high-ranking bureaucrat cannot be made an exception to the seniority rule. As far as the seniority rule dominates, civil servants must retire in an early stage of their

career in order to plunge themselves into the world of politics, where they have to face competition with other groups of politicians on an equal footing. There is no assurance that they will be promoted over the heads of fellow politicians. Civil servants of administrative vice ministerial rank naturally shun the risk and prefer to pursue their second career in the world of business or of some semipublic body. In this way, they are crowded out from the political scene. The percentage of high-ranking officials has shrunk radically. At the same time, the professionalization of politics has been accompanied by some loss of relevance in the distinction between party politicians and bureaucratic politicians. If a civil servant is reprofessionalized as a politician through the crucible of elections, he belongs to a cateogry of professional politicians. He is appointed minister not qua civil servant but qua politician. Sometimes, a bureaucratic politician is preferred over a party politician in order to assure the presence of some administrative capabilities in the cabinet. But the required quality is not necessarily closely connected with the field of specialization, nor with any general administrative technology acquired as civil servant. It only rarely occurs that a bureaucratic politician returns triumphally to his alma mater ministry as minister.

Professional politicians are trained after they are elected to the Diet for the first time. Every member of the Diet is assigned to one or more standing committees and special committees of the house to which he or she belongs. In addition to this, members of the LDP have a chance to become acquainted with fields of interest through activities in the Policy Research Council and other special research committees of the party. Each faction also offers a chance of becoming acquainted with a wide circle of important people. As new Diet members have roles both in the Diet and in the party, they expand their fields of interest. After the third return in the case of members of the lower house and after the first or second return in the case of the members of the upper house, they are appointed parliamentary vice minister. However, this does not lead directly to a ministerial post. Because Japan does not have junior ministerial positions, it is not necessarily clear whether a parliamentary vice minister is a member of the government or not. The parliamentary vice minister cannot attend the cabinet meetings on behalf of the minster in the latter's absence. Only another minister or the prime minister himself can act on behalf of a minister. In both ministries and agencies, the parliamentary vice minister is in charge of political affairs but stands outside the chain of command. Nonetheless, this position is an indispensable step in the political career. Still more important are the middle-ranking posts of party official or a Diet committee chair. Throughout the entire process, LDP members of

various origins are merged into a single category of professional politicians qualified to be ministers.

It is not so easy to assess the professionalization of politics along the dimension of representation vs. administrative efficiency. Professional politicians, including reprofessionalized ex-bureaucrats, are not amateurs: They are professionals. But of what? They are neither specialists nor administrative managers, and the short tenure of ministers reveals that they are not expected to be so. Professional politicians are a new species of men who are political generalists well versed in a wide range of nationally important fields. There is a stratification among them according to their ability as political generalists.

With the advent of a class of professional politicians, people speak of the "primacy of politics," without asking why this has occurred. In the age of high technology, it is a great contradiction that politics has precedence over administrative efficiency. But there are two kinds of societal problems that cannot be solved by administrative efficiency. One is a kind of problem that cuts across a narrow technical field, the solution of which requires a fresh view, unperturbed by established paradigms. Another is a kind of problem entangled with vested interests. The two interrelated kinds of problems are mostly insoluble, but they cannot be neglected. Only a group of professional politicians dares attack these problems, mobilizing both the experts' knowledge and the necessary political support and, finally, giving legitimacy to the solution. In so doing, the professional politicians are encouraged by the belief that they and only they represent the nation—and their constituencies as well. It would be an exaggeration to speak of an age of the primacy of politics, for the professional politicians have to depend upon persons with technical knowledge and administrative expertise in order to fulfill their own missions.

A COLLECTIVE PRINCIPLE AND DECISIONMAKING PATTERNS

In addition to general administrative missions, the constitution of Japan gives the cabinet the following functions: to administer the law faithfully, conduct affairs of state, and manage foreign affairs; to conclude treaties; to administer the civil service; to prepare the budget and present it to the Diet; to enact cabinet orders; and to decide on general amnesties, special amnesties, commutations of punishment, reprieves, and restorations of rights. These functions must be performed through cabinet meetings, presided over by the prime minister. Representing the cabinet, he submits cabinet bills, the budget, and other proposals to the Diet and reports to it on general national affairs and foreign relations.

However, one should remember that it is the cabinet as a collective body, and not the prime minister, in which the constitution vests executive power. Every decision made in the name of the state and nation must be made by the cabinet. There are three kinds of decisionmaking: a cabinet decision, an agreement in the cabinet, and a report to the cabinet. A final cabinet decision must be reached by unanimous vote. When the cabinet reaches an agreement, the prime minister plays a key role as its leader. Nevertheless, he cannot decide anything officially without carrying his colleagues together with him.

Under the Meiji Constitution, the prime minister was primus inter pares and could be no more than that. The present constitution restored him to the position of cabinet head, with strengthened powers, but the collective principle is retained. If he is to exercise supervision and control over administrative branches, he must do so in accordance with the policy guidelines decided by the cabinet. Unlike the chancellor of the Federal Republic of Germany, the Japanese prime minister cannot make policy guidelines by himself. If he is to make a decision on questions of jurisdiction between ministers, he must consult the cabinet in advance. Even though he can suspend the official measures or orders of any administrative organ, new measures to replace them must be decided by the cabinet.

The way a cabinet is managed may be characterized in terms of an aggregation model in which proposals from ministries and agencies are added up through a filter of political feasibility. A dominance model in which the prime minister gives a firm directive in advance and takes strong leadership is not theoretically unknown. Things may not be changed much by the incumbent's personality, although he can give the impression of a change of style. On some occasions, the prime minister preempts a decision of the cabinet by leaking his intent to the press or to fellow politicians. But his intent cannot have official effect unless it is recognized by the cabinet. Even a draft of his speech to the opening session of the Diet must be agreed to in cabinet meetings.

Every agenda is previewed in a meeting of administrative vice ministers and others, held one day before each cabinet meeting. An entangled matter must have been settled by the councillors of the Cabinet Office, or it will never come up to the cabinet table. The cabinet meeting's schedule is so tight that ministers busy defending their ministries' proposals are not inclined to interfere with the matters of other ministries and agencies, though they are not prohibited from doing so. For the sake of coordinating controversial policies a cabinet committee is preferred, which high-ranking officials of the ruling party and other important officials can attend according to circumstance. Still, it is unavoidable that the cabinet occasionally comes to a standstill,

for all cabinet members have in mind the faction they belong to, the ministry they preside over, and the constituency they represent, but not the cabinet whose members they are, and they are not, therefore, necessarily willing to follow the prime minister into the ditch.

The number of cabinet members is fixed at twenty by the Cabinet Law. This number was originally sixteen, but it has gradually been increased. All ministers, including the prime minister, are considered to have two roles, one political, and one administrative. In a political capacity, they are called ministers of state and are supposed to participate in national affairs as coequal members of the cabinet. In an administrative capacity, they are called ministers, directors general, or commissioners, depending on the type of administrative organ they head. In addition to the Prime Minister's Office, with the prime minister as its competent minister, there are twelve ministries, eight agencies, and one commission, each represented in the cabinet by their heads. Organizationally, the agencies and commissions are housed in the Prime Minister's Office. Whereas a minister can issue ordinances himself, a director general must ask the prime minister before doing so, presenting him a draft of the ordinance. This is only a technical difference. Because political and administrative roles are integrated in the person of a minister, every member of the cabinet enjoys one and the same status. Seats in the cabinet room are arranged according to the date of establishment of the organ over which the minister presides. Though one cannot deny that an office gives prestige to an incumbent, it is also true that an incumbent increases, or in some cases decreases, the prestige of the office. The ranking of ministers is fixed by their positions in the ruling party as professional politicians and not by the seat numbers in the cabinet room.

Notwithstanding the collective principle, the Japanese prime minister is not aloof from a worldwide trend in which the chief executive of a government, whether president or prime minister, stands in the frontline of social problem solving. He is exposed to national as well as international attention and publicity. This can be called the "limelight effect" of the chief executive. In response to rising expectations of the populace, chief executives are taking a more and more active role in policy decisions, irrespective of their intent. Japanese prime ministers can be classified into a group of those who like the limelight and a group of those who do not. Many past prime ministers were prudent enough to shun the limelight. Nakasone might have been a bit of an exception to this rule. He not only liked the limelight but also stood quite well in it. Because of this, he enjoyed an unprecedented high rate of popular support, in spite of a very shaky power base in the ruling party.

THE MAKING OF A JAPANESE CABINET

List of the Cabinets in Chronological Order

Yoshida I	May 22, 1946
Katayama	May 24, 1947
Ashida	March 10, 1948
Yoshida II	October 15, 1948
Yoshida III	February 16, 1949
	1st reshuffled, June 28, 1950
	2nd reshuffled, July 4, 1951
	3rd reshuffled, December 26, 1951
Yoshida IV	October 30, 1952
Yoshida V	May 21, 1953
Hatoyama I	December 10, 1954
Hatoyama II	March 19, 1955
Hatoyama III	November 22, 1955
Ishibashi	December 23, 1956
Kishi I	February 25, 1957
	reshuffled, July 10, 1957
Kishi II	June 12, 1958
	reshuffled, June 6, 1959
Ikeda I	July 19, 1960
Ikeda II	December 8, 1960
	1st reshuffled, July 18, 1961
	2nd reshuffled, July 18, 1962
	3rd reshuffled, July 18, 1963
Ikeda III	December 9, 1963
	reshuffled, July 18, 1964
Sato I	November 9, 1964
	1st reshuffled, June 3, 1965
	2nd reshuffled, August 1, 1966
	3rd reshuffled, December 3, 1966
Sato II	February 17, 1967
	1st reshuffled, November 25, 1967
	2nd reshuffled, November 30, 1968
Sato III	January 14, 1970
	reshuffled, July 5, 1971
Tanaka I	July 7, 1972
Tanaka II	December 22, 1972
	1st reshuffled, November 25, 1973
	2nd reshuffled, November 11, 1974
Miki	December 9, 1974
	reshuffled, September 15, 1976

Fukuda	August 2, 1976
	reshuffled, November 28, 1977
Ohira I	December 7, 1978
Ohira II	November 9, 1979
Suzuki	July 17, 1980
	reshuffled, November 30, 1980
Nakasone I	November 27, 1982
Nakasone II	December 27, 1983
	1st reshuffled, November 13, 1984
	2nd reshuffled, December 28, 1985

7
PATHWAYS TO INDIA'S NATIONAL GOVERNING ELITE

Richard Sisson

India's national governing elite during the postindependence period has its origins in the development of a distinctive political class prior to independence, a class formed in civil disobedience movements and the open umbrella that the Indian National Congress provided as well as in the legislative institutions that were successively infused with autonomous powers under the regimes created by the Government of India Acts of 1919 and 1935.[1] From 1920 to the achievement of independence in 1947, under these constitutional formats, there were held seven elections to provincial legislative bodies as well as to the central legislature, though the latter did not enjoy the powers and autonomy of the former. The provincial elections of 1937 in particular made evident the existence of a class of Indians devoted to politics as a vocation. This class was defined by shared commitment to two objectives: the forging of an Indian political community and the achievement of freedom for it, and the reform of representative institutions and the exercise of self-governance through them. It was composed of representatives from various social groups, was engaged with executive authority in both local and regional arenas, and was linked by the Congress party, hierarchically within, corporatively without.[2]

At independence the dominant segment of this political class constituted itself as a governing elite at both the national and provincial levels and was committed both to controlling the institutions and redesigning the purposes of the colonial state. Those who constituted the government at the national level included central figures and/or their associates and deputies from the highest echelons of the national Congress party organization together with invitees with special expertise

from major social groups not widely represented in the nationalist elite.[3] Those who constituted the national government had pursued their careers in national arenas; similarly, those who formed governments in the states, both existent and about to be created, had primarily pursued their careers in provincial arenas, though they had shared in the burden of the nationalist struggle.

During the critical years of constitution making from 1947 to 1950 and for the subsequent two years before the first national elections in 1952, these two segments of the governing elite met and constituted a linkage in India's fledgling federal system through the institution of the Constituent Assembly (from 1950 to 1952 renamed the Provisional Parliament), which had been indirectly elected by provincial legislative assemblies in 1946 and which included representatives from among governing elites in the Indian states. Representative institutions not only assisted and shaped the development of a nationalist elite in the preindependence period, but they also served as crucible in which coalition, fission, and realignment took place, transforming the nationalist elite into a governing elite anointed with nationalist legacy. In this chapter I shall explore the progress made by this governing elite, its contours, and its reconstitution since the passing of the old generation.

CONTEXT AND RULES

The concepts of *political class* and *governing elite* as used herein for India are quite concrete. The former, which shall not be directly investigated, encompasses those who engage in politics as their principal vocation. By governing elite I mean those who hold positions of ultimate formal authority in the state—in this case the Council of Ministers of the Government of India.

The present analysis focuses upon the post-Nehru or Indira period of Indian politics, stretching eighteen years across three decades. Indira Gandhi, or Indira, as I shall refer to her as did her political advocates and opponents alike, assumed the prime ministership after the unexpected death of Lal Bahadur Shastri in 1966. She maintained her position in the face of strong opposition from important state-level political leaders, collectively known as the Syndicate, whose support she had enjoyed in 1966, given their perceptions of her as a malleable leader who had never contested general elections or held a responsible public position for an appreciable span of time.[4] Nor did she appear to have an autonomous base of political support. Misperception of will and versatility together with election reverses of the syndicate and their supporters served as catalyst to their defeat in the succession contest after the fourth general elections in 1967. Those elections marked the

eligibility of a generation of voters still in swaddling at independence as well as witnessed the defeat of the Congress party in half the Indian states.

Indira's tenure (1966–1984) encompassed the development of a post-independence political elite, one whose comprehension of the nationalist movement was derived from texts and oral tradition rather than from experience in the streets, in legislative chambers, or within the walls of British jails. It also included four of India's eight national general elections. The size of the Indian electorate expanded during her tenure from 250 million to 400 million; the number of states increased from sixteen to twenty-two with electorates ultimately ranging in size from under 1 million to over 60 million. The number of seats in the Lok Sabha, the directly elected lower house of Parliament, increased from 494 to 542. Voter turnout fluctuated above 55 percent, reaching a high of 64 percent in 1984. Meanwhile there was a decline in party identification in the electorate, a rise of regionalist parties in the states, and an authoritarian interlude from 1975 to 1977 that terminated with the victory of the Janata coalition in the elections of 1977. In those elections the Congress party attracted but 35 percent of the vote.[5]

In the context of these changes in the electorate and the states, what has transpired with respect to the composition and function of the national governing elite? There are several analyses of the Council of Ministers during the Jawaharlal Nehru period, which encompassed the first part of free India's span; my concern in this chapter, is the Indira (Nehru's daughter's) years. One knows, for example, that cabinets of the Nehru period were composed of persons who had entered politics during the preindependence period, who had been involved in public affairs almost exclusively at the national level, pursued politics as a vocation, held tenure in the ministry for a minimum of a full parliamentary term and likewise the portfolio for which they had been given charge.[6] Both cabinet ministers and ministers of state tended to have had national political careers with the institutions of the Congress party organization continuing to perform a linkage role between Delhi, the federal capital, and the states as they had prior to independence and as had the Constituent Assembly during the critical years of state formation. State-level party leaders, when drawn into the national government, tended to move into it directly upon being elected to Parliament, but at that time they constituted only 11 percent of the total and did not enjoy control of core ministries. The principal movers in the governing elite during this period were the nationalist inheritors of executive authority at the time of the transfer of power and those drawn by them from Parliament after they had served a worthy apprenticeship there.[7] Their pathways to power were found in the na-

tionalist movement and a national arena; the pathways of their successors, as we shall see, have been much different.

I shall analyze the structure and function of India's national governing elite with the above canvas as context. I shall examine the elite's sociological character, its changing political origins, the pathways that have defined its recruitment and mobility, and its functions in India's federal system. In so doing I shall examine councils of ministers, both cabinet ministers and ministers of state, during Indira Gandhi's tenure as prime minister at six critical junctures and shall analyze changes that have occurred across them.[8]

SOCIAL RECRUITMENT: THE GOVERNING ELITE DURING THE INDIRA ERA

The Indian national governing elite during the Indira era included representatives from significant social and religious minorities, was highly educated, recruited from well-to-do, though not the most well-endowed, economic groups, and was composed of persons who either made politics a career or who possessed professional expertise that could be utilized by the state. These dimensions, however, have shown variation over time, and they tend to be distributed in a consistently distinctive fashion between cabinet ministers and ministers of state, as to suggest the existence of two separate strata.

As in many states, regionalism has continually been a fundamental issue in India's national politics—indeed from the beginning of the century. The data in Table 7.1 present the regional distribution in the Council of Ministers, and one finds that the eastern states of Orissa and West Bengal have had less than proportional representation in both cabinet and ministerial ranks, the periphery having had slightly more. In fact, the east also has had the most recent entrants into politics among members of the council, 83 percent having entered politics after 1952, whereas no other region has more than 30 percent. This newer postindependence segment of the governing elite is the result of the prime minister's effort to develop an expanded base of political support in states where Communist and regionalist parties enjoyed uncommon electoral success during the Indira era.

The governing elite during the Indira period also became increasingly representative of social and religious minorities, reflecting efforts to mobilize and maintain political support for core segments of the governing class from within these communities. The summary proportions for all ministries approximate the general distribution of religious communities, though Muslims are underrepresented by 4 percent, and the pattern of change has progressively approached congruency. For ex-

Table 7.1
Regional Distribution of the National Governing Elite in India, 1966-1980 (in percent)

	Total Population[a]	Councils of Ministers (N=196)	Cabinet Ministers (N=99)	Ministers of State (N=97)
North	44	45	43	47
East	12	6	4	8
West	14	16	18	14
South	24	23	24	22
Periphery	6	9	10	8

[a] Population (685 million), based on the 1981 census.

Note: The composition of regions is as follows: *North:* Bihar, Delhi, Haryana, Madhya Pradesh, Punjab, Rajasthan, and Uttar Pradesh; *East:* Orissa and West Bengal; *West:* Goa, Gujarat, and Maharashtra; *South:* Andhra Pradesh, Karnataka, Kerala, and Tamil Nadu; *Periphery:* Arunachal Pradesh, Assam, Himachal Pradesh, and Jammu-Kashmir.

Table 7.2
Ministers' Educational Achievement, 1966-1980 (in percent)

	Councils of Ministers (N=195)	Cabinet Ministers (N=99)	Ministers of State (N=96)
LL.B.	51	55	44
Postgraduate	22	15	31
B.A.	25	26	23
Matric	2	4	1

ample, from 15 percent minority representation in 1966, the proportion had expanded to 34 percent in the ministry formed after the 1980 elections—a proportion generally congruent with the composition of the larger society.[9]

Prior to Indira's formation of the 1980 ministry upon her return from parliamentary exile, some two-thirds or more of the members in each cabinet of the Indira era possessed a postgraduate degree (see Table 7.2). With the exception of 1967, over half had a law degree. Although cabinet ministers and ministers of state alike are well educated, there are marginal distinctions between them, the former being

Table 7.3
Occupational Distribution of Ministers, 1966-1980 (in percent)

	Councils of Ministers (N=196)	Cabinet Ministers (N=99)	Ministers of State (N=97)
Politics	39	58	19
Lawyers	28	25	31
Other professional	17	8	26
Merchant/industry	8	3	13
Agriculture	8	6	11

more likely to have been educated for careers in law while the latter are more likely to have been educated in other disciplines, especially business and the sciences; neither rank has been the province of those educated in the arts and humanities.

One also finds that the younger the ministers, the more highly educated they have tended to be, a pattern especially pronounced among those with nonlegal postgraduate specializations. The more highly educated also tend to have entered politics during the postindependence period; indeed nearly 60 percent of those with specialized advanced degrees, compared with 45 percent of the total sample, entered politics after the first general elections in 1952. The younger, highly educated have also tended to have established themselves in professional careers before entering political life.

Of cabinet ministers, 45 percent were sixty years old or older at the time of their incumbency, whereas only 18 percent of the lower-ranking ministers were. Ministers of state have continually been drawn from younger cohorts than have those in the senior cabinet stratum. This is not a function of mobility from lower to higher strata by which the logic of time would inflate the latter. Here are two distinct and separate strata representing two different age cohorts separately drawn. Indeed, 46 percent of all cabinet ministers were fifty years old or older when first elected to Parliament, compared to 20 percent for their junior colleagues—the former in many cases having pursued political careers in state politics before being drawn to the national arena, the latter having tended to commence and to pursue their political careers in the national arena alone.

The professional politicians together with lawyers constituted two-thirds of the governing class during the Indira era (see Table 7.3). These proportions remained rather steady until 1980, when the occu-

pational distribution of the new ministry became more dispersed with a decline in the number of professional politicians and an increase in the proportion of businessmen and landlords, a turn away by the prime minister from the socialist rhetoric of the prior decade—*garibi hatao,* "abolish poverty."

Distinctions between members of the cabinet and ministers of state in terms of their interest and experiential background, however, are substantial. The majority of cabinet ministers have been drawn from a class of professional politicians, and until a dramatic shift to other professionals in the ministry constituted in 1980, the proportion of professional politicians increased in linear fashion.

Ministers of state, in contrast, derived from a substantially different interest and experiential reservoir. The proportion who have been professional politicians, never high during the Indira regime, has shown continual decline; the proportion of those who have pursued professional careers, such as lawyers and other professionals, before entering public life has consistently constituted over half of the sample, while there has been a striking increase in the proportion of ministers whose occupations involve the employment of capital—industrialists, merchants, and landlords—who have turned to politics in midcareer, a majority of whom have come from the upper house, the Rajya Sabha.

What one finds is an informal arrangement of functional representation that during the colonial regime was a part of the formal electoral arrangements. Whereas representatives from social minorities have followed a path into the Council of Ministers through reserved constituencies in elections to the Lok Sabha, those from industrial, commercial, and professional backgrounds (other than law) are more likely to have found their way into the council through the indirectly elected Rajya Sabha than through the directly elected Lok Sabha. Morever, they tend to become lodged in the ranks of ministers of state rather than in the cabinet.

A substantial proportion of the governing class pursues politics as a lifetime vocation, though more recent entrants have pursued careers other than politics before entering the political arena as full-time players. But in terms of gainful lifetime pursuits, as in each of the other sociological dimensions, one finds a pattern of stratification and pathways to power that clearly discriminates between members of the cabinet and ministers of state—the former tending more to being lifetime practitioners of the political arts, the latter more inclined to have had greater experience in other careers, particularly careers in commerce and in the professions.

Table 7.4
Time of Ministers' First Election to Public Office, 1966-1980 (in percent)

	Councils of Ministers (N=194)	Cabinet Ministers (N=99)	Ministers of State (N=95)
Pre-1952	31	45	17
1952-1961	34	29	38
1962 on	35	25	45

THE GREENHOUSE OF THE GOVERNING ELITE

When and how have those who have come to constitute the national government become involved in political life and then engaged in politics as a major life pursuit? In what ways, if any, have these dimensions changed during the period under examination? Are there discernible distinctions within the class, or are critical matters of political engagement and career more or less randomly distributed?

A majority of those who served in the national Council of Ministers during the Indira regime entered politics during the nationalist movement, though my data show distinct patterns of change in this regard between the commencement and end of her tenure. In her "inherited" ministry of 1966, for example, nearly two-thirds of the ministry had entered politics before independence, with a majority having become politically active during or before the Quit India Movement of 1942. By the end of her tenure, however, more than half of the council had entered politics after independence.

In contrast to the time of entry into public life, however, nearly 70 percent of the governing elite first ran for office in elections under the constitution of independent India (see Table 7.4). Thus, whereas members of the national Council of Ministers as a whole became politically involved before independence, whether in movements of civil disobedience, party activism, student associations, or social reform movements, their sustained political engagement has been a postindependence phenomenon. As with the timing of ministers' political entry, successive ministries have been increasingly recruited from among those who first ran for public office after 1962. Whereas in 1966 a majority of the council had first run in elections before 1952, in 1980 a majority had first run in 1962 or later. One finds too that the majority of the national governing elite has tended first to run in elections to one of

the two houses of Parliament, with the remainder first running in elections to state and local governmental institutions.

Again, there is a marked contrast between members of the cabinet and ministers of state. Whereas an exploration of the composition of the national governing elite suggests two distinctive types, an analysis of the political careers suggest two distinct classes with limited mobility between them within this elite.

With respect to political entry, members of the cabinet during the Indira era were drawn consistently from among those who had entered politics *prior* to independence, though declining from over two-thirds at the outset to less than half after her return from temporary parliamentary exile in 1980. Ministers of state, in contrast, had become politically active primarily *after* independence, initially as a consequence of an appetite for electoral contest and subsequently through involvement in politically active voluntary associations.

A similar differentiation is found in the timing of initial election to representative bodies. In terms of longitudinal comparisons, in the case of the cabinet, over half in each ministry through 1971 had first run in elections to legislative institutions created during the colonial period. In the case of the cabinet appointed immediately after the 1980 elections, one of every three incumbents had first been elected to public office within the previous fifteen years—the years that define the Indira era.

This pattern of change is much more pronounced among ministers of state. Those who had first run in elections before 1952 practically disappeared after 1966, subsequently appearing only as episodic blips. Indeed, ministers of state elected during the 1950s also progressively declined, from a high of 56 percent immediately following Indira's first election to 17 percent immediately following her last. Initially these negative slopes were complemented by the increasing proportion of ministers who had been elected during the last phase of the Nehru era, that is after 1962; and although only 14 percent of the incumbents in 1971 had been first elected subsequent to Indira Gandhi's ascending to the prime ministership, by 1980 one-half of the ministers of state had entered legislative institutions after her assumption of the prime ministership.

There is also a contrast between cabinet ministers and ministers of state with respect to where they commenced their legislative careers. The proportion of cabinet ministers who first ran in elections to the legislative assembly of their state never declined below 42 percent and had a high of 69 percent, the proportion of ministers of state who did so never exceeded 33 percent and in three ministries declined to below 15 percent. Indeed, an average of 40 percent of cabinet ministers in

Indira Gandhi's ministries had served in state assemblies for more than one term. The equivalent proportion for ministers of state is 13 percent, and most of those who are encompassed by this segment enjoyed upward mobility and thus helped infuse the analogous cabinet segment with increased subsequent robustness. Ministers of state tend to begin, pursue, and finish their political careers in parliament, whereas cabinet ministers are more likely to begin and initially pursue their careers in state governments but then pursue and complete their public life in New Delhi.

Finally, it should be noted that the national governing elite has included leaders from the opposition, from socialist and regionalist parties. Overall, an average of 12 percent of the Council of Ministers has derived from the opposition, showing a slight increase in 1980 after remaining steady through the previous decade. A slightly larger proportion of ministers of state have spent part of their careers in the opposition than have cabinet ministers, though these proportions switched noticeably in 1980 when 24 percent of the cabinet had been members of non-Congress parties. The national leadership has shown an openness previously characteristic primarily in the states—evidence of the continuation of the operation of the Congress "system," though in altered form.

With respect to the strong preindependence origins of the governing class under the Indira regime, cabinet members had more, ministers of state, less. Although the proportion of those entering politics after 1962 had increased, the increase has been most pronounced among ministers of state. In terms of political engagement defined as effective electoral contestation, the ministers during the Indira era have come from a postindependence generation.

Most members of the national governing class have run in elections first at the national rather than at the state or local levels. This is especially true of ministers of state and less so of members of the cabinet, who tend to have first pursued a career in state politics, to have served in the state legislative assembly for more than a single term, and to have filled a mediating and linkage function between the state and national levels in India's complex federal system.

RECRUITMENT AND MOBILITY WITHIN THE NATIONAL ELITE

What range of political experience—whether in party, parliamentary, or executive institutions—do ministers have before their selection to ministerial rank? What period of time do they spend learning about and absorbing the values and folkways of the institution to which they

Table 7.5
State Government Experience of Members of Councils of Ministers, 1966-1980 (in percent)

	Councils of Ministers (N=196)	Cabinet Ministers (N=99)	Ministers of State (N=97)
Chief minister	15	26	4
State ministry	30	47	9
State assembly	38	56	18

are responsible and through which they govern? What is the length of tenure of incumbents once they assume their station? Is there a high mobility between ministerial strata within the governing elite?

Whereas members of the cabinet during the Nehru period were drawn from a class of politicians whose involvement in public life had been almost exclusively at the national level, ministers of cabinet rank under Indira Gandhi were increasingly drawn from state political arenas. Indeed a majority of cabinet ministers during this time was drawn from those who had served in the legislative assembly of their state (see Table 7.5). Furthermore, nearly half had served as a minister in the state government and 15 percent as chief minister. As in so many other dimensions, the difference between members of the cabinet and ministers of state again stands out. With the exception of 1967, over 50 percent of cabinet ministers had been members of state legislative assemblies or had served as state ministers, many having served for more than five years.

Striking too is the fact that cabinet members had held their positions prior to the extensive involvement of the prime minister in state political affairs, involvement that commenced after the 1967 elections and became pronounced during the 1970s. These were state-level leaders who had developed autonomous bases of political support in their states and had shown versatility as political "engineers" of governing coalitions. The chief ministers never developed a strong presence in the national governing class. Many of them were unceremoniously relieved of their positions when needs of governance or their will for power exceeded the scope of the prime minister's tolerance.

The career patterns of ministers of state contrast dramatically with those of cabinet rank. Only 18 percent of the ministers of state had served in the state assemblies (only in 1980 did the proportion exceed 25 percent). Likewise only 9 percent had ever served in a state ministry.

Table 7.6
Participation of Future Ministers in Parliamentary Committees, 1966-1980
(in percent)

	Councils of Ministers (N=185)	Cabinet Ministers (N=94)	Ministers of State (N=91)
Executive committee, parliamentary party	27	18	40
Standing committee of parliament	23	9	39

Only 4 percent had served as chief minister, no one having served during the decade of the 1970s.

Ministers of state have followed career lines that are distinctive. They have tended to commence and to pursue their political careers in national rather than state politics. Over 70 percent of the ministers of state had first run in elections to either the Lok Sabha or Rajya Sabha. Whereas cabinet ministers spent much of their apprenticeship for national position in state government, ministers of state spent most of their preparation in institutions within parliament (see Table 7.6). At least 30 percent of the ministers of state in each of Indira's governments had served on at least one major parliamentary committee. On average less than 10 percent of the cabinet ministers had so served. A large proportion of ministers of state and of members of the cabinet had served on the executive committee of the Congress parliamentary party (CPP).

A substantial majority of cabinet ministers during the Indira regime moved immediately and directly into the cabinet upon entering Parliament, almost all in less than a single session of Parliament, nearly two-thirds on average within one year of their initial election (see Table 7.7). Thus as a group, cabinet ministers have not had experience as backbenchers, absorbing the folkways of Parliament, and developing knowledge about ministerial performance through parliamentary debate and committee incumbency. A large proportion, over two-thirds, had also become members of the government of their state within two years of their election and thus did not have the equivalent experience in the state legislative assembly.

Over 70 percent of ministers of state, in contrast, served in Parliament for over two years before being inducted into the government. Indeed, over time an increasingly larger proportion of future ministers

Table 7.7
Years from Election to Parliament to Entry into Council of Ministers, 1966-1980 (in percent)

	Councils of Ministers (N=196)	Cabinet Ministers (N=99)	Ministers of State (N=97)
0-1	46	65	27
2-5	32	19	44
6+	22	16	29

of state served in Parliament two years or more. In 1980, 83 percent had served in Parliament six years or more, that is, they had served in at least two separate parliaments and had been elected to Parliament a minimum of two times before being selected for ministerial position. Likewise, in 1980, the prime minister selected as cabinet ministers persons who had served a longer period than normal in Parliament, more than half having been at least twice elected. This stands in striking contrast to the cabinets of the 1970s, when nearly three-quarters had been inducted into the cabinet immediately upon entering Parliament.

Cabinets during the Indira era have demonstrated uneven patterns of continuity, reflecting efforts on the part of the prime minister to maintain control of people in power and the political scaffolding essential for the cabinet's maintenance. On balance approximately 70 percent of the members of any Council of Ministers during the Indira era had been a member of a previous council.

There are several marked exceptions, however. The two councils in which ministerial continuity was highest were in 1966, the year Indira became prime minister upon the death of Prime Minister Shastri, and in the mid-1970s, just before and during the national emergency. These were years of crisis. After the 1967 national elections, however, Indira appointed a cohort of new ministers of state: One of every two had not served in any ministerial position before. Less than half of both the cabinet ministers and ministers of state had served in any ministerial position under Lal Bahadur Shastri. Immediately after the 1971 elections, in which Indira was returned with a two-thirds majority in Parliament, the prime minister reconstituted the Council of Ministers substantially and tended to maintain it until the national emergency declared in June 1975. Over half of the cabinet ministers were new in 1971, none having been drawn from among the ministers of state. A new team was substantially in place by 1974. The Council of Ministers

during the emergency, however, was changed substantially, with half of the cabinet having been changed between 1971 and 1976, none having been recruited from among ministers of state. In 1976, 80 percent of the ministers of state were new to their positions.

The major disjuncture in ministerial recruitment occurred in 1980, three years after the Indira government was unceremoniously routed from office in elections that brought an end to the national emergency. Here one finds only slightly over one-third of the new council having previously been ministers. The 1980 ministry marked a break in the composition of the governing elite, though it was not accompanied by a change in prime ministerial style.

It is 1971, however, that marks a point of pronounced renewal and the creation of an Indira stamp on the Indian governing elite. Over half of the cabinet was appointed anew with *no* mobility from ministerial to cabinet rank. Particularly striking is the fact that only 5 percent of those who were ministers of state before 1967 were retained in that capacity, and from 1974 on they disappeared altogether. With her 1980 ministry, Indira had nearly completely replaced the ministerial team she had selected in 1971. No cabinet members present in 1971 were present in 1980 nor any deputy ministers; no ministers of state in 1971 continued in that position in 1980; only 18 percent of the cabinet was composed of former ministers of state. The only permanent incumbent of the national governing elite during the Indira regime was the prime minister herself.

With respect to mobility from ministers of state to cabinet ministers there appears to be something of a "20 percent rule" that is operative. There was never a case during the period of Indira Gandhi's governance where 20 percent or more of any cabinet was composed of former ministers of state. Mobility from the rank of deputy minister to minister of state was similarly constrained, the proportion in this regard only twice exceeding 25 percent. These data and this analysis suggest that ministers of cabinet rank and ministers of state are very different political types, they perform different functions, they infrequently meet, and the pathways of their recruitment rarely commingled under Indira.

SUMMATION AND INFERENCES

The Indian national governing elite changed almost completely in its compositon and substantially in its political character during the Indira era. This elite was highly educated, increasingly so until 1980. That year marked an effort at ministerial renewal on the part of the prime minister and a turn away from the urbanity and political hauteur of previous ministerial cohorts. I have shown that the formation of an

elite transcended its preindependence origins, with increasingly larger proportions having initially run in elections after independence, although through the decade of the 1970s over half had preindependence political involvements.

This national elite has been regionally representative, showing a modest bias toward states where parties other than the Congress have ascended to a position of political dominance. Though the elite in its initial phase was unrepresentative of social and religious minorities, which during the first two decades after independence had extended to the Congress party substantial electoral support, representation of these groups increasingly approached congruency with the larger society. This occurred in inverse relationship with Congress's declining electoral performance in reserved constituencies and in those with a large Muslim electorate. Although these trends—together with the proclivity to appoint aspirants formerly in opposition—are interesting, they become more so to the extent that the inference that ministerial composition is directly related to Congress electoral fortune can be more completely substantiated.

Those enjoying the highest status and the greatest authority and power, members of the cabinet, tend to practice politics as a vocation and to have spent a considerable portion of their career in executive positions. Typically they have served in a state legislative assembly, state ministry, and, in a lesser proportion of cases, as chief ministers. They typically have not had experience in the working of legislative and parliamentary committees, they have not served on committees charged with monitoring executive action and performance but, much like the prime minister herself, entered the cabinet immediately upon their election to Parliament.

Those at the lesser rank of minister of state have more typically been parliamentarians, only a small proportion having commenced their public life in state elective politics. They have typically had a parliamentary career before entering the executive ranks and, before engaging in legislative politics, have typically pursued a career other than politics. And ironically they have been drawn in greater proportion from the Rajya Sabha, elected by state legislative assemblies and constitutionally a protector of states' rights, whereas their superiors have come from the Lok Sabha but are much more likely to have had a career in state politics.

Mobility between the strata of this governing elite has been limited. As might be expected, there has been no downward mobility between the strata; there has been but marginal upward mobility. Members of the governing elite tend to spend their period of ministerial habitation in one or another of these strata. Ministers of state, like their senior

colleagues, have tended to finish their ministerial career at the same rank as they entered it.

The different strata of the governing elite, however, perform different important political functions. Cabinet ministers, who enjoy control of major departments of the national government, constitute a web of linkages between the national and state political systems, tend to operate through the bureaucracy with which many have had prior dealings as ministers in their states, and have played an important role in maintaining political support for the national governing coalition.

Ministers of state, in contrast, have had the function of maintaining close liaison with Parliament and the various interests both within the Congress party and the opposition that have found expression there; they have functioned as a link between Parliament and a superordinate prime minister, who had never had the experience of sitting in either house of Parliament as a backbencher, and a cabinet largely devoid of parliamentary experience.

Ministers of state have also played an important role in prime ministerial strategies of developing support and managing conflict. These positions have been employed to bring into the cabinet persons with technical expertise, whether in science or economic policy. They have also been employed to reduce the range and intensity of political claims from within the inner circle. Ministers of state have been persons who, at the outset in any event, do not have aspirations for augmenting their power and creating an autonomous base of political support without prime ministerial blessings and do not bear a high price tag with respect to the allocation of valuable party goods—tickets for elections or positions in state governments for factional associates. These positions provide a focus of expectancy for younger generations of political aspirants and have tended to be held by persons who are politically dependent and who can serve as an alternative channel of political access to the prime minister as opposed to that provided by their more senior colleagues whose base of support in the states has usually been perceived as a threat to prime ministerial interests.

Finally, the national governing class has tended to become a substitute for party organization. Ministers of both strata have increasingly served as channels of access to national power, as arbiters of state-level disputes, and as the penultimate level of advocacy in the allocation of party tickets for elections to state assemblies and to the national Parliament, the prime minister being the final arbiter.

NOTES

An earlier version of this paper was presented at a meeting of the Research Committee on Political Elites, World Congress of Political Science, Paris, July 1985.

1. See Richard Sisson and Lawrence L. Shrader, "Legislative Formation in Preindependent India: The Issue of Prerequisites for Democratic Regimes," in Paul Wallace, ed., *Nation and Region in India* (New Delhi: Oxford University Press, 1986), pp. 197–218; Hugh Tinker, *The Foundations of Local Government in India, Pakistan, and Burma* (London; Pall Mall Press, 1954), especially Part 2; W. H. Morris-Jones, *Parliament in India* (Philadelphia: University of Pennsylvania Press, 1957), especially Chapter 2; and Reginald Coupland, *The Indian Problem: Report on the Constitutional Problem in India* (Oxford: Oxford University Press), 1944.

2. The development of this class can be traced through Anil Seal, *The Emergence of Indian Nationalism: Competition and Collaboration in the Nineteenth Century* (Cambridge: Cambridge University Press, 1968); John McLane, *Indian Nationalism and the Early Congress* (Princeton: Princeton University Press, 1977); Gopal Krishna, "The Development of the Indian National Congress as a Mass Organization, 1918–1923," *Journal of Asian Studies* 25 (May 1966), 413–30; and studies of provincial transformations such as John H. Broomfield, *Elite Conflict in a Plural Society* (Berkeley and Los Angeles: University of California Press, 1968); John Gallagher, Gordon Johnson, and Anil Seal, eds., *Locality, Province and Nation: Essays on Indian Politics, 1870–1940* (Cambridge: Cambridge University Press, 1968); and Sisson and Shrader, op. cit.

3. R. J. Venkateswaran, *Cabinet Government in India* (London: George Allen and Unwin, 1967); and for analyses of party and parliamentary elites during this period see Stanley A. Kochanek, *The Congress Party of India: The Dynamics of One-Party Democracy* (Princeton: Princeton University Press, 1968); and Morris-Jones, op. cit.

4. The authoritative analysis of this fascinating process is found in Michael Brecher, *Nehru's Mantle: The Politics of Succession in India* (New York: Praeger, 1966); and his subsequent "Succession in India, 1967: The Routinization of Political Change," *Asian Survey* 7 (July 1967), 423–43. At the time of the first succession Indira Gandhi was a member of the Rajya Sabha (the Council of States), indirectly elected by state legislative assemblies. She had served as president of the Congress party in 1959.

5. For a complete compendium of national election data see V. B. Singh and Shankar Bose, *Elections in India: Data Handbook on Lok Sabha Elections, 1952–1980* (New Delhi: Sage Publications, 1984). See also Richard Sisson and William Vanderbok, "Mapping the Indian Electorate: Trends in Party Support in Seven National Elections," *Asian Survey*, October 1983, 1140–58; and their "Mapping the Indian Electorate II: Patterns of Weakness in the Indian Party System," *Asian Survey* 24 (October 1984), 1086–97.

6. Richard Sisson, "Prime Ministerial Power and the Selection of Ministers in India: Three Decades of Change," *International Political Science Review* 2 (1981), 137–57; Norman Nicholson, "Factionalism and the Indian Council of Ministers," *Journal of Commonwealth Political Studies* 10 (November 1972), 1979–97.

7. Norman Nicholson, "Integrative Strategies of a National Elite: Career Patterns in the Indian Council of Ministers," *Comparative Politics* 8 (July 1975), 533–57. A useful study that delineates profiles of ministerial elites from

1962–1972 is Satish K. Arora, "Social Background of the Indian Cabinet," *Economic and Political Weekly* 7 (Special Number 1972), 1523–32.

8. Data used herein derive from the *Who's Who* published by both the Lok Sabha and the Rajya Sabha; Times of India, *Directory and Yearbook Including Who's Who;* and newspaper accounts at the time of cabinet formation and change. The analysis is also informed by interviews with members of the Council of Ministers and secretaries of ministeries, including two prime ministers and three principal secretaries of the prime minister's secretariat. Those interviewed include persons who have served as members of the Council of Ministers under each of India's five prime ministers. The database includes 196 members of the Councils of Ministers under review—99 cabinet ministers and 97 ministers of state with the following distributions by ministries: 1966 = 16/18; 1967 = 19/16; 1971 = 14/22; 1974 17/15; 1976 = 16/14; and 1980 = 17/12.

9. For analyses of decline in electoral support for the Congress party in minority constituencies see Lloyd I. and Susanne Hoeber Rudolph, "Transformation of Congress Party: Why 1980 was not a Restoration," *Economic and Political Weekly* 16 (May 2, 1981), 811–13; and Myron Weiner, *India at the Polls, 1980* (Washington, D.C.: American Enterprise Institute, 1983).

8
SELECTION OF CABINET MINISTERS IN IRELAND, 1922-1982

John Coakley and Brian Farrell

INTRODUCTION: IRISH GOVERNMENT MINISTERS

It is the object of this chapter to assess the Irish pattern of government composition in the light of general research findings relating to two perspectives. The first is trends in the evolution of the overall composition of this formally dominant portion of the political elite. The particular interest of the Irish case from the first perspective lies in its hybrid nature, sharing with its West European neighbors a common set of political values and a liberal democratic constitutional tradition but also sharing with developing and certain other marginal countries a postcolonial experience and a heritage of intense nationalism in what was long a predominantly agrarian society. The second section deals with the strategies used by heads of government in selecting a team of ministers charged with the fulfilment of important executive, policy-making and other political tasks. Here the Irish experience is important primarily as a case study of a small country functioning in the shadow of a large neighbor and within a political tradition derived from the Westminster model (see Farrell 1973).

The actual number of ministers is rather small, a fact that reflects both constitutional restrictions and political traditions. According to the constitution that marked the birth of the independent Irish state in 1922, the government was to consist of a maximum of twelve ministers; in 1937 a new constitution, which remains in force to the present, extended this to fifteen. The government is collectively answerable to the Dail (House of Representatives), from which most of its members must be drawn. The prime minister has, however, enjoyed a restricted right of appointment of ministers from the indirectly elected

Senate. The 1937 constitution, for instance, requires all ministers to be members of one of the two houses of Parliament, with a maximum of two drawn from the Senate.

The practice of government formation in Ireland has remained remarkably uniform since 1922.[1] Some of the general characteristics of these governments are summarized in Table 8.1, which also lists the three posttreaty, preconstitution, provisional governments. Twenty-one of the twenty-six governments formed since the 1922 constitution came into effect have taken office immediately after a general election. The practice has always been the same: On the Dail's first meeting after the general election, the item on the order paper immediately after the election of the speaker is the nomination of the prime minister. The prime minister, following his formal appointment, announces the composition of the cabinet, which is voted on en bloc. Although not required to do so, the prime minister by convention indicates the ministries to be allotted to his nominees; on occasion, planned future changes of allocation are announced. The whole process of government formation has normally been completed in a single day's parliamentary sitting; opposition tactics and not prime ministerial hesitation have been responsible for rare instances in which formal parliamentary approval has been delayed to the following day. Even before his selection, each prospective prime minister has finalized his list of ministerial appointees. On the five occasions on which the formation of a new government did not follow a general election (on the coming into effect of the constitution in 1922, following a technical government defeat in 1930, and as a consequence of a midterm change of leadership in the governing Fianna Fail party in 1959, 1966, and 1979), the procedure has been equally predetermined. One can notice that the overall size of the government increased gradually, rather than in step with the constitutional change, and attained the maximum size permitted by the constitution only in 1973.

Despite the relatively large number of ministerial appointments, the total number of individuals involved is quite low; only ninety-four persons have held ministerial office since the constitution of 1922 came into force. This reflects the extent to which prime ministers tend to leave their cabinets intact for a considerable length of time; only when there was a break after a long period of single-party government, as in 1932, 1948, and 1973, did a significant number of new members appear. The addition of junior ministers (or as they were known until recently, parliamentary secretaries) would result in a small increase in the number of cases. Provision was made in 1924 for the appointment of up to seven parliamentary secretaries, who had to be members of one of the two houses of Parliament (in practice they have always been

Table 8.1
Irish Governments, 1922-1982

Date of Formation	Government	Initial Composition					Dail Support
		Fianna Fail	Fine Gael[a]	Labour Party	Other	Total	
1/14/22[c]	Collins	0	8	0	0	8	49.0
8/22/22[c]	Cosgrave 1	0	9	0	0	9	49.0
9/9/22[c]	Cosgrave 2	0	11	0	0	11	45.3
12/6/22	Cosgrave 3	0	10	0	0	10	45.3
9/19/23	Cosgrave 4	0	11	0	0	11	41.2
6/23/27	Cosgrave 5	0	10	0	0	10	30.7
10/11/27	Cosgrave 6	0	9	0	0	9	40.5
4/2/30	Cosgrave 7	0	9	0	0	9	40.5
3/9/32	de Valera 1	10	0	0	0	10	47.1
2/8/33	de Valera 2	10	0	0	0	10	50.3
7/21/37	de Valera 3	10	0	0	0	10	50.0
6/30/38	de Valera 4	10	0	0	0	10	55.8
7/1/43	de Valera 5	11	0	0	0	11	48.5
6/9/44	de Valera 6	11	0	0	0	11	55.1
2/18/48	Costello 1	0	6	2	5[d]	13	45.6
6/13/51	de Valera 7	12	0	0	0	12	46.9
6/2/54	Costello 2	0	8	4	1[e]	13	50.3
3/20/57	de Valera 8	12	0	0	0	12	53.1
6/23/59	Lemass 1	13	0	0	0	13	53.1
10/11/61	Lemass 2	14	0	0	0	14	48.6
4/21/65	Lemass 3	14	0	0	0	14	50.0
11/10/66	Lynch 1	14	0	0	0	14	50.0
7/2/69	Lynch 2	14	0	0	0	14	52.1
3/14/73	Cosgrave	0	10	5	0	15	50.7
7/5/77	Lynch 3	15	0	0	0	15	56.8
12/12/79	Haughey 1	15	0	0	0	15	56.8
6/30/81	FitzGerald 1	0	11	4	0	15	48.2
3/9/82	Haughey 2	15	0	0	0	15	48.8
12/14/82	FitzGerald 2	0	11	4	0	15	51.8

[a] Dail seats held by parties participating in Government as percentage of total Dail membership at the beginning of the Dail session; the first two figures in this column are estimates
[b] Includes also the Pro-Treaty party or Cumann na nGaedheal (1922-1933)
[c] Provisional governments
[d] Two Clann na Poblachta, one Clann na Talmhan, one National Labour, one independent
[e] Clann na Talmhan

Dail deputies). The maximum number was increased to ten in 1978, when the post was renamed "minister of state," and to fifteen in 1980. Originally it was the practice to appoint between three and five parliamentary secretaries, but the number increased in the 1960s and since 1969 the tendency has been to appoint the maximum number permitted by law.

GENERAL CHARACTERISTICS OF THE MINISTERIAL ELITE

The radical nature of the political break in 1922 is illustrated strikingly in the comparison of the political elites before and after this date. Specifically, one may compare the ninety-four-member Privy Council of 1922 with the set of government ministers appointed from independence until 1982. The social characteristics of members of the two groups have changed little over time, and, by coincidence, there are the same number of people in each group.[2] The bodies are not, of course, strictly comparable; the functions of the Privy Council were much greater in the judicial and lesser in the administrative domain than the cabinet; the Privy Council's jurisdiction extended over all of the island, and it included a significant British element; its membership, nevertheless, came rather closer to embracing the totality of the Irish political elite of the time than did any government subsequently.

The Privy Council of 1922 was made up overwhelmingly of Protestants and of members of the landed gentry; only two of the government ministers appointed since 1922 have been Protestants, and no more than five could have been classified as members of the landed gentry. The Privy Council of 1922 comprised twenty-seven peers, nine baronets, and twenty knights; no holder of a title has been appointed to government since 1922. This break contrasts sharply with the much more gradual easing out of the landed classes that has characterized the British and German political elites (Guttsman 1974). It is clear that a revolutionary shift took place in the composition of the Irish political elite in 1922: An old establishment, closely linked to the traditional Protestant upper class and composed of a mixture of unionists and supporters of devolved government for Ireland within the United Kingdom, was replaced by a new counterelite drawn from the Catholic middle classes and standing for Irish independence.

The sharp change in the nature of the Irish political elite that took place in 1922 is underlined in the only comprehensive study of this group that has thus far appeared (Cohan 1972). In analyzing the backgrounds of all ministers and parliamentary secretaries appointed up to 1969, together with the Opposition front bench of the 1965–1969

period, A. S. Cohan drew a distinction between the revolutionary political elite, the forty-nine officeholders who had been involved in the independence movement and civil war of the 1916–1923 period, and the postrevolutionary elite, the remaining fifty-four. The members of the revolutionary political elite emerged through a series of interlocking nationalist movements that included the Gaelic Athletic Association, the Gaelic League, Sinn Fein, and the Irish Republican Army (IRA). Between them, the pro- and anti-treaty sections of the old Sinn Fein movement continued to control all cabinet posts until 1948, and their influence remained great thereafter. No member of the pre-1922 unionist establishment took ministerial office in the new state, and it was not until 1948 that the first government minister was appointed who had been associated even with the pre-1922 moderate nationalist movement.

Cohan's study suggested that there have been few differences in social background between the revolutionary and the postrevolutionary elites: They differed mainly with respect to recruitment paths, the postrevolutionary elite depending to a much greater extent than their predecessors on reputations gained locally in their constituencies rather than nationally as part of the independence movement. In general, he wrote, the elite has reflected the religious and regional distribution of the population, though there has been a disproportionate tendency for its members to come from urban areas. However, the education and occupational distribution of the elite is, predictably, atypical: University graduates and professional people were greatly overrepresented. By contrast, farmers, businessmen, and military personnel were more poorly represented than one might expect.

Cohan's analysis is broadly confirmed when ministerial appointments between 1969 and 1982 are added to the list. Some social characteristics of Irish ministers of the 1922–1982 period are summarized in Table 8.2. Although the time period is only a little longer than that considered by Cohan, the numbers of individuals is very much greater. This reflects the larger size of recent governments, the much larger number of junior ministers appointed, and the much higher degree of ministerial mobility. A distinction is made in the table between government ministers and junior ministers, and, for comparative purposes, the social characteristics of Dail deputies and of the general population are added.

A number of general points of qualification should be made about Table 8.2. In the first place, it may seem unrealistic to group together all ministerial appointees over a sixty-year period. This is not, however, a serious problem; we shall argue below that the social characteristics of this portion of the political elite have changed little over time. Second, the data relating to Dail deputies are not strictly comparable.

Table 8.2
Social Characteristics of the Irish Political Elite and of the Irish Population, 1922-1982 (in percent)

	Government Ministers 1922-1982 (N=94)	Junior Ministers 1922-1982 (N=80)	Dail Deputies 1922-1948 (N=518)	Dail Deputies 1982 (N=166)	Population[a] 1966
Occupational group					
Professional	61.5	38.1	29.6	41.6	7.7
Other nonmanual	30.2	31.7	37.9	43.4	32.1
Manual	1.2	2.5	5.5	2.4	29.1
Farmers	7.0	27.8	27.1	12.7	31.1
Selected occupations					
Lawyers	26.7	11.4	9.4	12.2	0.2
Teachers	23.3	11.4	9.6	22.3	1.8
Education					
Third-level	75.9	41.9	21.1	55.4	4.0
Secondary	20.3	50.0	33.6	41.0	30.6
Primary	3.8	8.1	45.3	3.6	65.4
Sex					
Male	96.8	97.5	97.7	91.6	50.2
Female	3.2	2.5	2.3	8.4	49.8

[a]1966 population was 2,884,000. Figures on occupation are expressed as percentages of the economically active population; on education as percentages of those whose full-time education had ceased.

Source: For ministers, see note 2; other data calculated from Ireland 1967-1970, Gallagher 1984, McCracken 1958, and Nealon and Brennan 1983.

The aggregate data stop in 1948, a point at which Irish society began a rapid transformation. In an effort to counterbalance this, we have included data on the composition of the Dail in 1982. Finally, it is not, of course, possible to provide aggregate data on the entire population that lived through this period. The compromise adopted here has been to report the structure of the population at an intermediate point, 1966.

In addition to confirming the general bias in the direction of prestigious occupational groups, the data on Table 8.2 confirm what has been called the "law of increasing disproportion": the tendency for the representation of high-status social groups to increase as the level of

political activity rises (Putnam 1976:33). Thus the proportions of those engaged in the professions and of those with third-level education rise significantly as one moves from the general population to Dail deputies, again as one moves from Dail deputies to junior ministers, and from junior ministers to government ministers.

Two categories are outstandingly overrepresented: lawyers and teachers. The large number of ministers drawn from these two professions reflects dependence on the Dail as a recruiting pool. As in other parliaments, lawyers have always been overrepresented in the Dail, for reasons similar to those that obtain elsewhere: Politics is a pursuit that attracts lawyers, and potential politicians in turn find the lawyer's skills a valuable acquisition (McCracken 1958; Farrell 1971b; Farrell 1984; Gallagher 1984). The overrepresentation of teachers is due to the fact that from 1922 to 1937 six Dail seats were allocated to Ireland's two universities, as well as the exceptional level of political involvement of teachers generally. The high political profile of teachers presumably reflects their role as opinion leaders in a society with a relatively low level of industrialization and a relatively new middle class. It is worthy of note that Irish ministers who have been teachers come predominantly from the primary and secondary school sectors rather than from the universities, a characteristic that sets them apart from the ministerial elites of other Western countries but that is consistent with the pattern in the Third World.

The occupational profile of the Irish ministerial elite in general resembles that of its counterparts in other Western democracies. If anything, bias toward the professions of law and teaching has been even more marked (they account respectively for 27 and 23 percent of all ministerial officeholders, as compared with corresponding figures for the whole Atlantic area of 21 and 16 percent), and manual workers have been even more poorly represented than in the rest of the Atlantic area (Blondel 1985: 43, 48). The underrepresentation of women is just as marked: 3 percent of Irish ministers have been women, the same proportion as in the rest of the Atlantic area. The age profile of incoming Irish ministers has, however, been strikingly different from that in other Atlantic countries: Over the 1945–1981 period, incoming Irish ministers were very young. A final observation that should be made about the Irish ministerial elite relates to their region of normal residence: The area of the capital city, Dublin, has been heavily overrepresented, though many ministers normally resident there may have had strong family or other personal ties with other parts of the country.

Age. The general characteristics of the Irish ministerial elite have changed little over time, although there has been a greatly accelerated rate of recruitment and displacement in the 1980s. Attention should,

however, be drawn to three areas in which there have been significant differences between governments. The first and most dramatic is age. The earlier Irish pattern of long ministerial service and aging governments, documented by Chubb (1974: 82–90), has changed radically. The low average age at which Irish ministers first came to office is to be explained not by any tendency (at least, until very recently) on the part of Irish prime ministers to value youthfulness as a criterion of ministerial selection but rather by Ireland's experience as a postrevolutionary society. Revolutionary political elites tend to be exceptionally young; on gaining power in a state, they tend to age collectively and, in the space of a couple of decades, they become exceptionally old (Putnam 1976: 195–197).

This trend can be seen clearly in Ireland (see Figure 8.1). In the 1920s the great bulk of ministers were under forty years old, but the average age of cabinet ministers rose dramatically through the state's first decade in existence. Eamon De Valera came to power in 1932 with a younger cabinet but was slow to recruit new members, and in his subsequent cabinets the proportion of ministers aged fifty or more rose steadily. By the 1940s Irish cabinets had a rather high average age, but from the 1960s on, with the passing of the revolutionary generation, there has been a more even and a more stable distribution of ministers among different age groups. Four changes of government in the 1979–1982 period involving significant new recruitment did not disturb this distribution; new entrants typically were in their early forties on first appointment.

Social Status. There has also been some variation in the social status of cabinet incumbents. Although the level of education of ministers (as measured, for instance, in terms of the proportion having received third-level education) has remained stable over time or could even be said to have risen, their occupational status has tended to fall. This may be examined in terms of such conventional measures of social class as the Hall-Jones index, which is used in Figure 8.2 to illustrate the changing class composition of Irish governments. In the seven-point Hall-Jones scale, the top position (class 1) is defined in terms of higher professional, administrative, and other elite categories.[3] The dominance of this group among the ministerial elite is clear. The proportion of ministers in this category was highest in the governments of the early 1920s, dropped sharply in the early De Valera governments and has since fluctuated around an intermediate position. The description of the change of government in 1932 as one "from government by Clongowes men to government by Christian Brothers' men" (implying a transition from former pupils of one of Ireland's elite secondary schools to former pupils of a religious order concerned with mass

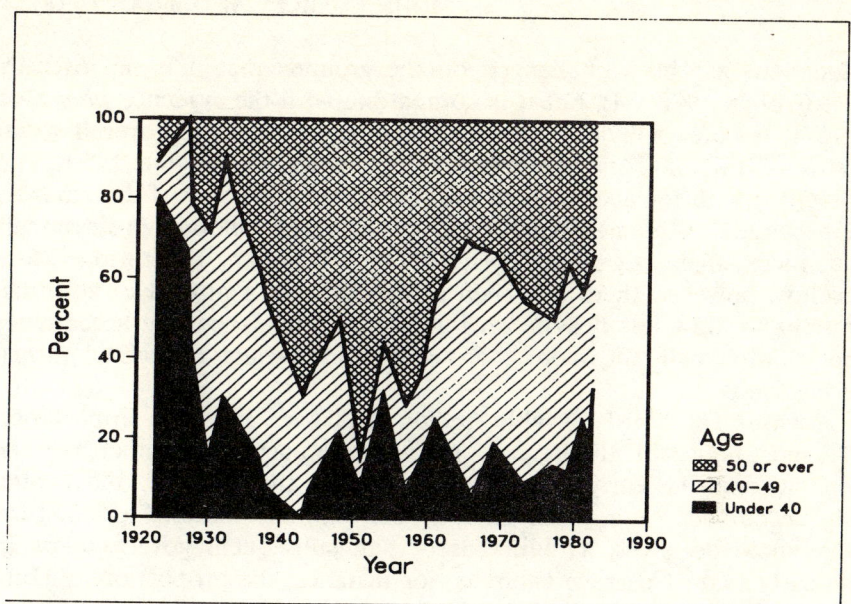

FIGURE 8.1
Cabinets by Age, 1922-1982

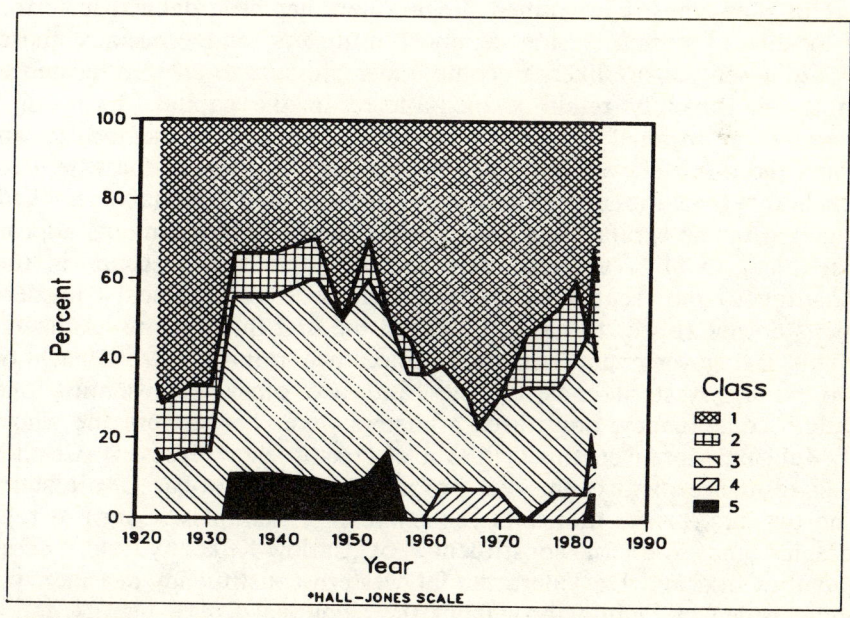

FIGURE 8.2
Cabinets by Social Class, 1922-1982

education) has been challenged on the grounds that it is not literally true (Cohan 1972: 34), but it is compatible with the evidence presented here. It is noteworthy that the most significant rise in the overall social status of Fianna Fail governments took place during the 1950s and coincided with the accession to prominence in the party of the "mohair suit brigade"—the new generation of upwardly mobile professionals that increasingly began to replace the revolutionary generation. More recently, however, there has been a tendency for Fianna Fail administrations to draw less heavily on this group, a tendency that accentuates the contrast with the more thoroughly middle-class Fine Gael ministerial teams.

Region. The third variable, region, has been of some importance. The most noticeable difference is not between parties but rather between generations. The early governments, despite the fact that the capital city accounted for a much smaller share of the national population, were more decisively Dublin based than subsequent governments. In the early Liam Cosgrave cabinets, for instance, the proportion of Dublin-based ministers exceeded 80 percent; in the pre-1948 De Valera governments it was still greater than 60 percent. Since then, however, Dublin-based ministers have constituted a minority in the cabinet, especially in Fianna Fail administrations.

This point must be qualified. Region here has been defined in terms of locality of normal residence; most ministers, and especially those with long service, are likely to come under pressure to take up residence rather than merely retain a pied-à-terre in the capital. Two other measures of regional origin are possible. The first is the locality in which the minister was born and brought up. In view of the extent to which the revolutionary elite was composed of individuals who had migrated to the capital, this would make the early governments appear much less Dublin centered. The second alternative measure is the constituency represented by the minister. Such geographical considerations do not appear to have influenced the first three prime ministers. In his last government Lemass selected two ministers from each of two remote western constituencies and two others representing one Dublin constituency; only three ministers were chosen from the whole of Munster. Moreover, this criterion of constituency represented rather than residence distorts the real proportion of Dublin-based ministers. The two first prime ministers are interesting examples: Cosgrave represented the southern constituency of Carlow-Kilkenny and subsequently Cork, and De Valera the far western constituency of Clare, yet both resided in Dublin throughout their political lives.

Such patterns of dual or multiple regional affiliation were characteristic of the first generation of parliamentary representatives. In the

postwar period, place of birth and upbringing, county of normal residence, and constituency represented were much more likely to coincide. The geographical distribution of later governments is therefore less ambiguous. Fianna Fail governments tend to be less Dublin centered than Fine Gael–Labour coalitions and are careful to give symbolic recognition to traditional sources of party support in the West and South. By comparison, the 1981 and 1982 Garret FitzGerald governments were so heavily weighted toward the capital that his first administration attracted the criticism that it was dominated by a "Donnybrook set," implying that a professional, intellectually fashionable, and economically privileged clique enjoyed a central role in the government (Farrell 1987).

CRITERIA FOR SELECTING MINISTERS

The general characteristics of the Irish ministerial elite as described above suggest a pattern not dissimilar to those of other Western democracies. The general pattern is itself essentially a cumulation of a series of appointments by incoming prime ministers. The decision criteria of these prime ministers are of interest for two reasons: first, because of the criteria's role in explaining the overall characteristics of the ministerial elite and, second, because of the intrinsic importance of the manner in which individual cabinets are formed.

The relative lack of scholarly interest in general principles of ministerial selection has already been remarked upon (Blondel 1982: 3–6). It is, however, appropriate in examining the Irish case to review the scanty evidence that has been brought forward relating to this process elsewhere. Case studies of the ministerial selection process in different countries tend to take rather varying perspectives on selection—social, psychological, or institutional, for instance—but some firm, widely accepted conclusions emerge. Broadly speaking, one can say that prime ministers seem to be subject to two types of considerations in selecting ministers: the personal qualities of individual ministers and the collective character of the cabinet as a whole.

A Comparative Framework

Experience. Three kinds of personal experience appear to be of significance. In many countries, three principal career paths to ministerial office may be identified: the civil service, the parliamentary party, and the party organization (Dogan 1989). The second of these has been of greatest importance in parliamentary democracies. Indeed, although European constitutions typically make no requirement that ministers

be selected from Parliament and may even prohibit simultaneous parliamentary and cabinet membership, the predominance of the parliamentary route is overwhelming. In the United Kingdom only a handful of cabinet ministers appointed in the 1868–1958 period were of "unorthodox," nonparliamentary origin (Willson 1959); in France the predominance of parliamentarians over the 1870–1978 period was even more marked, notwithstanding the requirement since 1958 that ministers resign parliamentary seats (Dogan 1989); the appointment of nonparliamentarians in the Federal Republic of Germany has been described as "exceptional" (Amphoux 1962: 222–224); and it has become an unwritten rule in Italy that cabinet members be selected from Parliament (Dogan 1981). Among the exceptions to this route in Western democracies are the Netherlands, where civil service experience has been extremely important, and the United States.

Further experience may also be required. In Britain a relatively long period of parliamentary service, including several years as a junior minister, is a normal prerequisite to cabinet office (see Chapter 5). In Italy a certain parliamentary seniority and junior ministerial experience are prerequisites, but too long a period in a noncabinet post (more than five years) implies a disqualification from promotion (Dogan 1981). In France, preministerial experience tends to be gained instead in parliamentary committees (Dogan 1989).

Ability. Political success is itself in part a function of a second consideration, ability. It is to be supposed that a minimum degree of ability is a prerequisite to cabinet office, but it should be noted that only in the United States has competence been seen as the most important characteristic (Burstein 1977). Studies elsewhere scarcely mention ability, and its importance has been explicitly questioned in the Italian case (Dogan 1981).

Reliability. Of rather more importance is the personal quality that might be described as reliability: the feeling of prime ministers that they can trust colleagues in conducting the affairs of their ministry and in relating to the cabinet within certain bounds of discretion. This has been identified as an important consideration in the United States, where personal friendship has frequently been a factor for presidents in making cabinet appointments (Burstein 1977). In France, a set of factors has been identified that presumably relates to the same characteristic: political inheritance, attendance at an elite school, involvement in the Resistance, and personal companionship (Dogan 1989).

A prime minister must also take account of the overall balance of his cabinet. Of greatest importance is, of course, the allocation of posts within coalitions between parties and within parties between factions. A prime minister rarely has control over the former, as it is typically

the subject of interparty agreement. Although a prime minister may not be able to alter the proportions of seats going to particular parties or factions, his capacity to select individuals within these constraints varies. Thus the German federal chancellor has sought to determine the personnel who have represented minor parties in coalitions (Amphoux 1962: 224–227), but the Italian prime minister is typically helpless in the face of nominations from particular factions, though these cannot veto other appointments (Dogan 1981). Australian cabinets, similarly, tend to consist of a balance of factions (Headey 1974: 254–258).

A balance may also need to be maintained between other types of categories. Of most widespread importance is region, a consideration that is particularly important in Germany and Italy. Other important ascriptive characteristics are religion (for example, in Germany and Switzerland) and language (for example, in Belgium and Switzerland). All three of these are of major significance in the formation of Canadian cabinets. Finally, reference should be made to the possibility that certain ministries are reserved for holders of special qualifications (for instance, in law, agriculture, or military matters).

Importance of Various Criteria in Ireland

Experience. To what extent have these considerations mattered in the Irish case? As in other countries, political experience additional to that specified in the constitution has been necessary. Of greatest importance is what has been referred to as "consecration by universal suffrage" (Dogan 1989). It has always been possible in Ireland to appoint ministers who are not Dail deputies, and the prime minister's theoretical freedom of choice in this respect since 1937 has been greater than a casual glance at the constitution would suggest. The prime minister is entitled to appoint up to two ministers from the Senate, and because he also appoints eleven senators of his own choice, he can in effect appoint any two citizens to the cabinet by simultaneously appointing them to the Senate. The right of appointment from the Senate has been used on only three occasions. De Valera appointed a senator as his minister for posts and telegraphs in 1932 and reappointed him in 1933. Again in 1957, when the minister for education lost his Dail seat in the general election, De Valera nominated him to the Senate and to the Government as minister for agriculture. The most recent case was in 1981, when FitzGerald appointed a prominent member of his party to the Senate and to the senior Ministry of Foreign Affairs.

There are distinct political drawbacks to the use of Senate nominations in government formation. Ambitious Dail backbenchers are

disgruntled, the Opposition is likely to interpret such a nomination as indicating lack of confidence or competence, and the absence of a popular mandate may be controversial. There is a practical procedural disadvantage: The new Senate does not take office until some months after the new Dail has convened, and if a senator is appointed to the Government his post must be filled for this interim period on a provisional basis.

Although a lengthy period of Dail service normally precedes a ministerial appointment, it is by no means a prerequisite. No fewer than four ministers have been appointed without any previous parliamentary experience. Still less necessary is service as a junior minister, though it is of some importance. In the early years of the state, the office of junior minister was not regarded as a rung on the ladder of promotion. Of seven parliamentary secretaries appointed during the 1924–1927 period, only one went on to become a minister, despite the fact that this was a period of exceptional ministerial turnover and that two other ministers were appointed who had never been parliamentary secretaries. Under the long period of uninterrupted De Valera government (1932–1948), however, the junior ministry became an established step in promotion: After the creation of the initial 1932 government, no one became a minister who had not previously been a parliamentary secretary. Yet junior appointments were not a sufficient condition of promotion: Three of De Valera's parliamentary secretaries remained for at least a decade at their posts (and one for a full fourteen years) without promotion, whereas a number of newcomers were promoted to the cabinet in a few years. Since then, however, the junior ministerial step has been bypassed in a number of cases; it is no longer a condition of promotion.

Ability. It is much more difficult to assess the extent to which ability has been a factor in determining the membership of governments. The first generation of the Irish political elite were "politicians by accident," divided by a constitutional issue that was largely symbolic. The original bonds of loyalty that created that revolutionary generation became the partisan ties that separated them into two opposing groups. Ability was not the critical criterion for recruitment or promotion; political reputation or influence, loyalty, and proximity to the leader were the functional prerequisites. Given the competitive character of the Irish electoral system and the extent of intraparty rivalry, there is less emphasis on professional, technical competence than on political skills in recruiting the political elite. In the cases that have been quoted (the Labour appointments in the 1973 coalition and economic appointments under Jack Lynch in 1977 and FitzGerald in 1982) the promise of technical expertise has often been offset by political inexperience.

Reliability. In contrast, reliability—although difficult to measure with any precision—has undoubtedly been a significant factor in appointments. Dependence on this criterion has been attributed in particular to De Valera, who not only appointed comrades-in-arms, who gave him strong personal loyalty, but also retained them in office for inordinately long periods (Farrell 1971a: 27). Later leaders seemed less concerned with valuing friendship or loyalty over other criteria. But perhaps because of an evident growth of factionalism in the period from 1975-1985, the most recent prime ministers have been inclined, where possible, to select party colleagues who share their own distinctive philosophies. An examination of ministerial selection by FitzGerald and Charles Haughey suggests that reliability has become an increasingly important criterion for government selection (Farrell 1987).

Balance Between Parties. The balances of forces in various cabinets between relevant categories is rather easier to measure.[4] Distribution of seats between parties has been of significance in the five instances of coalition government. On the first occasion, in 1948, one seat was allocated to a formal independent (who was a former senior member and future leader of Fine Gael) and the remaining ones were allocated with mathematical accuracy among five parties, each getting its exact share of seats in terms of its Dail strength. This pattern was altered in the three-party coalition of 1954, when Fine Gael took one seat fewer than its strict entitlement and the Labour party one more. This bias in favor of Labour has been maintained in three other coalitions. The Fine Gael-Labour cabinet ratio of 10:5 in 1974 could be seen as departing from the 11:4 ratio of the Dail parties, but when the cabinet posts were allocated in 1981 and 1982 on an 11:4 ratio, the relative sizes of the Dail parties would have suggested 12:3 or even 13:2 as more appropriate.[5] Allocation of posts among parties has been relatively uncontroversial, and Fine Gael, which has always taken the prime ministership and the ministry of finance, has never hesitated in being generous: The Labour party leader has always been deputy prime minister in these coalitions. Interparty bargaining on coalition formation, of course, also covers policy matters, and trade-offs may have taken place in this area (Gallagher 1980).

Balance Between Factions. The relatively high degree of party unity over most of the period has made the distribution of seats between factions of little significance in Ireland. The principle was quickly established that the party leader has the ultimate say in ministerial appointments. In the case of single-party governments, this means the prime minister; in coalitions, the prime minister's role is greatly circumscribed. He nominates ministers from minor coalition parties on the advice of the leaders of these parties, and experience has shown

that this two-tiered system of control greatly weakens the prime minister's authority over any ministers that are not in his own party. Particularly in recent years, however, internal divisions within the parties have become more marked. From the late 1960s through to the 1970s the senior ranks of Fianna Fail exhibited a marked cleavage between a moderate group, initially a majority headed by Jack Lynch, and a more vociferously nationalist group, becoming a majority under Charles Haughey (Garvin 1981; Farrell 1987). There was a comparable shift within Fine Gael as the initial conservative majority headed by Liam Cosgrave was displaced by a progressive tendency headed by Garret FitzGerald. Like other socialist parties, the Labour party has always suffered from left-right tensions, and these have focused in recent years on attitudes toward coalition, the Left favoring an independent policy outside government.

In the past, prime ministers and party leaders have appeared to be unchallenged leaders of monolithic political groupings. However, some sensitivity toward factions can be identified both under Lemass and Cosgrave, whereas Lynch at both the beginning and the end of his leadership phase had to cope with a factionalism that threatened his authority. That factionalism, exhibited in an increasing tendency to "leak" to the media, a reluctance to accept the discipline of the parliamentary whip, and occasional direct challenges to the leadership, has become more marked in the 1970s and 1980s. The most conspicuous manifestation was in the Haughey government of 1979–1981, which was, in effect, a coalition of two factions. So powerful was the position of the minority faction that its leader, George Colley, was even able to breach one of Mattei Dogan's unwritten rules of cabinet formation in Italy: Colley was given a veto over appointments to the Ministries of Justice and Defence.

Other Factors. Striking a balance between different social categories has been of little importance in the formation of Irish cabinets. It should be clear from the discussion above that region has not been of great importance: Although a greater regional spread would be revealed if constituency represented rather than place of normal residence were considered, Dublin and the East have tended to have had disproportionately high representation in cabinets (Farrell 1987). In the absence of major regional divisions, prime ministers have not felt under pressure in this respect, but it is noteworthy that the 1975–1986 coalition governments (and notably the first FitzGerald government, of 1981) have been alleged to have had insufficient representation from the West. Despite its importance in the past as a political factor, religion has been of no significance in determining the composition of cabinets. Only two ministers have been Protestants; there is no convention similar

to that which operates in the Irish Supreme Court by which at least one of its five members has traditionally been a Protestant (Gallagher 1980:9). Neither has language been of any significance: No particular effort has been made to ensure that the tiny (2 percent) Irish-speaking minority is represented in government. However, to the degree that special qualifications have been important, knowledge of Irish has been a prerequisite to appointment as minister for the Gaeltacht (Irish-speaking districts), and some degree of proficiency in Irish has also been expected of the minister for education.

Considerations that have been important as criteria for selecting ministers in other countries have been of uneven importance in Ireland. There are also, however, a number of factors that have been of some significance in Ireland that have scarcely been commented upon elsewhere. Two additional social categories have emerged as important in recent years, especially in the FitzGerald governments. The first is *gender:* since 1977, a woman has always been appointed to at least a junior post. Second, *age* has been of some importance. In a country with an extremely young population (in 1981 61.7 percent of the population was less than thirty-five years old), there has been a tendency to ensure that several young ministers have been appointed. Indeed, in the FitzGerald governments, youth and promise have outweighed age and experience in determining appointments.

Another consideration that requires mention is the political payoff. Although there appears to be some popular expectation that high achievers in electoral terms should be rewarded, actual instances of possible cabinet appointments on this basis are few. But personal support in internal party battles is more likely to lead to reward. This was said to be true particularly of the two Haughey governments. However, an examination of the FitzGerald governments exhibits a tendency toward a restrictive perception of qualification for office in another domain: There is some evidence of a tendency to dispense with ministers who do not share his philosophy (Farrell 1987). Another variant of the political payoff is the political investment: There is some evidence that cabinet posts may have been allocated to marginal constituencies in recent years in the hope of enhancing the government's electoral prospects locally in the long term. The evidence, however, suggests that such electoral considerations are more likely to determine the choice of junior ministers than of full government members. Another factor of significance in Ireland, but now apparently less influential, has been the tendency toward familial relationship in government appointments. To some extent this reflects both the small scale of the Irish political system and the dominance of the first generation of parliamentarians. Although familial relationship continues to be a sig-

nificant characteristic of the parliamentary elite, it is noticeably less marked among more recent government appointees.

CONCLUSION

The first, rather unsurprising, conclusion to be drawn from this study is that the Irish ministerial elite, like its counterpart elsewhere, is a privileged group in social and economic terms. It does, however, exhibit certain characteristics that set it apart from the ministerial elites of other Western democracies. The most important is its evolution over time. A revolutionary break took place in the social continuity of the Irish ruling class in 1922 with the passing of the traditional ruling oligarchy. The new elite was rather more homogeneous than ministerial elites in other Western societies, elites that lost their aristocratic basis more gradually; differences between parties and over time, though significant, were less marked in Ireland than elsewhere. The single characteristic of the elite that did change rapidly was characteristic of postrevolutionary societies: its average age.

The social group that forms the pool of eligibles from which government ministers are drawn in Western societies is, of course, extremely large. Answers to the question of how individual ministers are selected from this pool are rather indefinite and show a good deal of variation from country to country. It has been suggested above that the pool of eligibles is narrowed considerably by the existence of certain hurdles that minister-aspirants must cross, and that the final selection is then based on calculations of internal cabinet balance. In Ireland the near requirement of Dail membership dramatically limits the number of candidates for office: Fifteen ministers (or thirty, if junior ministers are included) are to be selected from an average of about eighty Dail deputies who constitute the parliamentary majority. If certain standards of ability and reliability are also demanded (not to mention the question of availability—not all backbenchers necessarily welcome the prospect of ministerial office), it can be assumed that prime ministers' freedom in balancing cabinets among various political or social categories could be severely restricted. An Irish prime minister may, then, be forced to choose between giving priority to individual characteristics and balancing the interests of different groups. In this, however, his range of options differs only in degree from that of the prime ministers of other liberal democratic states.

NOTES

This is a revised version of a paper presented at a meeting of the Research Committee on Political Elites at the XIIIth World Congress of the International Political Science Association, Paris, 15–20 July 1985

1. For the general political background, see Chubb 1982; the process of prime ministerial selection is discussed in Coakley 1984; and the evolution of the Irish party system is described in Gallagher 1985.

2. The discussion of the characteristics of Irish government ministers in the remainder of this section draws on an analysis of my computer file of biographical data on the ministers, based on official records of appointments, parliamentary and other directories and other sources.

3. The application of the Hall-Jones scale to Irish occupations follows the adaptation of the scale in MacGreil 1977: 594–600. The seven categories are formally defined as follows, in descending order: (1) professionally qualified and higher administrative, (2) managerial and executive (with some responsibility for directing and initiating policy), (3) inspectional, supervisory, and other nonmanual (higher grade), (4) inspectional, supervisory, and other nonmanual (lower grade), (5) routine grades of manual work and skilled manual, (6) manual, semiskilled, (7) manual, routine.

4. On Irish coalition governments see Cohan 1979 and Farrell 1983.

5. The three best-known formulas for proportional allocation of places (the largest remainder, d'Hondt, and St-Lague systems) each result in an allocation among the five parties in the 1948 coalition identical to the allocation actually agreed on, and in 1954 to a 9:3:1 allocation to Fine Gael, Labour, and Clann na Talmhan. In 1974 the first two of these suggest an 11:4 distribution between Fine Gael and Labour, whereas the St-Lague system suggests 10:5; and in both 1981 and 1982 the largest remainder and St-Lague systems suggest a 12:3 division, whereas the d'Hondt formula suggests a 13:2 ratio.

REFERENCES

Amphoux, Jean, 1962. *Le chancelier fédéral dans le régime constitutionnel de la République Fédérale d'Allemagne* (Paris: R. Pichon et R. Durand-Auzias).

Blondel, Jean, 1982. *The Organisation of Governments: A Comparative Analysis of Governmental Structures* (London: Sage).

———, 1985. *Government Ministers in the Contemporary World* (London: Sage).

Burstein, Paul, 1977. "Political Elites and Labor Markets: Selection of American Cabinet Members, 1932–72," *Social Forces* 56 (1): 189–201.

Chubb, Basil, 1974. *Cabinet Government in Ireland* (Dublin: Institute of Public Administration).

———, 1982. *The Government and Politics of Ireland*, 2nd ed. (London: Longman).

Coakley, John, 1984. "Selecting a Prime Minister: The Irish Experience," *Parliamentary Affairs* 37 (4): 403–417.

Cohan, A. S., 1972. *The Irish Political Elite* (Dublin: Gill and Macmillan).

———, 1979. "The Open Coalition in the Closed Society: The Strange Pattern of Government Formation in Ireland," *Comparative Politics* 11 (3): 319–338.

Dogan, Mattei, 1989. "Career Pathways to the Cabinet in France" in this volume, chapter 1.

———, 1981. "La sélection des ministres en Italie: dix regles non-écrites," *Revue internationale de science politique* 2 (2): 189–209.

Farrell, Brian, 1971a. *Chairman or Chief? The Role of Taoiseach in Irish Government* (Dublin: Gill and Macmillan).

———, 1971b. "Dail Deputies: 'The 1969 Generation,'" *Economic and Social Review* 2 (3): 309–327.

———, 1983. "Coalitions and Political Institutions: The Irish Experience," in Vernon Bogdanor (ed.), *Coalition Government in Western Europe* (London: Heinemann Educational Books, for the Policy Studies Institute).

———, 1987. "Government Formation and Ministerial Selection," in Howard R. Penniman and Brian Farrell (eds.), *Ireland at the Polls 1981–82* (Washington, D.C.: American Enterprise Institute for Public Policy Research, and Durham, N.C.: Duke University Press).

Farrell, Brian, (ed.), 1973. *The Irish Parliamentary Tradition* (Dublin: Gill and Macmillan).

Farrell, David, 1984. "Age, Education and Occupational Backgrounds of TDs and 'Routes' to the Dail: The Effects of Localism in the 1980s," *Administration* 32 (3): 323–341.

Gallagher, Michael, 1980. "The Composition of Goverments in the Republic of Ireland 1959–1980," Paper presented to the ECPR conference.

———, 1984. "166 Who Rule: The Dail Deputies of November 1982," *Economic and Social Review* 15 (4): 241–264.

———, 1985. *Political Parties in the Republic of Ireland* (Dublin: Gill and Macmillan).

Garvin, Tom, 1981. "The Growth of Faction in the Fianna Fail Party, 1966–1980," *Parliamentary Affairs* 34 (1): 110–123.

Guttsman, W. L., 1974. "Elite Recruitment and Political Leadership in Britain and Germany Since 1950: A Comparative Study of MPs and Cabinets," in Ivor Crewe (ed.), *British Political Sociology Yearbook, Vol. 1: Elites in Western Democracy* (London: Croom Helm).

Headey, Bruce, 1974. *British Cabinet Ministers: The Roles of Politicians in Executive Office* (London: George Allen & Unwin).

Ireland, 1967–70. *Census of Ireland, 1966,* 7 vols. (Dublin: Stationery Office).

McCracken, J. L., 1958. *Representative Government in Ireland: A Study of Dail Eireann 1919–1948* (London: Oxford University Press).

MacGréil, Michael, 1977. *Prejudice and Tolerance in Ireland* (Dublin: College of Industrial Relations).

Nealon, Ted, and Seamus Brennan, 1983. *Nealon's Guide: 24th Dail & Seanad: 2nd Election '82* (Dublin: Platform Press).

Putnam, Robert D., 1976. *The Comparative Study of Political Elites* (Englewood Cliffs: Prentice-Hall).

Willson, F.M.G., 1959. "The Routes of Entry of New Members of the British Cabinet, 1868–1958," *Political Studies* 7 (3): 222–232.

9
SELECTION BY LOT IN ANCIENT ATHENS

C. Fred Alford

Mass male participation in the administration of the state is rarely mentioned among the political achievements of the Athenian polis in the late fifth and early fourth centuries B.C. Usually cited are the great speeches in the assembly and law courts, the direct democracy, and the large citizen juries. In this chapter I shall show why mass—perhaps even universal—citizen participation in the administration of the state should not be overlooked. As an organizational feat, this participation is a significant achievement in its own right. Indeed, precisely because the administrative system of Athens was designed to be run by average citizens, it was sophisticated and highly differentiated. Mass participation, moreover, possessed political significance. It reinforced the Athenian democrats' control over the assembly, giving them de facto as well as de jure control over the policy of the state.

Most of us learn about the polis from the classical philosophers, playwrights, and orators, who were generally concerned with matters more abstract and universal than the administration of the state. Mass participation in the mundane tasks of administration simply does not readily fit the categories through which the ancient state is generally approached. In my approach to this issue I try to follow the advice of Moses Finley in his *Politics in the Ancient World:* "Inquiry into the ancient state and government needs to be lowered from the stratosphere of rarefied concepts, by a consideration not only of ideology . . . but also of the material relations among the citizens or classes of citizens as much as those more commonly noticed between the state and the citizens."[1] By the relations among classes Finley was not referring to a Marxist approach to classical politics but rather to an approach that

sees the politics of the polis as being much like any other politics: a struggle among groups for interest and advantage. This chapter stresses the concrete link between participation and interest.

It has been argued that the Athenian democrats had an intuitive grasp of what Robert Michels over two millennia later was to call the "iron law of oligarchy." More clearly than we, the Athenian democrats saw how an autonomous administration always risks rendering democratic control a mere formality. It will be recalled that Michels's "iron law" states that the necessity for democratic (though not only democratic) institutions to delegate responsibility internally naturally leads to the development of a cadre of leaders. By virtue of their knowledge and position, leaders are generally able to manipulate the opinion of their followers or ignore it. The leadership is free to do so because it possesses a de facto monopoly over all those things that contribute to the control of an organization, such as knowledge, skills, status, channels of communication, and money. The iron law is a theory of irresponsible leadership, according to which the leaders of organizations are effectively free of direction and control by their followers. The iron law applies to labor unions, political parties, and the state. It is a characteristic of organized social life in general. "It is organization which gives birth to the dominion of the elected over the electors, of the mandataries over the mandators, of the delegates over the delegators. Who says organization, says oligarchy."[2]

Whether or not the iron law is an organic necessity, as Michels suggested, the tendency he described seems characteristic of almost all social life above a modest level of complexity. However, the Athenian polis of the late fifth to middle fourth centuries sharply mitigated the impact of the iron law, and not merely because the polis was a direct democracy. This was itself not a major factor. The democratic assembly delegated large amounts of responsibility to more than one thousand magistrates. It allowed the Council of Five Hundred (Boule) to control the agenda of the popular assembly, a responsibility that gave the council the sole right of introducing legislation. Yet neither magistrates nor council ever became independent of the assembly, challenged its authority or control, nor became a power base for popular leaders.

Although the Athenians involved perhaps almost all citizens in the administration of the state, this involvement did not mitigate the iron law simply by making most Athenians more or less competent administrators. More likely the opposite was the case: Mass citizen participation inhibited the development of a skilled caste of administrators who could successfully challenge the assembly. Whereas enough is known about Athenian institutions to support this claim, remarkably little is known about how the Athenian democrats understood and

valued the democracy. Because the democrats did not write down their political theory (or at least it has not been discovered), we cannot be certain what function they intended universal participation to serve. To be sure, A.H.M. Jones exaggerated when he stated, "It is curious that in the abundant literature produced in the greatest democracy of Greece there survives no statement of democratic political theory." There exist several surviving works that contain material pertinent to the political theory of the democracy.[3] However, these works are not always helpful in understanding the significance of the institutional structure of the democracy. To understand how the Greeks understood the concept of *arete* (often translated as excellence or virtue), for example, it is possible to examine the use of the term by a number of authors in a variety of contexts over a period of time. The result can be surprising. For instance, A.W.H. Adkins has shown that the fifth century "Greek in the street" might well consider embezzlement, revenge killing, and the successful imposition of tyranny as instances of *arete*.[4] In studying institutions—which do not speak for themselves—we lack this hermeneutic context. As we also lack an unambiguous theoretical statement of the significance of institutions for the democrats, our risk of tacitly substituting contemporary experience for the Greek context is high. However, the consequence of not taking this risk is to fail to address the significance of a fascinating institution—mass citizen participation in the administration of the polis—that enabled the Athenians to keep a remarkably complex administrative structure utterly subordinate to the democratic assembly. Knowing all the risks involved, I shall explain the meaning of mass citizen participation by examining the institutions that made it possible. I shall support my argument with classical sources when possible.

Several sets of terms require clarification. The type of oligarchy with which Michels was concerned may be called an oligarchy of expertise: Above all it is the knowledge and skills gained by officeholders that allow them to manipulate or ignore their followers. However, when applied to Athens the term *oligarchy* generally has a different connotation: It refers to the power and influence of the great families; oligarchies of blood and wealth these might be called. In addition, the term *oligarchs* is frequently used to refer to Athens' wealthiest 5,000 to 9,000 male citizens. Conversely, the term *democrats* is frequently (and very loosely) used to refer to the other 30,000 or so male citizens over eighteen. Unless otherwise qualified (as it frequently will be), the term *oligarchy* will be employed in Michels's sense.

It is generally recognized that the history of Athenian constitutional reform since Solon can be seen in terms of a movement to prevent oligarchies of blood and wealth from monopolizing political power. The

emergence of a decentralized and nontenured administration can readily be seen as part of this traditional political struggle, even before oligarchies based upon expertise became a widespread possibility, perhaps for the first time in the age of Pericles (beginning about 461 B.C.). What I seek to add to this familiar argument is that during the age of Pericles the Athenian system of decentralized administration came to serve an additional purpose: It prevented the development of oligarchies of expertise, which might have threatened the de facto supremacy of the assembly, which the democrats controlled with their numbers.

Just as important, the system of universal participation prevented the orators, who possessed a monopoly on a certain type of expertise—the skills of rhetoric—from combining this monopoly with one of the skills of administration. In other words, the Athenian administrative system prevented an oligarchy of blood and wealth, skilled in the techniques of rhetoric, from becoming an oligarchy of administrative expertise as well. If the great families had come to monopolize administrative expertise as they came to monopolize rhetorical expertise, they would have threatened democratic rule to a far greater degree than they actually did. That my argument unavoidably involves a certain inference of intent from function (that is, because it is apparent how universal participation prevented the emergence of oligarchies of expertise, we can assume that the democrats intended this) has been noted above. However, even if the democrats did not intend this, my argument will have identified an important latent function of universal participation.[5]

HOW WIDESPREAD WAS PARTICIPATION IN ADMINISTRATION?

Aristotle claimed that during the era in which Pericles was a general, "more than 20,000 men were eating public bread" (*Constitution of Athens* [hereafter, *CA*] 24). That is, they were receiving state pay as soldiers, sailors, dock guards, jurors, and so forth. Among these 20,000 were 500 council members, 700 domestic magistrates, and perhaps 300 magistrates of colonies of Athens. Though it is widely held that Aristotle exaggerated (at least insofar as he wrote as if all magistrates served constantly, the jury of 6,000 was perpetually in session, and the city constantly at war), it can be readily shown that there were at least 1,000 active domestic magistrates.[6] Using this figure, it can be demonstrated that most—and perhaps almost all—citizens must have served as magistrate for one year.

The Council of Five Hundred, in addition to its function of introducing legislation to the assembly, acted as chief magistrate (*CA* 47–50.1). Control of the council rotated among the ten tribes of Athens,

so that a subcommittee of 50 would comprise the active membership for one-tenth of a year, called a *prytany*. Subcommittees of the council were chosen by lot. Among these was the subcommittee of 10 *logistai*, who audited the financial magistrates each *prytany*, and 30 men who sat in the marketplace and invited citizen complaints against any magistrate. Another subcommittee of 10 had oversight of ship construction; 10 determined if the horses of the cavalry were properly maintained; 10 reviewed claims of the disabled and "war orphans" (those approved received two obols per day). Additional subcommittees of the council were mentioned by Aristotle at *CA* 43–49. A group of 30 assemblers (*syllogeis*) drawn from the council was mentioned by other sources. They controlled admission to the assembly, and in the fourth century distributed payment for assembly attendance.[7] Few of these administrative positions were full-time, but most required a substantial commitment. It seems reasonable to conclude that from the Council of Five Hundred, there were at any one time at least 160 who could be considered active magistrates. (Why the council was itself not an autonomous power center will be discussed later.)

The nine archons were traditionally the most prestigious magistrates, and in the period under consideration were also chosen by lot. Other important magistracies were the ten treasurers of Athena; the ten *poletai* (who let state contracts, mining rights, and the right to collect taxes); ten receivers, or *apodektai* (who received money generated by the *poletai*). Other magistracies included: a board of ten that took care of the sanctuaries; ten city commissioners (who controlled the prices of flute girls and regulated the location of dung heaps, among other tasks); ten superintendents of markets; ten inspectors of weights and measures; thirty-five inspectors of the corn supply; ten commissioners of trade; eleven prison wardens; five to introduce small claims cases to the courts; a board of forty to sit as a small claims court (disputes under forty drachmas); five road commissioners; twenty auditors (who performed a year-end financial audit of those magistrates who controlled money, and who should not be confused with the auditors drawn from the council); ten in charge of sacrifices; ten in charge of annual religious rites; ten commissioners of the quadrennial games (they served a four-year term). Also chosen by lot was the chief clerk of the council and another to record the laws (*CA* 47–54; 60). Other sources mentioned ten inspectors of the dockyards.[8] A special category of magistrates was the arbitrators, men sixty years of age who had just completed forty-two years of military eligibility. They arbitrated cases involving more than ten drachmas and prepared for trial those cases that could not be

successfully arbitrated. Perhaps thirty to forty actually heard cases.[9]

There were additional offices to be filled. U. von Wilamowitz-Moellendorff suggested that the trierarchs (wealthy citizens who maintained a ship of the fleet for a year) could be considered magistrates because they were appointed to office.[10] However, the trierarchy will not be considered a magistracy here. Neither will the 500 dock guards, nor the 50 guards of the Acropolis, whom Aristotle mentioned, be considered as magistrates (*CA* 24). Nor will thoroughly unpolitical offices, also frequently chosen by lot, such as the judges of the theatrical contests (Lysias, "On a Wound by Premeditation," 3), be considered as magistracies. However, it does seem appropriate to include the magistrates of the local demes, or districts (there were over 100, and perhaps as many as 140). J. W. Headlam suggested that there might well have been over 35 offices per deme.[11] The political structure of the deme, with its own assembly, elections, officers, priests, festivals, and public records, mirrored that of the polis. There were also a number of offices to be filled at the tribal level. However, following Wilamowitz, I shall count only the *demarch* and treasurer for each deme, which gives a conservative figure of 280 deme magistrates.

In addition to the secretaries, there were also clerks and messengers attached to the various colleges (Demosthenes, "The Embassy," 249). Wilamowitz's reckoning suggested that 350 clerks would be a reasonable estimate. Often they were *metics* (foreigners) or freedmen, who made their living as clerks, but sometimes they were citizens, as Aeschines was (Demosthenes, "The Crown," 261). The law prohibited these clerks from holding a particular office for more than one year; therefore, they rotated from office to office (Lysias, "Against Nicomachus," 29). It is generally believed that despite this yearly rotation, these clerks maintained a certain continuity in the administration and frequently instructed the yearly officeholders in their tasks.

The result is 1,010 offices, broken down into the following categories:

160	council members (those considered active magistrates at any one time)
246	ordinary magistrates, chosen by lot
25	secretaries of the major colleges
35	arbitrators
34	elected military officials (*CA* 61)
45	other elected officials (includes no special commissions—*CA* 43.1)

280	deme magistrates
185	citizen clerks, minor secretaries, and messengers,

1010[12]

Unless otherwise noted, offices were filled by lot.

Considerable attention has been paid to the particular offices not merely to establish their number, although this is an important consideration. The number of offices, as well as the areas of life that were administered, serve to dramatically demonstrate that the administrative system at Athens was sufficiently complex and differentiated that the iron law of oligarchy could have readily emerged had measures not been taken to prevent it. A city that regulated the price charged by flute girls, controlled the location of drain pipes and dung heaps, and regulated the price and quality of foodstuffs in the markets (not to mention Athens's administration—in the fifth century—of an empire of over one hundred dependent communities throughout the Aegean) was not an ancient city with a primitive bureaucracy. However, whether 1,010 administrative offices is many or a few depends almost entirely on the population available to fill them. Population estimates for the fifth and fourth centuries vary. For the year 431, most estimates fall between 38,000 and 45,000 male citizens over eighteen years. Fourth century figures were lower. A. W. Gomme set the male citizen population (eighteen–fifty-nine years old) in 400 at 22,000 (the result of the plague and twenty-eight years of war); by 323 it had recovered to perhaps 28,000.[13] Especially relevant is the death rate, which Jones estimated was uniformly high from ages twenty to sixty throughout the entire period under consideration. Of 500 men of twenty, not many more than 100 survived until sixty years of age.[14]

The age of majority was thirty for council members and probably the same for most magistracies (Xenophon *Memorabilia* 1.2.35).[15] Although there is considerable disagreement over the total population of Athens, there is more agreement on the distribution. Two recent estimates agreed that those of nineteen years would constitute 3 percent of the population, those thirty-one would constitute 2.3 percent, and those sixty years of age 0.6–0.9 percent.[16] If we apply these percentages to the high estimate of 45,000 male citizens over eighteen, this gives 1,035 citizens aged thirty-one. As the term of office was generally one year and the officeholder could generally not succeed himself (the generals are a notable exception), this age cohort could be expected over the next forty years to fill one thousand offices. Otherwise expressed, over a forty-year period a population of about 45,000 would have to fill about 40,000 positions, if we assume that each office was

held by one man for one year. This ignores, of course, the fact that many might have held more than one office, whereas others held no office at all. However, these calculations do not take full account of the high death rate. The 1,035 citizens in the age cohort of thirty-one would be reduced to 405 by age sixty (using 0.9 percent). One could compare losses due to the high death rate with the likelihood of an individual being chosen more than once (or not at all), but the data are so imprecise as to make this not especially fruitful. In any case, it appears that there were about as many offices to be filled as citizens available to fill them.

Calculations similar to these have been frequently performed for the council, less often for the magistracies. A. Zimmern conservatively estimated that with a citizen body of 40,000, 2 of 5 citizens would sit on the council at some time. G. Glotz put it more casually: Every reputable citizen of moderate means could expect to sit on the council once in his lifetime.[17] These are extraordinary facts. Virtually every citizen would serve as a magistrate, and about half would sit on the council. Surely no other polity has achieved such remarkable levels of citizen participation. Why did the Athenians organize the polis so? Before addressing this question, it is necessary to confront one more preliminary issue. Did the democracy actually work as its formal institutional structure suggests it did?

Corruption and fraud at the deme level was apparently quite widespread. Aristotle claimed that it was corruption of the lot system within the demes that caused the selection of most magistrates (all but the council) to be moved to the tribal level (*CA* 62.1). Most common was apparently one deme's selling its place to another (there was a complicated double-lot system for some offices, in which the preliminary selection took place in the demes) (*CA* 8.1, 55.1). Or the *demarch* might discourage multiple candidates for a single office, thus virtually guaranteeing that a particular individual would be chosen.[18] Another illegality was practiced as well. The Solonic exclusion of the *thetes* (the lowest class) from certain offices was ignored in the fourth century, though the law was apparently never changed.[19] It also appears that the wealthy were somewhat—but not vastly—overrepresented on the council, and probably among the archons as well.[20] If all this constituted corruption, it may well be that most citizens were comfortable with a certain slackness in the system. The slackness made it more likely that those of modest means would serve in the relatively well-paying minor magistracies, whereas the wealthy would be more likely to serve in the more demanding, but less well-paying, positions (*CA* 62.2). Johannes Sundwall's research demonstrated that almost all the dock inspectors—an ordinary magistracy, but one of considerable importance (they were

responsible for the condition of the fleet)—were not men of wealth, and few appear to have served in any other major office.[21]

WHY UNIVERSAL CITIZEN PARTICIPATION?

There was fraud, bribery, and widespread winking at certain manipulations of the lot system. The influence of wealth was not absent. However, there is little evidence that the institutions outlined by Aristotle did not work roughly as described. But why did they work this way in the first place? Not all explanations see the issue in terms of Athens' success in mitigating the iron law of oligarchy. Among these explanations are the following:

1. The many offices were a way of distributing the wealth of Athens among its citizens by paying them fairly well for what amounted in many cases to token service (Pseudo-Xenophon *Constitution of the Athenians* 1.2–3).

2. The many offices, distributed by lot as they were, helped mitigate intense factional conflict by granting the oligarchs a place in public life (Isocrates, "Areopagiticus," 23). A group that lacked a "parliamentary majority" in the assembly was not entirely excluded from office.[22] Were there but few offices, the democrats would have been required to control them all in order to rule the democracy. In fact, the lot system, rotation in office, the large number of offices, and the eligibility of almost all citizens for almost all offices, can be considered as component parts of a single institution: one that involved a maximum number of citizens in office. When democracy is defined as the type of constitution that assigns offices by lot, as it was by democrats and oligarchs alike, it is generally this compound of practices that is meant.[23] That the lot per se was not democratic is shown by its use by the oligarchical government of 400 at Athens (Thucydides *History* 8.70).

3. Another explanation of the large number of offices, again associated with an explanation of the lot, is that the democrats had an almost literal understanding of democracy. Democracy meant shared participation in the administration—as well as the governance—of the state (Thucydides, 2.40; Aristotle *Politics* 1317b2–3, 15–25). However, this is not so much an explanation as a definition, which does not answer the question of why the democrats assumed it, if in fact they did. Such an explanation could be read as suggesting that the democrats were so civic-minded as to value participation purely for its own sake, for its symbolic value. Such a perspective idealizes the average democrat unnecessarily. The functional explanation invoked below helps to explain this otherwise somewhat puzzling extension of the meaning of

democracy to include shared participation in the administration of the state.

4. If one considers the institutional requirements of involving even a relatively small number of average citizens in the administration of the polis, then another explanation (not necessarily incompatible with the others) of virtually universal participation suggests itself. A structural requirement of involving *some* average citizens in office may have been to involve almost *all* average citizens. If this can be shown, then the easier question of why some average citizens were involved can be addressed shortly. For the average citizen to share in the administration of the polis, it seems necessary that administrative tasks be radically simplified. The large number of offices would reflect the principle of the assembly line: Because untrained workers were to perform what was collectively a quite sophisticated task—the administration of Athens—it was necessary that the task be broken down into simple parts. C. Hignett asserted that the lot was used to appoint most magistrates because the offices were relatively unimportant. However, E. S. Stavely seems to have been correct when he wrote that this has the emphasis backwards.[24] The fact is that the offices were individually unimportant so that the lot could be employed in the first place. Each office was made relatively unimportant (each magistracy was composed of a college of ten individuals) so that each could be filled with average citizens without subjecting the city to the risk of utterly incompetent officials (it is generally agreed that the *dokimasia,* or scrutiny, examined only the probity of a candidate, not his merit or ability).[25] An effect—perhaps almost a side effect—of simplifying the magistracies was that over one thousand offices were created. Coupled with the relatively small citizen population, plus rotation in office, this led to virtually universal participation.[26]

Other aspects of the institutional structure served brilliantly the function of allowing Athens to be run by rank amateurs. The college system acted to flatten the extremes that might be produced by the luck of the draw. The performance of a board of ten would presumably tend toward the mean level of its members. Such an arrangement also increased tenfold the number of offices. Many boards shared functions that we today would probably combine. For instance, one board (*poletai*) let state contracts, another (*apodektai*) received income from them, and both were required to perform their functions before the council and people, in a plaza in front of the council chambers (*CA* 47–48). This arrangement served not merely to increase the number of jobs or to promote honesty. It served another function as well. Magistrates were subject to severe liability, personally and collectively, if they were convicted of defalcation, malfeasance, or even incompetence.[27] A prac-

tical condition of involving average citizens was that their responsibility, and thus their liability, be mitigated.

It has been suggested that the responsibilities of many magistrates were so onerous that sortition acted as a form of conscription to office, which otherwise few would wish to hold.[28] In any case, most magistracies demanded no special abilities.[29] The treasurers of Athena, for example, supervised the security of the treasures of Athens, a responsible assignment, but one requiring little financial acumen (*CA* 47). Even the duties of the king archon, the most prestigious magistrate, were not necessarily especially taxing.[30] Most boards, such as the building inspectors, oversaw the work of architects and contractors elected or appointed by the assembly. Such oversight required a certain practical wisdom but little expertise. Indeed, such boards might be said to embody the Aristotelian principle that the tenants, not the contractor, are in the end the best judge of a building's construction (*Politics* 1282a 10–20).

Why did the Athenians involve any average citizens at all in the administration of the state, it might be asked. Far fewer professional administrators could surely have done the job more efficiently, a practice we follow today. Well-educated slaves and *metics* were also available and might well have performed most of the administrative tasks themselves (as a sort of indentured civil service) in the absence of supervision by the colleges of magistrates. One need not turn to the vague explanation that democracy meant participation in administration by average citizens. A more concrete function was served by citizen participation. This function did not require universal citizen participation. It only required substantial citizen participation. However, the tendency that led from the latter to the former has already been explained. Had average citizens not participated in the administration of the polis, administration would likely have become the province of a caste of mandarins. Citizen participation in the administration of the polis prevented familiarity with the skills of statecraft from becoming the province of a few, as the skills of persuading the assembly had become.

THE ORATORS

The Athenian assembly was led by a group that indeed possessed a monopoly upon a certain type of leadership skill: the orators, who commanded the skills of rhetoric. It may seem surprising that the iron law operated most powerfully in the assembly, which was characterized by direct democracy and the right of every male citizen to address the assembly (*isegoria*). However, it would not have surprised Michels. Toward the beginning of *Political Parties,* Michels considered the "bril-

liant attempt" by Moritz Rittinghausen "to get a real basis for direct legislation by the people." Against Rittinghausen's proposal for direct democracy, Michels argued not merely that it is impractical but that it would fail to mitigate the iron law, as it "failed to provide any guarantee against the formation of an oligarchical camerilla." Whereas direct democracy may (depending upon how it is organized) deprive the leaders of their role as functionaries, and in this way prevent their self-aggrandizement, it provides no protection against the development of a cadre of orators who can sway the crowd through specious argument.[31] Indeed, many more pages in *Political Parties* are devoted to the psychological susceptibility of the mass (which Michels at some point speculated might even be genetic[32]) than to the strictly organizational factors contributing to oligarchy.

At Athens the influence of sophistic thought was at its peak. Arguments employing an extreme materialism and stressing likelihood and expedience were considered powerfully persuasive by most citizens. At the same time, such arguments were beyond the ability of the average citizen to construct for himself. Special training in the skills of rhetoric was required in order to wield such arguments, and such training was affordable only by the wealthy: oligarchs in the traditional sense. Those who commanded such skills constituted precisely the type of "oligarchical camerilla" to which Michels referred. Yet although the orators at Athens were indeed oligarchs in Michels's sense as well, they failed to constitute an oligarchy; that is, they failed to constitute a leadership group that was effectively free of citizen control. One cannot find this distinction—oligarchs without oligarchy—in *Political Parties*, but it is a useful one. It describes well how Athens mitigated the iron law: not by eliminating cadres of leaders and not by widely distributing leadership skills—the skills of rhetoric were not learned by holding administrative office—but rather by depriving Athens's leaders of a permanent and institutionalized power base, including that found in the possession of or control over administrative office.

The orators were without political office of any kind. Though some orators were also generals, it was not necessary to be a general in order to be an influential orator, as the case of Cleon demonstrated (Thucydides *History* 5.2). (Furthermore, the office of general was itself not secure: The position was elective, the term was one year, and although a general could succeed himself, he could be removed at any time by a vote of no confidence in the assembly, which was apparently not uncommon.) It is a truism that increasing the security of tenure in office frees the representative from the immediate demands of his constituency. Indeed, it is upon such truisms that the iron law of oligarchy is built. However, at Athens the orators had no term of office

at all.³³ An orator's power existed only as long as he could convince the assembly of the rightness of his policies. Under such circumstances, many orators—including those, such as Pericles, who came from great families—were remarkably responsive to the wishes of the democratic majority. Indeed, it is really to this that the classical philosophers objected; that is, they claimed that the leaders of Athens gave the majority of citizens what it wanted, rather than what was good for it.³⁴ Such a position is defensible, but it should be recognized for what it is: a complaint that Athens was insufficiently oligarchic in Michels's sense.

COUNCIL OF FIVE HUNDRED

It seems unlikely that those orators at Athens who represented the democratic faction would have continued to be responsive to the majority of citizens had this majority been an inactive and uninformed mass. However, it would be a misleading idealization to suggest that Athens avoided the worst effects of the iron law because most male Athenians were able, informed, and involved. Though this is part of the story, the larger part is that Athens mitigated the iron law by separating political leadership from the offices that ran the state, thus rendering the political leadership directly dependent upon its ability to continually persuade the assembly of the rightness of its policies. Conversely, Athens rendered it impossible that administrative officers themselves might foment an oligarchy of expertise. Athens did so by subdividing these offices into functional units, thus preventing any office from monopolizing great power, and by staffing these offices with average citizens. This leads to an interesting conclusion: The supremacy of the assembly (which the democrats controlled with their numbers) was maintained not so much by raising the administrative abilities of the average democrat as by lowering the capacity of the average magistrate. Virtually universal participation, coupled with stringent scrutiny and substantial and sometimes arbitrary penalties for failure, presumably produced large numbers of mediocre and timid magistrates. However, this too was functional: Magistrates lacking in initiative would be even less likely to garner power to themselves. The result was that magistrates remained subordinate to the council, and the council remained subordinate to the assembly.

Consider what a feat it was to prevent a body that controlled the agenda of the assembly and introduced every piece of legislation to it from becoming an autonomous center of power. What amounted to monthly rotation in office (the *prytany* system), coupled with the lot, prevented the development of a coterie of skilled and experienced

councilmen. What is more, the development of a sense of corporate identity among council members was forestalled. (There is no evidence that the overrepresentation of the wealthy on the council made any difference in this regard.) The same can be said for all magistrates. Council and magistrates remained, in effect, subcommittees of the assembly. The Athenian system separated utterly political leadership from the offices that ran the state. In fact, there exists widespread agreement that the council never became an autonomous power center.[35]

The supremacy of the assembly was not, to be sure, maintained by institutional structure alone. In some measure it was the result of a culture that had little respect for administrators. The most skilled and those with the greatest advantages did not become administrators. They generally became orators. Permanent civil servants were frequently slaves, *metics,* or freedmen. It was a mark of poverty, or perhaps a servile character, to have served in such a position. Demosthenes never allowed Aeschines to forget that he had once earned his living as "secretary and attendant of petty magistracies" (Demosthenes, "The Crown," 261; see also "The Embassy," 70, 200, 249).[36] However, this aspect of the culture was reinforced by institutional structure. If any citizen could serve in virtually any magistracy, then the office itself was diminished in dignity. If a citizen's brother-in-law served as archon, and his son as council member, these offices would likely be lacking a certain aura for him. It is perhaps for this reason that there were special laws against insulting magistrates (Demosthenes, "Against Meidias," 32).[37]

CONCLUSION

It has been argued that virutally universal participation in the administration of the city was part of a power struggle through which the democrats maintained the supremacy of the institution (assembly) that their numbers controlled. The democrats' participation in the actual administration of the city served, whether intended or not, to prevent the development of oligarchies of administrative expertise. Moreover, universal participation prevented the orators from establishing any sort of institutionalized power base within the administration. Similarly, universal participation prevented the orators from monopolizing the skills of administration as they had come to monopolize the skills of persuasion. One suspects that had the orators been able to monopolize both, they would have indeed constituted a powerful "oligarchical camerilla." That the administrative structure of Athens is not generally considered a major achievement—at least in comparison with the vitality and openness of debate in the assembly and law courts—reflects

in large measure the success of the Athenian system on its own terms. It was able to utterly subordinate its administrators to the assembly.

If it is the case that virtually universal participation in the administration of the state was part of the democrats' power struggle for actual (and not merely de jure) control of the state, then participation may have been viewed by the average democrat much like military service is frequently viewed today: as a necessary personal sacrifice in the interest of the larger group. In this case the larger group was the democrats. At Athens, intense feelings of loyalty were generally directed toward associations smaller than the polis.[38] That administrative service to the state was compensated does not contradict this claim about loyalty. Soldiers in Western European countries are paid modestly even when drafted. The lot may have acted to implement what was in effect a form of compulsory service.[39]

If the "Greek in the street" saw his participation in the administration of the polis as part of the struggle between democrats and oligarchs (in the traditional sense) then the agonal framework of Greek life would not have ignored this aspect of life either. Indeed, participation would represent the redirection of this competitive spirit along more cooperative lines. There was little opportunity for individual glory in the administration of the state.[40] It may seem ironic that the democrats won this contest in significant measure because their numbers ensured that most of them would perform their administrative tasks in a mediocre fashion. However, if the administration of the state is seen to be in a perpetual and generally successful struggle for power with its citizens, then this irony loses its force. In the Athenian polis the struggle between administrators and the assembly was potentially more explosive than today because that struggle tended to occur together with the struggle between democrats and oligarchs (in the traditional sense). This coincidence may have heightened the democrats' awareness of the degree to which an administration that is not successfully subordinated to the popular assembly risks making democracy merely a procedure under which elite groups vie to manage the state's affairs.

The immediacy and intensity of Athenian democracy dramatically demostrates the level of political involvement necessary to mitigate the iron law of oligarchy. Indeed, one might hypothesize that a level of participation comparable to that of Athens can only be achieved when the following two conditions are met (other conditions must also be met, of course, such as those having to do with size and political openness): (1) Politics must be absolutely central to the life of a particular group (rather then, for example, the private pursuit of wealth); (2) the connection between participation and interest must be direct and palpable. Constrast this with the widespread avoidance of jury

duty in the United States. The connection between jury duty and interest is abstract at best and for many simply negative; that is, the stipend for jury service is insufficient to make up for lost wages. The Athenian experience suggests something else as well, which is really the obverse of the preceding considerations. It suggests that a small group's monopolization of administrative skills is itself a political act, of fundamentally the same type (though of course vastly less violent) as a revolution or coup. That the monopolization of administrative skills is not usually seen in this light, but is instead generally seen as the natural consequence of large-scale political and bureaucratic organization, reflects perhaps a certain alienation from politics with which the Athenians were not familiar.

However, this recognition is unlikely to make the operation of the iron law less remorseless in the modern world, even within groups of comparable size to the Athenian polis (such as some labor unions, professional associations, small towns, political associations). The Athenian experience also suggests what an enormous commitment of political will, coupled with what was really massive political mobilization, is necessary to combat the effects of the iron law. Few societies in history have enjoyed politics sufficiently to make the effort. In modern times those societies that have been sufficiently politically mobilized to make the effort have not been sufficiently democratized for the effort to lead to greater political freedom. The cultural revolution in China during the late 1960s is a prime example. The Athenian combination of extensive political mobilization, coupled with widespread popular commitment to democratic institutions, put it in a unique position to combat the iron law in the name of democracy.

NOTES

Citations of classical sources are given in the text in the form that is usual in classical studies.

1. Moses Finley, *Politics in the Ancient World* (Cambridge: Cambridge University Press, 1983), 49.
2. Robert Michels, *Political Parties,* trans. Eden and Cedar Paul (Glencoe, Ill.: The Free Press, 1958), 27–45; 417–419. Quote, p. 418.
3. Quote from A.H.M. Jones, *Athenian Democracy* (Oxford: Basil Blackwell, 1957), 41. Among works pertinent to the political theory of the democrats are several of the tragedies (Aeschylus's *Suppliants* and *Eumenides,* Sophocles' *Antigone,* and Euripides' *Suppliants*) and comedies (Aristophanes' *Knights* and *Wasps*); Herodotus's *History* (the "constitutional debate"); Thucydides' *History* (Pericles' funeral oration, the speech of Athenagoras, the description of the

oligarchic revolt of 411); the *Constitution of the Athenians* by the "old oligarch" (pseudo-Xenophon); the early dialogues of Plato (especially the *Apology* and *Protagoras*), and Xenophon's *Memorabilia*. What we lack are not statements pertinent to the democracy but rather a systematic defense of democratic political theory. The difference is revealed by the difficulty of interpreting some pertinent statements. Just one example: Aeschylus's *Eumenides* has been read as a protest against the democrats' attack on the aristocratic areopagus. However, an interpretation with Aeschylus supporting the democrats' reforms seems equally plausible, as R. Bonner suggested, in *Aspects of Athenian Democracy* (Berkeley: University of California Press, 1933), 9. A common strategy, employed by Havelock and Jones, is to read the philosophers' criticisms of democracy from right to left, as it were; that is, the democrats presumably asserted what the philosophers criticized. Though Havelock sought to "control" this method by using fragments from the historical Thrasymachus, for example, the method has obvious defects. See Jones, *Athenian Democracy,* 42–43; Havelock, *The Liberal Temper in Greek Politics* (London: Jonathan Cape, 1957), 230–239.

4. A.W.H. Adkins, *Moral Values and Political Behaviour in Ancient Greece* (New York: W. W. Norton and Co., 1972), chaps. 4–5.

5. "*Manifest functions* are those objective consequences contributing to the adjustment or adaptation of a system which are intended and recognized by all participants. *Latent functions,* correlatively, being those which are neither intended nor recognized." From R. Merton, *Social Theory and Social Structure,* rev. and enlarged ed. (Glencoe, Ill.: The Free Press, 1957).

6. Wilamowitz and Zimmern both easily arrived at a figure of well over 1,000 paid offices, not including jury duty, military service, or attendance in the assembly. They counted dock guards and the like, because the two were addressing a slightly different issue: not how many magistrates per se, but how many paid positions there were. See U. von Wilamowitz-Moellendorff, *Aristotles und Athen* (Berlin: Weidmannsche Buchhandlung, 1893), vol. 2, 201–211, and A. Zimmern, *The Greek Commonwealth,* 5th ed. rev. (Oxford: Clarendon Press, 1931), 174–177. A different counting procedure (e.g., he excluded deme magistrates) accounts for Jones's vastly lower estimate of 350 domestic magistrates, in *Athenian Democracy,* 6, 136, n. 9. More recently, Mogens Hansen argued that Aristotle's figure of 700 domestic magistrates (*CA* 24.3) is "probably right." Indeed, Hansen went on to list a large number of magistrates not included by Aristotle, but known from other sources, including a board of magistrates empowered to buy sacrificial animals and another in charge of Athenian coinage and the mint. In fact, Hansen operated from what he noted is a "technical and restricted definition of arche (office)." Were he to include some of the offices mentioned above, such as arbitrators and deme magistrates, his figure would easily exceed 1,000. See "Seven Hundred Archai in Classical Athens," *Greek, Roman, and Byzantine Studies* 21 (1980), 151–154.

7. G. Glotz, *The Greek City,* trans. N. Mallinson (New York: Barnes & Noble, 1965), 189, gave the inscription source.

8. J. W. Headlam *Election by Lot at Athens,* 2nd rev. ed., ed. D. C. MacGregor (Cambridge: Cambridge University Press, 1933), chap. 6.

9. *CA* 53. Not only is it not clear how many arbitrators would actually hear cases, but it is not clear how many arbitrators there were. It has generally been assumed that the arbitrators were drawn only from those of hoplite ("middle-class") status, but as P. J. Rhodes argued, *CA* 53.4 seems to imply that the arbitrators were drawn from all classes. See "Ephebi, Bouleutae and the Population of Athens," *Zeitschrift für Papyrologie und Epigraphik* 38 (1980), 191. Rhodes went on to note that the only complete list of arbitrators numbers 103 (*Inscriptiones Graecae,* vol. 2–3, 2d ed., inscription no. 1926). However, this figure is from the year 325/324. It is generally agreed that the population in 431 was considerably higher. Presumably the number of arbitrators would have been higher too. In any case, it should be apparent that my estimate of 35 is quite conservative.

10. Wilamowitz, *Aristotles und Athen,* vol. 2, 203. Pseudo-Xenophon, "Constitution of the Athenians," 3.4.

11. Headlam, *Election by Lot,* 166–167. J. Traill, "The Political Organization of Attica," *Hesperia,* supplement 14 (1975).

12. It is generally agreed that the number of new fourth-century offices roughly equals the number of discontinued fifth-century offices; i.e., the number of offices remained constant during the entire period under consideration. Jones, *Athenian Democracy,* 136 n. 9. Hansen, "Seven Hundred Archai," 166.

13. Jones, *Athenian Democracy,* estimated 40,000 male citizens over eighteen in 431 (8–9, and appendix). A. W. Gomme, *The Population of Athens in the Fifth and Fourth Centuries* B.C. (Chicago: Argonaut, 1967), estimated 43,000 male citizens between eighteen and sixty in 431 (26–28). However, in "The Number of Athenian Hoplites in 431 B.C.," Mogens Hansen suggested that Gomme's estimate for 431 is too high because the number of *metic* hoplites "was probably much higher than that accepted by Gomme and Jones." *Symbolae Osloenses* 56 (1981), 23–24. All estimates for the year 431 utilize Thucydides' assessment of the strength of the Athenian army at the outbreak of the Peloponnesian War as a major source (*History,* 2, 13, 6–9).

14. Jones, *Athenian Democracy,* 82–83.

15. Hansen, "Seven Hundred Archai," Appendix 1: "The Minimum Age for Archai," 167–173.

16. E. Ruschenbusch, "Die soziale Herkunft der Epheben um 330," and "Die soziale Zusammensetzung des Rates der 500 im 4. h.," both in *Zeitschrift für Papyrologie und Epigraphik* 35 (1979), 173–175; 177–180. Rhodes, "Ephebi, Bouleutae and the Population of Athens," 191, 194–195, and notes.

17. Zimmern, *The Greek Commonwealth,* 164. Glotz, *The Greek City,* 183. Jones noted that with a few serving twice the council could have been manned from hoplites—slightly less than 40 percent of the citizen population according to Jones' estimate—alone (*Athenian Democracy,* 106). However, this is but a different way of saying the same thing. But cf. Rhodes, "Ephebi, Bouleutae and the Population of Athens," 193–196.

18. E. S. Staveley reviewed the different possible modes of corruption, in *Greek and Roman Voting and Elections* (Ithaca, N.Y.: Cornell University Press, 1972), 108–117. Aeschines' accusation that Demosthenes was appointed to the council by bribery, not the lot, is classic (Aeschines, "The Treaty," 3).

19. *CA* 7.4. However, C. Hignett offered another interpretation of this passage: that the upper classes had become impoverished after twenty-seven years of war. See *A History of the Athenian Constitution to the End of the Fifth Century B.C.* (Oxford: Clarendon Press, 1952), 226.

20. Johannes Sundwall calculated that if the composition of the council had been due to mere chance, only about 6 percent of its members would have been wealthy. In fact, sixty-one (or 12 percent) appear to have been wealthy, and sixty appear to have been well-to-do. Sundwall estimated that about 375 out of 500 members in any one year were men of means. In *Epigraphische Beiträge zur Sozial-politischen geschichte Athens im zeitalter Demosthenes* (Leipzig: Druck von. G. Kreysing, 1906), 1-18. See also Headlam, *Election by Lot*, 200. Apparently it was not uncommon for the wealthy to volunteer to serve on the council (Lysias, "Against Philon," 33). This would obviously mean that the lot was not being strictly observed.

21. Sundwall, *Epigraphische Beiträge*, 35ff. Headlam, *Election by Lot*, 206.

22. H. Müller-Strübing, *Aristophanes und die historische Kritik* (Leipzig: B. G. Teubner, 1873). Glotz, *The Greek City*, 213. Headlam criticized this view in *Election by Lot*, 16-19.

23. Aristotle *Rhetoric* 1365b31; *Politics* 1294b7-8; Euripides *Suppliants* 406-408; Herodotus *History* 3.80. The close connection between the lot and rotation in office among all citizens was suggested by Theseus in *Suppliants*.

24. C. Hignett, *A History of the Athenian Constitution*, 230. Staveley, *Greek and Roman Voting and Elections*, 55.

25. V. Ehrenberg, *The Greek State* (New York: Barnes and Noble, 1960), 68; Headlam, *Election by Lot*, 96-101; Staveley, *Greek and Roman Voting and Elections*, 57-60; *CA* 55.3-5.

26. Headlam, writing before the rediscovery of Aristotle's *Constitution of Athens*, seems to have been the first contemporary author to assert what I have called the assembly-line theory. See *Election by Lot*, 90-91; 138; 142. Jones asserted a similar principle, *Athenian Democracy*, 104.

27. Antiphon the orator told how one year all but one of the Hellenotamiai (treasurers of the Delian League) were put to death for defalcation. Later they were discovered to have been innocent (Headlam, *Election by Lot*, 95). Even Pericles was fined for malversation (Plutarch, "Pericles," 23).

28. Headlam, *Election by Lot*, 94-95. Staveley, *Greek and Roman Voting*, 40.

29. See the nice summary of a case study, based upon inscriptions, of the dock inspectors, by Böckh, in Headlam, *Election by Lot*, chap. 6. Their knowledge of ship construction and seamanship must have been considerable, but no more so than that possessed by most who have grown up in a seaport, and have served in the navy.

30. In "Against Andocides," 4, Lysias claimed that if Andocides should be chosen king archon by lot, he would do little but make sacrifices and offer prayers.

31. Michels, *Political Parties*, 27-30.

32. Arthur Mitzman, *Sociology and Estrangement* (New York: Alfred Knopf, 1973), 323-325.

33. Some have found this difficult to believe and have suggested that the generals constituted a secret government of Athens. Jones showed how weak the evidence is in this regard, *Athenian Democracy,* 124–129.

34. Plato *Gorgias* 518–519. Cf. *Republic* 488b–493e.

35. Jones, *Athenian Democracy,* 118. Headlam, *Election by Lot,* 64. P. J. Rhodes, *The Athenian Boule* (Oxford: Clarendon Press, 1972), 63–64. A. W. Gomme, *More Essays in Greek History and Literature* (Oxford: Basil Blackwell, 1962), 179.

36. Jones, *Athenian Democracy,* 104.

37. Glotz, *The Greek City,* 223. Ehrenberg, "Losung," in *Pauly's Realencyclopädie der classischen Altertumswissenschaft,* vol. 13. Hrsg. von Wilhelm Kroll (Stuttgart: J. B. Metzlersche Verlagsbuchhandlung, 1926), 1481.

38. Adkins, *Moral Values and Political Behaviour,* 131–132. The parochial character of Greek loyalty was expressed by various characters in Plato's dialogues, such as Meno (*Meno* 71E), and Polemarchus (*Republic* 331e–332d).

39. Headlam, *Election by Lot,* 94–95. Staveley, *Greek and Roman Voting,* 40.

40. Adkins, *Moral Values and Political Behaviour,* chaps. 5–6. A wild competitiveness in search of individual glory was the Greek disease. The career of Alcibiades is a classic example.

10
IRREMOVABLE LEADERS AND MINISTERIAL INSTABILITY IN EUROPEAN DEMOCRACIES

Mattei Dogan

The negative effects of ministerial instability have been greatly exaggerated. In the same way as fever is only a symptom of a sickness, ministerial instability is only one of the most visible manifestations of an institutional disequilibrium. It is not high temperature that provokes illness, and in the same way it is not ministerial volatility that destabilizes a political system. In the literature on unstable democracies, the diagnosis of the problem has been inappropriately formulated, permitting a confusion between the stable regime with revolving governments and the instability of the regime itself. A comparative analysis of regimes characterized by high governmental turnover should obviously search behind the accidents of history for what these regimes have had in common.

The scope of this chapter is not to analyze the causes of governmental instability. Several works have already been devoted to this topic (von Beyme 1981; Hermens 1951; Soulie 1939). Rather, I will try to show why ministerial instability has not in reality had the disastrous effects that it has been accused of by many political scientists and historians in various countries and especially in the United States.

I can state my argument simply: The negative consequences of ministerial instability are limited because it is normally accompanied by the maintenance in power of a core of political leaders who ensure the continuity of state leadership. The instability of cabinets and the stability of the core ministerial personnel are usually inseparable phenomena. This concomitance is the focus of my comparative analysis.

The literature on cabinet stability/instability and its relations to the fragmentation of the party system or parliamentary fractionalization has neglected the notion of ministerial core. Even authors who have an intimate knowledge of Western Europe, even scholars who have tested empirically the causes and consequences of ministerial instability, have not considered the stability of many leaders when they measured cabinet turnover. No wonder most of their correlation coefficients explain "a tenth" or "one-fifth of the variance" (Taylor and Herman 1971). Cabinet turnover does not, contrary to what Lijphart suggested, "measure the health of a system" (Lijphart 1968, 72). Klaus von Beyme is one of the few authors who felt the importance of the stability of people as opposed to the instability of cabinets, but he treated this issue too briefly (von Beyme 1981, 882–83). When one measures the core, it seems obvious that cabinet instability has a different significance and that it does not engender the same consequences depending on whether it is countervailed by a ministerial core or not. The importance of the core varies from country to country, as will appear in the following analysis.

In regimes with governmental instability a change of government does not, most of the time, mean the replacement of all outgoing ministers by newcomers. If instability devoured all ministers, it would not last long because the leaders—instead of benefiting from instability—would be its victims. One can observe two types of ministers in these regimes: a core of quasi-irremovable or recurrent leaders and a much larger number of politicians who hold a fraction of power for a short period of time. I shall call the group of irremovable leaders the "governmental nucleus" and the ministers of a day, "ephemeral personages." Around the solid rock, many moths flutter and perish as they reach the flame of power. Between the two, there is an intermediate category.

The governmental nucleus includes ministers who hold the most important positions and who remain in power most of the time. This delimitation excludes secretaries and under secretaries of state and other junior ministers, whatever their official title in various countries, even if they exercise governmental functions for a long time. The prime ministers, even if they remain in power for a short period of time, are included in the governmental nucleus. Without such a notion of governmental nucleus, it will be difficult to explain why, in spite of the ministerial dance, the French Third Republic lasted for seventy years and how, in spite of an equivalent ministerial instability, democracy has flourished in Finland since 1917 and in Italy since 1945.

Who belongs to the ministerial core? In most democracies, a significant proportion of ministers participate in only one cabinet. After the

first appointment, the selection of cabinet ministers continues. The question of how a politician becomes a minister raises a second question of why many former ministers do not succeed in returning to power. An ambitious minister who is not reappointed is a politician eliminated from the inner circle by his rivals or enemies in his party or in parliament. For a variety of reasons, many are never reappointed: Some are defeated in elections, some lose their influence within their party, some retire from politics more or less voluntarily. Whatever the reason, it could be admitted that reappointment is a confirmation of the first selection, a new stage in the selection process. A third or a fourth appointment as minister appears as a kind of superselection. It is beautiful to be a minister. It is still better to remain one or to become one again.

The formation of an inner circle within the party is called, since Robert Michels, the iron law of oligarchy. Theories of coalition building help to understand the formation of inner circles in parliament. At the governmental level, the inner circle takes the form of what I call the ministerial core, which functions like a centrifuge separating the leaders from the average parliamentarians. From all evidence, ministers are very unequal. We must distinguish between those who left their mark on history and those who just made an appearance in the political arena. The duration of ministerial service is a good criterion, even if it is certainly not the only one.

A political career could be very long without ever reaching the highest levels—thirty years in parliament and only three months as minister, for instance. The opposite is extremely rare but does occur with technocrats. Fame can also be built as leader of the opposition, without being in government. These opposition leaders obviously belong to the leadership core and have to be included in the ministerial nucleus, regardless of the length of their executive service. Some examples are Otto Bauer in the Austrian First Republic, Georges Clemenceau during two decades, Stjepan Radic in interwar Yugoslavia, Pietro Nenni and Palmiro Togliatti in Italy, or Gil Robles in the Spanish Second Republic.

Power is implicit in the notion of ministerial core because those who survive ministerial crises are selected again by their peers. The survivors are more prestigious than those eliminated in the process. Reappointment reflects a strengthening of political influence. It also supposes, in most cases, advancement to a higher rank—based on acquired experience—from a technical ministry to a more important one (from Transportation to Finance, for instance). There is, within the cabinet, a hierarchy, generated in large part by seniority. In most

cases the key members of the ministerial core are simultaneously becoming more powerful at the summit of their political party.

The existence of a ministerial core can be explained by the fact that political parties tend to delegate their leaders to government. This is particularly true in regimes with proportional representation and rigid lists of candidates, which favor well-organized and centralized parties controlled by leaders who tend to perpetuate themselves at the summit of their party.

A ministerial core is generated even in democracies characterized by governmental stability. For instance, over a long period in the Netherlands (1848–1956), 225 of the 334 ministers participated in only 1 cabinet, 58 in 2 cabinets, 33 in 3 cabinets, and 18 in 4 or more cabinets. In terms of years of service, the 76 ministers who remained in power more than four years weigh as much as the 258 whose length of service was less than four years. In this case, if one considers a length of four years as a possible criterion, 23 percent of ministers constituted the ministerial core (Dogan and Sheffer-Van der Veen 1957-1958). It is clear that the significance of a ministerial core is much higher for democracies with governmental instability than for the others.

The ministerial core fulfills a function different from that of the interlocking directorates in consociational democracies. In the Netherlands of yesteryear, the "intrabloc overlapping membership in the governing bodies of the bloc institutions [were] clear symptoms of the cohesiveness of each of the four elites" (Lijphart 1968, 60). There are interlocking directorates in most multiparty systems. In Italy, for instance, there is a Catholic interlocking directorate (which includes the Episcopacy, Catholic Action, Coltivatori Diretti), a Communist one (including the strongest labor union), a Socialist one, a Liberal one. A ministerial core is an "intimate" locus of power where delegates of the interlocking directorates face each other as peers behind closed doors. The few most important cabinet ministers, who meet in a kind of supercabinet to choose among crucial options, all belong to the ministerial core. When the prime minister meets with the leaders of the opposition to discuss matters concerning national defense or foreign policy, as is often done in France, he meets with the members of the possible alternative ministerial core. Most of the time two generations are represented in a ministerial core: the old stars, some dying but still brilliant, and the new stars, more influential than prestigious. The first group transfers power to the second, in a manner too slow to appear in parliamentary debates, but which is sometimes revealed by perspicacious observers.

I will first try to circumscribe the governmental nucleus and its stabilizing role under the French Third Republic. Next, I will put forth

evidence about the group of stable and influential ministers during the French Fourth Republic, leaving in the shadow those who speedily passed through. Then I will analyze the group of key men in Italy where the core appears in all its beauty. Finland, with its peaceful revolving government, also provides an example of a ministerial nucleus. Interwar Czechoslovakia is an interesting case of strong leadership beyond the ministerial turnover. The Weimar Republic and the Austrian First Republic offer examples of strong ministerial cores even if immersed in a deeply split political class. Next, I will deal with regimes where the ministerial dance was not conducted by a core of strong dancers: the Spanish Second Republic, the chaotic Portuguese First Republic, the incipient Polish Republic after World War I, and interwar Yugoslavia. Finally, I will look at Greece, which experienced a succession of regimes rather than ministerial instability.

This tour is partly a pilgrimage to the cemetery of European democracies. According to an erroneous belief held by even some historians, twelve democracies collapsed before World War II because of internal unrest and unstable government. In fact, in several countries the democratic game was discharged from outside by invasion, for instance, the French Third Republic, Czechoslovakia, and Estonia. Other democracies collapsed for a variety of reasons, but governmental instability was not among the important ones because it was compensated for by the existence of a strong ministerial core.

THE GOVERNMENTAL NUCLEUS DURING THE FRENCH THIRD REPUBLIC

Under the Third Republic (1870–1940), there were 106 cabinets with an average length of eight months (see Table 10.1). A total of 631 ministers received 2,082 appointments, but a quarter of these appointments, or 516, went to 35 men who participated in more than 10 governments. Opposite them are 366 ministers, 58 percent of the total, who belonged to but 1 or 2 governments, and who totaled only 485 appointments. On balance, the political weight of those 35 men seems heavier than that of the 366 others.

Other criteria could also be adopted in order to weigh governmental offices. For instance, the 502 ministers who participated in no more than 4 governments and who ran up a total of 917 appointments do not suffice to make up for the weight of 129 ministers who were appointed five or more times and who totaled 1,135 appointments.

One comes up with the same type of results when considering not the number of appointments but the length of office-holding: 420 ministers, two-thirds of the total, held their offices less than two years.

Table 10.1
Parliamentary Seniority Before First Appointment and Length of Ministerial Career, French Third Republic, 1870-1940

Ministerial Duration	Years Between First Election and First Appointment					
	Under 4	5-6	7-14	15	Non MPs	Totals
Less than 90 days	24	21	29	14	16	104
3 to 6 months	16	2	19	4	6	47
6 to 12 months	36	28	36	19	19	138
12 to 18 months	21	7	28	14	9	79
18 to 24 months	17	6	16	8	5	52
24 to 36 months	22	11	20	9	6	68
36 to 48 months	11	4	9	4	1	29
more than 3 years	48	21	37	11	0	114
Total ministers	192	100	194	83	62	631

Together, they ran up a total of about 3,600 months of duty. On the heavier side of the balance, there were only 75 men who remained in power more than four years each and who were power incarnate for more than 4,300 months. Among the 75 ministers, the silhouettes of 24 persons, who maintained themselves in the government for more than seven years, stand out; in the middle of them, a monument of 10 men, each with more than ten years: Briand, Delcassé, de Freycinet, Sarraut, Leygue, Barthou, Ribot, Doumergue, Cheron, and Queuille.

These 75 persons made up what I call the governmental nucleus, which pushed out into the cold those with ephemeral terms of office. The core men were, in one sense, interdependent and interchangeable. Ministerial crises hardly affected them, and they easily passed from one ministerial department to another, thus showing that they were virtually irremovable—not because they were particularly competent in a given field, but because of their multiform political breadth. To these 75, one must add some others who kept power less than four years but were nonetheless preeminents, or still others whose influence is certified by historians. The criterion of four years seems, in effect, too rigid. In order to circumscribe this nucleus better, some adjustments must be made, in particular, by including some prime ministers and ministers of finance who remained outside, such as Gambetta, who reigned only 77 days.

During certain periods, this nucleus took on a clear color. Thus, out of the 91 men who participated in more than 6 governments between 1899 and 1940, 47 were Radicals and 22 others were their next-door neighbors on the floor of Parliament. In other words, three-quarters of the most stable ministerial personnel were recruited from the ranks of the Radicals and the Radical Left. The name *Radical Republic* is well justified.

Of the 56 prime ministers of the Third Republic, 22 headed 2 governments or more. If we consider the most unstable period, 1920–1940, we count 42 cabinets but only 19 prime ministers, almost all of whom were ministers either before or after their prime ministership. Briand directed 10 governments and participated in 15 others; Sarraut belonged to 25 cabinets; Eynac, 22; Leygue, 20; Queuille, 20 (and later 10 more in the Fourth Republic); Daladier, 18; Chautemps and Barthou, 17 each; de Monzie, 16; Delcassé, Maginot, and Steeg, 15 each; de Freycinet, Painlevé, Bonnet, Pietri, Bourgeois, Flandrin, and Loucheur, 14 each; Laval, 13; Cheron, 12; Ribot, Tirard, Rollin, Berard, Tardieu, Develle, and Dalimier, 11 each; Clementel, Rouvier, Poincaré, Doumergue, Besnard, and Paul-Boncour, 10 each.

The importance of the governmental nucleus is also shown by the personification of certain fundamental issues: Briand and European security; Poincaré and financial stability; Ferry and colonization; Combes and anticlericalism. Of course, the personification of a policy was a mild phenomenon in comparison with the personalization of power itself under the Fifth Republic's presidential regime. But such personification of a policy took on particular significance in the context of cabinet instability. The Third Republic's ministerial instability (106 cabinets in seventy years, 42 between 1920 and 1940) masked the remarkable permanence of a core of men that assured the continuity of the state, in spite of incessant change and reshuffling.

By contrast, the instability of ephemeral individuals is remarkable. Nearly half the ministers, exactly 289, remained in power for less than a year: 138, between seven and twelve months, 47, between three and six months, and 104, less than ninety days. (In counting the 104 of less than ninety days, I exclude the short-lived final government of the Third Republic.) To the 289 ministers with less than a year, we must add 131 others who were able to stay in power more than one but less than two years; still another 97 were able to keep their positions between two and three years. Only 114 governed more than three years (see Table 10.1). Among the latter were 75 persons who constituted the nucleus that I have just traced. At the time when their ministerial careers terminated, the majority of ministers were still in the prime of life: 373—that is, 60 percent—were less than fifty-nine years old when

they quit a government for the last time, with or without the hope of returning.

On one side of the balance, there are 114 personalities who remained in power more than three years, on the other side, a comparable number of ephemeral personages of less than ninety days. Among the latter we count 44 who climbed to power only to fall after less than thirty days, like mayflies born at nine o'clock in the morning on a summer's day only to die at five in the evening. Most of them were only under secretaries of state. In short, the existence of a core of 75 personalities (or 114 if we adopt more generous criteria) is an important element in explaining the functioning of the Third Republic and of its achievements despite chronic governmental instability.

KEY RULERS OF THE FOURTH REPUBLIC

At first glance, the picture is depressing. Among the 24 cabinets of the Fourth Republic, 2 resigned on the day of their presentation to the National Assembly (Robert Schuman II and Queuille II); 5 remained in power only a few weeks (de Gaulle, Blum, Marie, Edgar Faure I, and Pflimlin); 11 were so-called semi-annual, lasting between five and eight months; only 6 lasted more than 300 days (Ramadier, Queuille I, Pinay, Laniel, Faure II, and Guy Mollet).

Nevertheless, ministerial instability has been a phenomenon with much less significance than generally admitted, because change of government did not necessarily mean change of the ministerial team, parliamentary majority, or political orientation. It was simply a new crystallization of the same parliamentary majority around a new group of ministers, which included few newcomers and which proposed a program where only the order of priorities was changed.

I will try to show that apparent instability covers a relative stability, even a profound stability. It is necessary to proceed with such an analysis step by step. Among the 227 members of the government, 128 reached cabinet level, and 99 more were secretaries of state. The 227 ministers of the 24 cabinets were appointed to a total of 776 ministerial positions, but 250 of these appointments, or nearly one-third, went to only 23 men, each of whom participated in 9 or more ministerial combinations. An equivalent number of appointments, 208, went to 138 persons who participated in at most 3 governments, representing two-thirds of all ministers. The other 66 ministers each belonged to more than 3 and less than 9 cabinets. If we place on one side of the balance of ministerial responsibilities the political weight of these two-thirds of all ministers and on the other side the weight of the 23 statesmen, the latter appears much heavier.

A similar calculation can be done for the length of the ministerial service: 37 ministers remained in power a total of 120 months, and an equivalent number of ministers, exactly 40, remained in power—some irremovably—for 1,900 months, almost 16 times longer.

One way to delimit the governmental nucleus is to count those ministers appointed to at least 6 cabinets.

Pflimlin—16 cabinets
Schuman, Bourges-Maunoury—14
Moch, Morice—13
Thomas—12
Bidault, E. Faure, Mitterrand, Bacon—11
Queuille, Marie, Lacoste, Jacquinot, Letourneau, Maroselli, Schneiter—10
Pleven, R. Mayer, Teitgen, Claudius-Petit, Louvel, Coste-Floret—9
Pineau, Buron, Brune, Lejeune—8
Pinay, Gaillard, D. Mayer, Gazier, Bonnefous, Colin, Ribeyre, Petsche, Tanguy-Prigent, Biondi, Hugues, de Chevigne—7

In total, 39 personalities are in this list. Among them, 10 remained in power more than five years, another 10, more than four years. To them should be added the following presidents: Auriol, Blum, Coty, Gouin, Ramadier, Guy Mollet, Mendès-France, and Herriot.

Another aspect worth stressing is the stability of the same people in the same office:

Foreign Affairs: 2 incumbents, Bidault and Schuman, in 17 cabinets over a period of ten years (November 1945–June 1954)
Interior: 4 ministers, Depreux, Moch, Queuille, and Brune, in 17 cabinets (June 1946–July 1953)
Industry and Commerce: 3 ministers, Croizat, D. Mayer, and Bacon, in 19 governments over a period of ten years (January 1946–February 1956)
Agriculture: 3 ministers, Tanguy-Prigent, Pflimlin, and Laurent, in 18 cabinets
Public Works: 3 ministers, Moch, Pineau, and Pinay, in 13 cabinets over a period of seven-and-a-half years
Colonies: 4 ministers, Letourneau, Coste-Floret, Moutet, and Jacquinot, in 20 cabinets over eight years
Education: 2 ministers, Naegelen and Marie, in 10 cabinets
Housing: Claudius-Petit, in 8 successive cabinets
Health: Schneiter, in 7 successive cabinets.

Another interesting aspect is the survival of ministers from one cabinet to the next, but in a different department. Other politicians returned to power after a more or less voluntary "retreat." If we set aside the cabinets presided over by de Gaulle, the homogenous Socialist cabinet directed by Blum, and the cabinets of Pleven and Laniel, in the remaining cabinets the number of new men was limited to 1, 2, or occasionally 3 or 4 politicians, exceptionally 5 or 6, most of whom were former secretaries of state. In 2 cabinets, Bourges-Maunoury and Queuille III, no newcomers were included. Nevertheless, the Pinay cabinet, made up of 16 old-timers and only 1 newcomer, was in terms of economic policy, one of the most important changes in the sequence of cabinets.

The 24 cabinets included a total of 58 vice presidents of the Council of Ministers and ministers of state without portfolio. These 58 appointments were held by 20 individuals, 14 of whom were, at other times, in charge of one or more of the most important ministerial departments. The vice presidents of the council and the state ministers illustrate the persistence of some ministers from one cabinet to the next. In the de Gaulle cabinet of November 1945, there were 4 ministers of state representing as many political colors: Auriol, Jacquinot, Francisque Gay, and Thorez. The latter 2 became vice presidents in the following cabinet presided over by Gouin who, in his turn, became vice president in the cabinet of his successor, Bidault, who also recalled to power another 2 former vice presidents. Ramadier surrounded himself with 5 former vice presidents or ministers of state, among them 1 former president of the council, 1 former vice president, and 3 leaders of parliamentary groups. The Marie cabinet included as vice presidents a former president of the council, Blum; a former vice president, Teitgen; and as ministers of state, a former president, Ramadier, and one future president, Queuille. From the second Schuman cabinet to the Guy Mollet cabinet, every vice president of the council was a former president, with the exception of Guy Mollet, who later became president, and Teitgen, who made the vice presidency a personal speciality. During the seven years from the Gouin cabinet to the Pinay cabinet every president of the council had belonged to the cabinet both of his predecessor and of his successor, either as vice president or as one of the 3 or 4 most important ministers. The sole exception to this is the homogeneous Socialist government presided over by Blum. This situation resulted from the fact that the government was always a coalition, wherein each party in the parliamentary majority was represented by some of its most important leaders. Support without participation was the exception, not the rule.

Because of the needs of the political coalition and because of the well-known phenomenon of the monopolization of some departments by certain parties, who usually favored the same men, the presidents of the council were not able to choose the heads of the ministries freely. Men with various skills were numerous enough. Bourges-Maunoury was minister of national defense, finance, industry, interior, and finally, president of the council. Morice moved from education to the merchant marine, from public works to commerce and industry. Mitterrand was successively minister of veterans, information, colonies, the Council of Europe, interior, and justice; Pineau was as eclectic: food, public works, finance, and foreign affairs; so was Pflimlin: public health, economy, agriculture (where he was irremovable for a long time), commerce, Council of Europe, colonies, and finance, and finally president of the council. It would be easy to multiply the examples.

The fact that 15 of the 39 individuals in the governmental nucleus belonged to the small Radical party is another aspect of continuity. We should also take into consideration the stability of some higher civil servants, such as Jean Monnet, who played a role at least as important as many ministers. After all, the continuity of policy in many domains, and in spite of ministerial crises, is impressive. Furthermore, there was some continuity from the Third Republic to the Fourth Republic. Certain ministers of the Fourth Republic had also exercised governmental functions under the third: Blum, Gouin, Mendès-France, Laniel, Queuille, Marie, Ramadier, Schuman, Reynaud, Jacquinot, Petsche, Moutet, Moch, Delbos, as well as Presidents Auriol and Coty. All were active Resistants during the war (see Chapter 1 in this volume).

The stability of ministers at the head of the 15 most important departments was in France almost as remarkable as in Great Britain: 87 against 65 (Dogan and Campbell 1957, 331). As astonishing as this would seem, the number of new men brought by five or six reshuffles of the same British cabinet is as large as the number of new men in 5 or 6 new French cabinets. In France between August 1951 and March 1957, 31 parliamentarians were promoted to the cabinet for the first time. In Britain, during a period of equal length, October 1951 to May 1957, 33 politicians were so promoted (Dogan and Campbell 1957, 340). In Britain during the same period as the French Fourth Republic (August 1945 to May 1958), 75 persons became members of the cabinet, half of whom were promoted to this dignity by reshufflings of the cabinet. The stability of individuals was not so impressive as the stability of cabinets.

It is time to reconsider some harsh judgments about the Fourth Republic. How can one explain the achievements of this regime in so many fields? If the Fourth Republic had had greater cabinet stability,

would it have more easily found a solution to its colonial problems, Algeria in particular? The United States plunged into the same kind of errors in Vietnam, as did Portugal with its irremovable government.

Briefly stated, during the Fourth Republic, a stable nucleus remained solidly anchored to power. Out of 227 ministers, 150 participated in at most 3 governments, accumulating 245 appointments, whereas those 23 ministers who participated in at least 9 governments ran up a total of 240 appointments. The fact that the same men directed the same departments, and also the allocation of certain positions to men recruited from the same party, added to the firmness of the governmental core. The notion of ministerial nucleus is essential to understanding how the Fourth Republic functioned and succeeded in so many fields.

The transition from the Fourth Republic to the fifth was accomplished according to provisions in the constitution, in spite of the dramatic circumstances of the Algerian war. Changing a constitution does not necessarily mean that the regime is unstable. Sweden rewrote its constitution in the late 1960s and early 1970s, as have many other parliaments, but no one defines Swedish democracy as unstable.

THE GOVERNMENTAL NUCLEUS IN THE ITALIAN PARTY DEMOCRACY

Italian democracy was characterized by ministerial instability even under the monarchy. Between 1900 and 1914, 12 cabinets followed each other; there were another 7 cabinets between June 1919 and October 1922. In the democracy restored after 1945, ministerial instability immediately reappeared.

From June 1945 to August 1983, from Parri to Craxi, Italy was ruled by 43 cabinets. During these thirty-seven years, the regime was dominated by the Christian Democratic party, without which no cabinet was conceivable. All prime ministers except Parri and Spadolini were Christian Democrats (see Chapter 4 of this volume). Here I will analyze only the ministers belonging to this dominant party, but it is clear that the distinction between ministerial core and ephemeral personages is just as significant for the other parties, Social Democratic, Socialist, Liberal, and Republican.

From 1945 to 1983, 660 individuals occupied ministerial positions, 446 of whom belonged to the Christian Democratic party. The chronic ministerial instability that characterized the Italian political regime was balanced by the stability in power of key men, and even by the quasi-immovability of some of them. In effect, the 36 ministers who participated in 8 cabinets or more as full ministers (and in other governments as under secretaries of state), add up to more than 500 appointments.

For instance, Colombo remained permanently in power, with only a four-year interruption, between 1948 and 1982: 25 times as minister, once as prime minister, and 6 times as under secretary of state. Andreotti belonged to 27 governments: 5 times as prime minister, 16 times as minister, and 6 times as under secretary of state. Rumor was present in 23 governments, nearly without interruption, for more than twenty years, after having been general secretary of the Christian Democratic party for two years. Moro was prime minister for six years. By assassinating him, the terrorists of the Brigate Rosse wanted to eliminate a symbol. They understood the importance of the governmental nucleus.

For 43 cabinets, there are only 16 prime ministers. After De Gasperi (the Italian Konrad Adenauer), who led 8 cabinets, 4 leaders each led 5 cabinets: Moro, Rumor, Andreotti, and Fanfani; 4 other leaders headed 2 cabinets: Segni, Cossiga (both of who became presidents of the republic), Leone, and Spadolini. These leaders also participated in other cabinets as ministers.

The stability of individuals is particularly visible at the head of the principal departments. Thus, all the ministers of the interior except 4 (Taviani, Restivo, Gui, and Rognoni), were former prime ministers or en route to this position. From 1945 to 1983, Italy had 15 ministers of foreign affairs: 10 were previously or later prime ministers, the 5 others being men of the stature of Sforza (Liberal), Saragat (Social Democrat), Piccioni, Medici, and Ruffini. Gonella was in charge of the Ministry of Justice in 8 successive governments, after having assumed responsibility for public instruction in 5 governments. Andreotti was minister of defense in 8 governments. Taviani was minister of interior 7 times, minister of defense 5 times, minister of the treasury and budget 5 times, and minister of the Mezzogiorno 4 times. Vanoni was minister of finance for four years. Colombo, after having had the responsibility for industry through 4 governments, directed the treasury in 13 governments over seven years. Honor to the great leaders: De Gasperi was prime minister for eight years, and Moro for six. In addition, during the intervals when these personalities were not charged with ministerial responsibilities, they were at the head of the dominant party or were presiding over one of the assemblies. Hence, they controlled the government.

These men had known each other for many years, some from their youth. They launched themselves in politics during the first years of the republic. They remained present in the Roman political forum for twenty or thirty years, permanently in Parliament, with some discontinuities in government, and alternatively in the leadership of their party. They pursued their route together, in spite of political rivalries.

Consequently, they make up a political class in the sense that Gaetano Mosca gave to this notion.

The length of governmental functions exercised by the 36 most important Christian Democratic ministers exceeds the longevity of the career of most of the principal ministers in the so-called stable democracies, except Sweden and Norway.

Gravitating around this governmental nucleus, there are 286 under secretaries of state, whose collective influence was much more modest than that of the 133 full ministers. Most of them remained in government for just a short time; they only passed through. They were, from the ministerial point of view, ephemeral politicians, even if they were meanwhile, particularly in their constituencies, prestigious and powerful. If we put the political weight of the 86 most stable Christian Democratic personalities, in terms of the number of appointments, on one side of a scale, it would be much heavier than the other side with 330 ephemeral ministers and under secretaries of state.

Some foreign observers of the political game in Rome worry about ministerial instability; others denounce the immovability of men in power. Italian political scientists do not worry; a scholar such as Norberto Bobbio, for instance, wrote, "Where the government is weak, the society is stronger and also freer" (Bobbio 1981, 19). This paradox is fictitious because, in a multiparty system with one dominant party organized in factions, the two phenomena—instability and immovability—are intimately bound together.

MINISTERIAL INSTABILITY IN THE FINNISH SEMIPRESIDENTIAL SYSTEM

Finland lives by the rhythm of annual ministerial minicrises: 64 cabinets in 66 years, from March 1917 to May 1983. The regime is semipresidential. The president, elected for six years, can be reelected and disposes of real powers. Kekkonen became president after having been prime minister of 5 cabinets, between 1951 and 1956. Such a personalization of power, beginning with Mannerheim and continued with Paasikivi, illustrates a stability and continuity more profound than the instability of cabinets. Because of the semipresidential character of the political system, the nature of the ministerial core is somewhat institutionalized. In addition to Kekkonen, 2 prime ministers, Sorsa and Kallio, headed 4 cabinets, 4 prime ministers led 3 cabinets, and 10 prime ministers, 2 cabinets.

The ministerial core emerged clearly during the period 1917–1973. One minister, Virolainen, has participated in 15 cabinets; another, Miettunen, in 13 cabinets; a third, Karjalainen, in 11 cabinets; a fourth,

Torngren, in 10 cabinets. All 4 have also been prime ministers. Fourteen ministers were appointed 6 times or more, accumulating a total of 117 appointments.

On the other side of the balance, there are 118 ministers, representing one-half of the total number of 226 ministers between 1917 and 1973, who participated in only 1 cabinet. These 118 ministers remained in power for a short time: 15 ministers less than 100 days; 43 between 100 and 200 days; 40 between 200 and 400 days; and 20 between 400 and 500 days. Altogether they held their position 3,370 days, much less than Karjalainen's 4,887 days, Virolainen's 4,573 days, Torngren's 4,270 days, or Miettunen's 3,779 days. Of a total of 445 ministerial appointments during the period 1945–1973, there were only 176 newcomers and 269 reappointments of old-timers (Yrjola 1973, 19).

Eight cabinets among 64 consisted exclusively of "experts," and 17 cabinets did not include any "expert" at all. In all others, there were 1, 2, or 3 higher civil servants. Thus, only 8 times in 66 years was it difficult to build a parliamentary majority. Most of these cabinets of "experts" survived a short time: 6 less than 150 days, 1, 170 days, and 1, 269 days. Several times the solution has been minority government (Social-Democrat in 1926, 1948, 1972, Center in 1959 and 1961).

The parties have been, from the beginning of the republic, well organized and centralized. They delegated their representatives to government. As the leaders of the parties were almost immovable, they tended to appoint and reappoint themselves. When the most important leaders were not included in the cabinet, they controlled it from outside. The power of party leaders generated at the same time ministerial instability and a stable ministerial nucleus.

The Finnish political system has succeeded in building an equilibrium between presidency, parliament, and government, in which the stability—uninterrupted or recurrent—of party leaders in the cabinet, along with the length of the presidential mandate, created an antidote to possible noxious effects of ministerial turnovers.

CZECHOSLOVAKIA: STRONG LEADERSHIP BEYOND MINISTERIAL TURNOVER

In the twenty years from the declaration of its independence to the first stage of the Nazi invasion (November 1918 to September 1938), Czechoslovakia had 17 cabinets, with an average duration of fourteen months; 82 ministers accumulated 259 appointments (see Table 10.2). Half of these appointments went to 19 personalities, who participated in more than 5 cabinets each. Eduard Benes was present in all cabinets from the first to the fifteenth, as minister of foreign affairs and once

Table 10.2
Ministers and Number of Appointments, Czechoslovakia, 1918-1938 (17 Cabinets)

Ministers	Times Appointed	Total Appointments
33	1	33
14	2	28
7	3	21
9	4	36
6	5	30
4	6	24
2	7	14
1	8	8
3	9	27
1	11	11
1	12	12
1	15	15
82		259

as prime minister, until his election in 1935 as president of the republic after Tomas Masaryk's death. Milan Hodze was also present in all cabinets except 2, 3 times as prime minister. Jan Sramek remained continuously in power from 1922 to 1938. Franz Spina, Rudolf Bechyne, and Ivan Derer belonged to 9 cabinets each, virtually uninterruptedly. Emile Frank participated in 8 cabinets, Ludovig Czech and Jan Dostalek in 7 cabinets without interruption. Antonin Svelha was present in 6 cabinets, in 3 as prime minister, until his death in December 1933, and Jan Cerny was also in 6 cabinets, in 2 as prime minister (and in 2 more after September 1938). Jan Malypetr, after having directed 3 cabinets, was elected president of the Chamber of Deputies in November 1935. Tomas Masaryk, Benes, Svelha, and a few other ministers were also active in the informal government prior to Czechoslovakian independence. Several ministers, including Jan Masaryk (who either committed suicide or was assassinated after the Communist takeover in 1947), continued to serve in the government in exile in London between July 1940 and April 1945.

In the Petka, a steering committee superior to both cabinet and Parliament, the principal leaders met. "It started as a coalition of the leaders of the five main Czech parties and later became an inner cabinet" (Lijphart 1977, 33). Among the 82 ministers, only 33 participated in a single cabinet and only 14 in 2 cabinets. The 33 ministers

who made only 1 appearance served less time than the 3 leaders with the longest ministerial careers. In spite of this impressive continuity in power of a group of strong leaders in a kind of cartel, one finds Czechoslovakia ranked in several publications, because of the superficial criterion of ministerial turnover, among "unstable" democracies. But if one considers that the same men remained in the same positions for a long time across reconstructions of the cabinet, sharing executive responsibilities for a longer period than in any other democratic government in the world at that time outside Great Britain, one should admit that in the case of Czechoslovakia—as in the other countries analyzed here—the notion of ministerial nucleus is indispensable for a correct measure of ministerial durability.

In the 1930s Czechoslovakia had one of the fifteen highest GNPs per capita in the world. Democracy in this country had deep roots from the start: The democratic institutions did not collapse. The superficial ministerial turnover played no role in the loss of Czechoslovakia's independence through circumstances well known to all.

THE WEIMAR REPUBLIC: THE IMPOTENCE OF THE MINISTERIAL CORE

In the Weimar Republic, there were 20 governments in the fourteen years between February 1918 and January 1933, and 4 of these governments were presided over by the same man (Marx); 5 other leaders directed 2 governments each (Wirth, Luther, Muller, Stresemann, and Bruning). It would be superfluous to retrace a well-known history here; it is sufficient to indicate that the ministerial core appears clearly. Eighty-five politicians were appointed to a total of 267 positions in these 20 governments. But on the heavier side of the scale we have 14 leaders, each of whom participated in at least 4 cabinets; on the other side, 65 politicians appointed only once or twice. One minister, Gessler, participated in 14 cabinets as minister of defense; another, Brauns, participated uninterruptedly in 13 cabinets as minister of labor; Stresemann was in charge of foreign affairs in 9 cabinets; Luther, Wirth, Schmidt, Giesberts, and Curtius each belonged to 5 cabinets; Graf von Kanitz, Oeser, Groener, and Schatzel to 4 cabinets; 7 other ministers participated in 3 cabinets, and 24 in 2 cabinets each.

Among these 20 governments, 5 were led by nonparliamentarians: Cuno, Luther I and II, von Papen, and von Schleicher. Of a total of 267 ministerial appointments, 108 (40 percent) went to nonparliamentarians, 58 of whom were not even party members (Schmidt-Jortzig 1972, 343). It was not so much the frequent change of government that weakened the Weimar Republic as the recruitment of so many ministers

from outside of Parliament. In the last 2 cabinets of the Weimar Republic (von Papen and von Schleicher), none of the ministers were parliamentarians.

The breakdown of democracy in Germany is one of the most important events of the twentieth century and one that has not yet finished challenging the social sciences. In the analysis of this disaster, over a score of different factors could quite easily be included. However, ministerial instability was not considered an important factor in this collapse by authors such as Karl Dietrich Bracher, Richard Hamilton, and Juan Linz. The governmental nucleus was not able to overcome the other adversities the system faced. The collapse of the Weimar Republic resulted from the accumulation of many factors: the regime's lack of legitimacy in the eyes of many Germans; world economic crisis and high unemployment; impoverishment of the middle classes by inflation; national frustration engendered by the loss of the war; fragmentation of parties and the rise of the Extreme Right, favored by proportional representation; deep ideological cleavages, too frequent elections, and so on.

> On 31 January 1933, the day Hitler became Reichskanzler, there were 6,014,000 unemployed . . . one quarter of whom were below twenty-five years of age. Many young people never made the transition into a stable working life. They were particularly easy to mobilize into militia-like organizations and were available for street demonstrations and fights . . . [creating] an atmosphere of civil war, especially the storm troops (S.A.) and the Rote Frontkampferbund of the Communists. For the young and unemployed men they provided clothing, food, and most of all, a feeling of belonging and comradeship that meant a meaningful structuring of their daily life (Lepsius 1978, 57).

Ferdinand Hermens concurred, arguing that if the Weimar Republic had adopted the single-member constituency, instead of proportional representation, the polarization of the party system would have been avoided, since neither the Nazis nor the Communists would have received as much as 40 percent of the votes cast in any constituency. As late as September 1930, the democratic parties—the Social Democrats, the Center party, and its ally the Bavarian People's party—had secured a plurality in 296 of the 400 possible constituencies (Hermens 1951, 74).

AUSTRIA: ROTATION OF CABINETS AROUND A ROCK OF LEADERS

In Austria, twenty-two cabinets followed one another in the fifteen years between October 1918 and September 1933, with the continuous pres-

ence of a group of leaders in the cabinet. Five cabinets were directed by the same man, Ignaz Seipel; 2 leaders, Karl Renner and Johann Schober, directed 3 cabinets; 3 leaders, Mayr, Ramek, and Buresch directed 2 cabinets each. There were 11 prime ministers in 22 cabinets. But in reality, 1 cabinet was stillborn, and 4 cabinets had as prime ministers politicians proposed and influenced by Seipel, the leader of the Christian Social party, who directed 5 cabinets himself, and who played a determinant role during more than half of the republic's brief existence (see Table 10.3).In these 22 cabinets, 97 ministers held 269 positions. Seven leaders accumulated one-quarter of these appointments (see Table 10.4). Among them were Carl Vaugoin, who participated in 16 cabinets, in 1 as prime minister; Resch, in 15 cabinets as minister of social affairs; Schurff, in 9 as minister of industry and commerce; Grunenberger, in 8. But the most important leaders were not those with the longest ministerial careers. Seipel himself was officially present in only 6 cabinets and Schober in only 5. Two ministers became presidents of the republic after having participated in only 1 cabinet (Hainisch) or 3 cabinets (Miklas).

The ministerial core was very strong and there was, in comparison with the other countries considered here, a relatively small number of ephemeral ministers. Only 37 individuals participated in 1 cabinet and only 16 in 2 cabinets; many of these persons were civil servants. Only the first 4 cabinets were based on a coalition between the Socialist and Christian Social parties. The great socialist leaders, Viktor Adler and Otto Bauer, had the opportunity of participating in only 1 or 2 cabinets. The ministerial core was reinforced by a series of constitutional amendments in December 1929, which increased the power of the president especially in regard to the appointment of ministers. But this change came too late.

As indicated in Table 10.3, ministerial crises were resolved within a few days; only on two occasions were more than two weeks necessary to find a new chancellor and cabinet. Such a brevity of ministerial crises reflects the strength of the ministerial core, which was very efficient in rearranging personnel as priorities changed.

Was ministerial turnover a source of concern for the political leaders and for the best observers of the Austrian First Republic? There is no evidence of such a concern in the best biography of Ignaz Seipel, by Klemens von Klemperer, nor in Martin Kitchen's *The Coming of Austrian Fascism,* nor in Victor Germains's *Austria of To-day,* published before the collapse of the regime, nor in Charles Gulick's *Austria From Habsburg to Hitler.*

Why, then, the collapse of democracy? Several books have attempted to answer this question, and almost all stress the deep ideological cleavages of Austrian society and of its ruling class, exacerbated by the

Table 10.3
Austrian Cabinets, First Republic, 1918-1933

Cabinet	Date Installed	Length (Days)	Resulting Crisis (Days)	Notes
Renner I	30 October 1918	124	12	A
Renner II	15 March 1919	216	0	A
Renner III	17 October 1919	237	26	A
Mayr I	7 July 1920	136	0	A
Mayr II	20 November 1920	192	20	B
Schober I	21 June 1921	219	0	C
Breisky	26 January 1922	1	0	D
Schober II	27 January 1922	118	7	E
Seipel I	31 May 1922	321	1	F
Seipel II	17 April 1923	218	0	F
Seipel III	20 November 1923	354	12	F
Ramek I	20 November 1924	420	1	G
Ramek II	15 January 1926	273	5	G
Seipel IV	20 October 1926	210	1	F
Seipel V	19 May 1927	684	1	F
Streeruwitz	4 May 1929	144	1	H
Schober III	26 September 1929	364	5	I
Vaugoin	30 September 1930	60	5	J
Ender	4 December 1930	194	4	K
Buresch I	20 June 1931	221	2	L
Buresch II	29 January 1932	98	14	L
Dollfuss I	20 May 1932	489	0	M

A: Coalition
B: Interim
C: Proposed by Seipel. Cabinet predominantly filled by civil servants
D: Stillborn cabinet
E: Cabinet composed mostly of civil servants
F: Seipel reign (five cabinets)
G: Seipel behind the scenes as kingmaker
H: "Seipel's Tool"
I: Vienna's former chief of police made prime minister under the threat of civil war
J: Seipel's lieutenant, recommended by Seipel
K: Including former prime ministers Schober and Vaugoin
L: Anti-Seipel minority government, including former prime minister Vaugoin, future prime minister Dollfuss, and many "experts"
M: Including former prime ministers Ender, Buresch, Vaugoin, and future prime minister Schuschnigg. Lasted until 21 September 1933

electoral system of proportional representation. The international environment should not be forgotten. When, in August 1932, the two principal protagonists, Seipel and Schober, died within two weeks of one another, Adolf Hitler had already obtained 37 percent of the popular vote in Germany. Engelbert Dollfuss and Kurt von Schuschnigg were then preparing themselves to face the forthcoming Nazi subversion within Austria.

SPAIN: A DIVIDED POLITICAL ELITE EMBARKS THE COUNTRY ON THE ROAD TO CIVIL WAR

Spain had 18 cabinets and 8 prime ministers in the five years between the dictatorship of Primo de Rivera and the civil war (April 1931 to July 1936). Six of these cabinets had the same leader, Alejandro Lerroux Garcia; another man, Manuel Azana y Diaz, had responsibility for 4 cabinets, and 2 others, Manuel Portela Villadres and Joaquin Chapaprieta Torregrose, each had 2 cabinets. In most of the cabinets the number of newcomers was very low: in 7 cabinets, only 1, 2 or 3 new men; in 5 cabinets, between 4 and 6 new ministers; only in 4 cabinets were more than one-half of the ministers newcomers (Linz 1975, 172). In these 18 cabinets, 92 ministers were appointed altogether 213 times. Some of them held the same position continuously. Ministerial instability reflected in part the antagonism between the republican government and the church and army. It also resulted from anarcho-syndicalist agitation, from the maximalist attitudes of socialists, and from the intransigence of regional nationalisms. The ministerial dance was only the foam produced by profound movements under the waves. The average duration of cabinets was 100 days; 9 cabinets lasted less than 60 days (Linz 1975, 172). In spite of the governmental nucleus, the alternative was dictatorship of the Right or of the Left, as all parties clearly perceived. A strong polarization occurred between the elections of 1933 and 1936: The Center fell from 224 to 40 seats, the Left increased from 100 to 280 seats, and the Right remained almost stable.

DEVOURING CABINET MINISTERS: THE PATHOLOGICAL CASE OF THE PORTUGUESE FIRST REPUBLIC

In Portugal, from October 5, 1910, to May 30, 1926, that is, 188 months, there were 45 cabinets with an average life of 4 months each; 28 cabinets lasted less than 100 days. This is the highest level of governmental instability in the history of democratic regimes: 226 persons were appointed a total of 446 times (see Table 10.6). Only

Table 10.4
Ministers and Number of Appointments, Austrian First Republic, 1918-1933
(22 Cabinets)

Ministers	Times Appointed	Total Appointments
37	1	37
16	2	32
20	3	60
11	4	44
6	5	30
3	6	18
1	8	8
1	9	9
1	15	15
1	16	16
97		269

Table 10.5
Ministers and Number of Appointments, Spanish Second Republic, 1931-1936
(18 Cabinets)

Ministers	Times Appointed	Total Appointments
43	1	43
19	2	38
10	3	30
10	4	40
4	5	20
3	6	18
1	7	7
1	8	8
1	9	9
92		213

Table 10.6
Ministers and Number of Appointments, First Portuguese Republic, 1910-1926
(45 Cabinets)

Ministers	Times Appointed	Total Appointments
120	1	120
55	2	110
24	3	72
12	4	48
4	5	20
7	6	42
2	7	14
2	10	20
226		446

about 3 dozen of these 226 were military men; the political game was primarily a game played by civilians. About half the cabinets fell because of parliamentary conflicts, some because of popular unrest, and a few following a military coup (Schwartzman 1981, 157).

Portugal contrasts with the other democracies analyzed here on two grounds. First is the lack of ministerial core. Eleven ministers received a total of 76 appointments; this means that 5 percent of the ministerial personnel received 17 percent of the total appointments. This is not enough to constitute a ministerial core, a governmental rock. The fact that Antonio Maria da Silva directed 6 cabinets; Bernardino Machado and Domingos Pereira, 3 cabinets; and 4 others, 2 cabinets each, did not compensate for the hemorrhage of ministers. "Political leaders—while they included some talented and intelligent men—too often lacked courage, and failed to unite and to cooperate for the public good. . . . Parties lacked distinct, clear programs, in part because personalities often were substituted for issues and ideas" (Wheeler 1978, 167). "The first constitutional president, Arriage, was virtually forced to resign after the 1915 Revolution. . . . The third president, Machado, was dismissed by a military junta . . . and Pais, a president elected for the first time by universal male suffrage rather than by Congress, was assassinated after only one year" (Wheeler 1978, 155–156). On the other side, 120 individuals were appointed only once each and 55 but twice (see Table 10.6). Ministers spent much energy and ambition to arrive in power, where they remained, on average, a few weeks.

The second contrast between Portugal and the other democratic regimes with low cabinet durability appears in the turmoil that characterized the First Republic, an experiment that was a pathological degeneration of democracy. In the standard history of that period, Douglas Wheeler's *Republican Portugal,* one can find on most pages words such as "coup d'état," "bombing," "emergency," "brief civil war," "murder," "assassination," "semihysteria of the congress," a prime minister perceived as "king of the mediocres." Thirty-three parties came and went. There were no fewer than ten recorded coup d'état attempts that reached the streets between 1921 and 1926 (Wheeler 1978, 203). "Severe civil disorder, violence, labor strife and insurrection among the military became increasingly common" (Wheeler 1978, 155). Congressional instability was equally serious. "Of four congresses elected beginning in 1911 . . . only two served out their full term . . . the other two were summarily disbanded by executive fiat following military coups in 1917 and 1919" (Wheeler 1978, 155–156). The escudo was devalued 400 percent in 1920. The Weimar Republic, Austria, and the French Fourth Republic were also characterized by political unrest, but it is a question of degree. In the German, Austrian, and French cases, the political unrest resulted from a polarization of the system and the division of the country into two or three camps. There was some "logic" to the political fights. In the Portuguese case, there was simply chaos.

It is true that when Portugal adopted the democratic regime in 1910, there were only about 15 pluralist democracies in the entire world. The prerequisites for a democratic regime were not met in this relatively poor, semiliterate agricultural country. Because of the concentration of agricultural land in the hands of a privileged class, one would have expected to have a democratic game limited to this elite. But, if we believe the historians, Portuguese and foreign, it seems that the elite itself was immature. There are examples of countries where a small elite was able to play the democratic game in spite of the backwardness of the masses.

Why did no governmental core appear? Many reasons could be given. For instance, the electoral system, by handicapping the organization of strong parties, left the battlefield open for ambitious individuals. Whatever the reasons for the absence of a core of strong leaders, one must ask if it is a simple coincidence that chaos developed in the absence of a ministerial core. The causal relation seems clear. In many countries chaos tends to generate, after a period of time, strong leadership; as a matter of fact, the sixteen chaotic years in Portugal were followed by the most stable single one-man dictatorship in the twentieth century. There was no alternative. The military put an end to this spectacle in

1926, and in 1932 Antonio Salazar seized the power he was to hold until 1968.

Let us compare the two extreme cases of Czechoslovakia and Portugal. Over a similar period, twenty years and fifteen years, eight months, respectively, there were 17 cabinets in the first country against 45 in the second. For the Czechoslovakian cabinet, which usually consisted of 16 members, we count 82 ministers; for the Portuguese cabinets, much smaller, comprising on average 6 members, we have 226 ministers. A ministerial nucleus appears in both regimes, a strong one in Czechoslovakia and a very weak one in Portugal. They belong to opposite types in terms of power and leadership core.

POLAND: PARLIAMENTARY OMNIPOTENCE AND MINISTERIAL WHIRLPOOL

Poland was "governed" for seven years (November 1919 to May 1926) by 16 cabinets with an average duration of five months, twenty days. However, the number of cabinets is not the most important aspect of this parliament-centered regime, but rather, the manner in which "the Diet pretended to decide at any moment the political composition of the cabinet. . . . For one-half of this period cabinets were formed by civil servants, which indicates that it was impossible to establish a formal coalition of parties" (Hermens 1951, 87). The system of proportional representation engendered from the beginning twelve Polish parties and two ethnic minority parties. A few years later, there were fourteen Polish parties and eight minority parties. During the entire parliamentary period, "no less than eighty parties sprouted up, though not all were in existence at the same time" (Hermens 1951, 87).

Two governments lasted less than a week, another one month, and a fourth two months. The most durable cabinet, led by Grabski in 1924–1925 and lasting almost two years, was an extraparliamentary cabinet composed mostly of higher civil servants. The short-lived cabinets of 1921–1923 were overthrown because they were unable to halt the fall of the value of money. In total, 170 ministers were appointed 317 times, on average less than 2 appointments per minister. The majority of them kept their position for less than three months and the number of appointments by reshuffle of the cabinet was relatively high, demonstrating the capacity of the parliament to change the composition of the cabinet at any time.

Chodzko, a medical doctor, participated in 10 cabinets, always as minister of public health; another expert, Darowski, participated in 8 cabinets as minister of labor; Raczynski remained minister of agriculture in 7 cabinets and General Sosnkowski was also in 7 cabinets, as

Table 10.7
Ministers and Number of Appointments, Poland, 1918-1926 (14 Cabinets)

Ministers	Times Appointed	Total Appointments
97	1	97
35	2	70
25	3	75
6	4	24
2	6	12
3	7	21
1	8	8
1	10	10
170		317

minister of war. One leader, Witos, directed 3 cabinets, and 2 others headed 2 cabinets each, Grabski and Ponikowski.

Seven leaders were appointed a total of 51 times. This is a small core group even compared with the 97 ministers who belonged to only 1 cabinet (see Table 10.7). The absense of a ministerial core is in a sense surprising, given the enormous importance of the Union of Polish Youth (the Zet) for Polish political thinking: Four-fifths of all the leading politicians of the republic came from its ranks (Roos 1972, 100).

The National Democrats had weakened the position of the president, thinking that Josef Pilsudski, the most noted leader, might have become a candidate. Pilsudski, in view of the powerlessness of the presidency, decided not to let his name be put forward: He refused to have himself be enclosed in a "gilded cage." He withdrew to his modest estate at Sulejowek—as de Gaulle, for similar reasons, was to retire to Colombey-les-deux-Eglises. In 1923, Pilsudski resigned even from the post of chief of the general staff.

The Socialist party played an important role in the breakdown of the regime. The Socialists accepted a share in governmental responsibilities in 1926 in the Skrzynski cabinet in order, it was said, to save the state and the working class from catastrophe. But they soon withdrew their two ministers and went into opposition because they thought that the "curative measures" being taken were imposing a burden on the workers and small farms. The Skrzynski cabinet, having lost its majority, resigned on May 5, 1926.

Meanwhile, General Zeligowski, devoted to Pilsudski and minister of war in the Skrzynski cabinet, had brought regiments attached to

Pilsudski to near Warsaw, where they were ready for the putsch on May 12, 1926. Then the Socialist party called for a general strike and, with the help of the railway worker's union, hindered the transportation of governmental troops to the capital; the president and the cabinet resigned in the night of May 14-15, 1926 (Roos 1961, 112). The Polish experience appears, from a comparative point of view, as an exception that proves the rule, because the absence of a governmental nucleus produced a chaotic situation. The return of Marshal Pilsudski to power became inevitable.

YUGOSLAVIA: FRAGILE COALITIONS IN A MULTINATIONAL STATE

In the ten years between September 1918 and December 1928, 12 governments followed each other, but 3 cabinets were directed by the same leader, Pasic, 2 by Protic, and another 2 by Davidovic. In total, there were 7 prime ministers, with a deeply split political class around the king, who incarnated the regime. The democratic apprenticeship was not an easy task in this essentially multinational state, which constantly risked coming apart. There were several important political parties, among them the Radicals (under Pasic and Protic), the Democrats, and the Peasant group led by the Croat Radic, none of which could obtain a majority in the Parliament. Radic adopted a fatal policy of abstention from Parliament, and Pasic dissolved the Croat Republican Peasant party and imprisoned Radic.

Pasic died in 1927 and Radic was killed in June 1928 by a deputy belonging to the Radical majority. In Zagreb, the opposition began to organize a countergovernment in Croatia, and the Democratic party withdrew from the government led by a Slovene leader Korosec, in December 1928. "The crisis was no mere cabinet crisis, such as the country had experienced twice a year for ten years. It was a crisis of the state. . . . The parliamentary system had been broken down" (Clissold 1966, 174). King Alexander asked Croat leaders Macek and Pribicevic their views on the "amputation of Croatia and Slovenia from the state," suggesting a solution as in the case of Norway and Sweden in 1905. But the Serbian parties strongly opposed a policy of federalism. The king was obliged to renounce the parliamentary game and wait for a maturation of the nation through better integration of the several ethnic communities. Parliament was dissolved and the constitution abolished in January 1929. A few months later, the official name of the state was changed from Kingdom of the Serbs, Croats, and Slovenes to Yugoslavia. The ethnic cleavages of the political class

prohibited the building of a ministerial core, which would have helped the functioning of the democratic system.

GREECE: UNSTABLE REGIMES RATHER THAN UNSTABLE GOVERNMENTS

In Greece, the parliamentary regime was reestablished in the aftermath of each world war, resulting the first time in a rapid succession of governments, 14 in five years (1920–1924), and the second time in 15 cabinets over a similar length of time (1945–1949) under 6 different prime ministers, with 5 dissolutions of the legislature before the expiration of its term. In the fourteen years between these two periods (1925–1939), 14 cabinets succeeded one another. For the period 1946–1967, 10 percent of ministers held 45 percent of the ministerial positions, measured in minister-months (Legg 1969a, 301). At certain moments the king symbolized permanence of the regime, and at other moments, the power to be destroyed. The country has known a succession of regimes more than a succession of ministerial cabinets. Greece's turbulent history cannot be retraced in terms of cabinet instability.

However, even in this unstable country, "Karamanlis held office as Prime Minister for a total of fourteen years—longer than any British Prime Minister since Gladstone, and perhaps longer than any Prime Minister of a democracy in the twentieth century. He won twelve personal elections, held five different ministries, and formed seven governments, each of them based on a single party. He dominated the political scene in Greece to a degree rivalled only by Elevtherios Venizelos" (Woodhouse 1982, Preface).

CONCLUSION

Among the 12 regimes analyzed here, four types can be distinguished. First are the systems that have fulfilled the basic functions of the democratic game and that were or are successful in many ways: the French Third Republic, the French Fourth Republic, interwar Czechoslovakia, the Italian Republic, and Finland. Even the Weimar Republic was not a failure, in spite of the hyperinflation of the early 1920s, until the depression.

The second type consists of the regimes such as the Weimar Republic and the Austrian First Republic, which broke down for a variety of reasons, but not because of ministerial instability: There was at the same time a countervailing ministerial core. Historians have not suggested government instability as a major cause of the collapse. The Austrian First Republic was undermined from within by profound

vertical cleavages of its society (but similar cleavages in neighboring Czechoslovakia did not endanger the system from within).

The existence of a governmental nucleus was not sufficient to save these fragile democracies because the ministerial instability that the governmental nucleus had to counterbalance was not the principle reason for the breakdown of the democratic regimes. Even if they had known a relative stability of ministers, they might not have escaped, for various reasons, the installment of an authoritarian or dictatorial regime.

In these two countries, the governmental nucleus had been an element of continuity, but one that interacted with other factors promoting instability. These factors, by their cumulative effects, finally provoked the breakdown of the democratic regime. The existence of a ministerial core can compensate for governmental instability, but it cannot countervail other weaknesses of the political regime.

The third type consists of the chaotic democracies: the Spanish Second Republic, the Portuguese First Republic, the incipient Polish Republic, and interwar Yugoslavia, where ministerial instability was not compensated for by the existence of a ministerial core. They collapsed in absence of external war, global depression, or invasion. These regimes had not fulfilled the "prerequisites of democracy," that is, a relatively high economic, social, and cultural development permitting real political participation. At that moment, these countries were, according to several indicators such as illiteracy, urbanization, infant mortality, and development of the mass media, at a level similar to that of Tunisia or Taiwan today.

Greece belongs to the fourth type. The situation in Greece was reminiscent of that in some Latin American countries, where the crisis of the regime was a more serious phenomenon than ministerial instability.

Ministerial Mobility Index

More empirical research is needed before determining a criterion for international comparisons. At this stage it might be helpful to suggest an "index of ministerial mobility." In Table 10.8, nine countries have been selected for this purpose. The size of the cabinet being different in the various countries, it is necessary to take into consideration the number of ministerial positions in order to calculate such an index. By dividing the number of ministers during a given period by the average number of positions in the cabinet, we obtain an indicator of the number of ministers per position. In Finland, for instance, each ministerial department has been occupied, on average, by 19 individuals over the sixty-six years considered.

Table 10.8
Index of Ministerial Mobility

	Number of Ministers	Positions per Government (Median)	Ministers per Position	Total Period (Years)	Index: Ministers per Position per Year (x100)
Czechoslovakia	82	16	4.8	20	24
Finland	226	12	18.8	66	28
Italy	660	60	11.0	37	30
France, Fourth Republic	227	33	6.9	14	49
Weimar Republic	85	12	7.1	14	51
Austria	97	10	9.7	15	65
Spain	92	14	6.6	5	132
Poland	170	15	11.3	8	141
Portugal	226	6	37.6	16	235

As the historical periods vary from country to country, we have to divide this indicator by the number of years covered. We finally obtain an index of ministers per position per year (in order to eliminate decimals, the index has been multiplied by 100). The index is the lowest for Czechoslovakia, Finland, and Italy, and the highest for the Portuguese First Republic, Poland after World War I, and the Spanish Second Republic.

Bureaucracies

One further dimension which must be mentioned in conjunction with the efficiency of the ministerial core is the presence of a strong and competent central administration. France and Austria are well-known examples of competence of the higher public administration, but this is also the case in Germany and Finland and in interwar Czechoslovakia. A competent state apparatus adds continuity to that provided by the ministerial core. Among the seven cases belonging to the first and second types, only one, Italy, does not have the privilege of a highly efficient senior civil service.

However, the cases of the third and fourth types had weak central administration, even more or less corrupt ones, such as the incipient Polish state, the Portuguese First Republic, interwar Yugoslavia and Greece. Only Spain could be characterized as an exception, but even there, the higher civil service did not reach the level of the French or Austrian central bureaucracies.

Socialists

Treading among the tombstones of 10 democracies, one is struck by the contrast among the Socialist leaders concerning the defense of the regime. In some countries, they were wise enough to perceive the peril. The German Socialists were a cornerstone of the Weimar coalition, and the French Socialists defended the democratic regime at the critical moment more than their formal ideology would have led them. In contrast, the responsibility of the Spanish and Polish Socialists in the breakdown of democracy has to be admitted by any fair observer. It is not coincidental that the French and German ministerial cores included the Socialists, while the Polish Socialists were excluded. In a curious reversal, the leaders of the Spanish Popular Front excluded the leaders of the Center-right.

Interest Aggregation and Decisionmaking

It would be useful to formulate the problem of ministerial instability and its accompanying governmental nucleus in terms of interest aggre-

gation and the locus of political decisionmaking, taking these two notions in the senses given them by Gabriel Almond, G. Bingham Powell, Robert Dahl, and others. The way in which interests are aggregated and the place where political decisions are made vary from one political system to another. Decisions can be made by the electorate whenever a single party or a coherent coalition of parties obtains a parliamentary majority, as in a two-party system. The referendum is another example of decisionmaking directly by the electorate. In the neocorporatist countries, some decisions are made outside of parliament in permanent commissions where consensus is negotiated. In the consociational democracies, the sites of decisions are often outside of parliament in powerful councils. In a federal system, the national parliament is discharged of some functions, and the authority to make many decisions is located at the regional level. In some regimes, it is the cabinet that is the center of gravity as, for instance, in Britain under the two-party system, or in Germany whenever one of the two big parties holds, by itself, a majority in the Bundestag. The decline of the national parliament as a site of interest aggregation and as a decisionmaker is a general phenomenon in competitive democracies, except in precisely those regimes characterized by ministerial instability.

If parliament remains the normal site of decisions, instead of becoming the place for ratification of compromises and of solutions developed elsewhere, programs arrive in parliament unfiltered by negotiations. Programs are proposed to parliamentarians without being sufficiently prepared by the executive power and without a potential majority. In these circumstances, ministerial instability becomes a system of government. The ministerial team is changed according to changing political priorities, particularly when the various parliamentary cleavages do not coincide.

Yet the leaders of these parties are precisely those sitting in the cabinet. They determine not only the order of priorities and consequently the duration of the government but also the selection of representatives to be appointed to the cabinet. In this selection process they are themselves in a privileged position, able to designate themselves as ministers. These self-designations operate according to sophisticated but unwritten rules.

Most of the European countries have found, after rather long experience, a certain constitutional equilibrium. The Netherlands, Belgium, and Austria have adopted consociational systems in order to counterbalance certain consequences of proportional representation and after having experienced serious crises that endangered national unity or civil order. In Austria after the war the most important decisions were made by a small extraconstitutional coalition committee (*Koalition-*

sausschuss) on which the top Catholic and Socialist leaders were represented (Lijphart 1977, 33). Sweden and Norway have progressively built neocorporatist systems as a remedy to ministerial instability (23 cabinets in Sweden between 1900 and 1936), transforming Parliament into an organ of ratification of decisions made elsewhere by the representatives of various interests. Austria and the Netherlands are becoming more neocorporatist and less consociational. Germany, having learned the lessons of the Weimar Republic, has introduced into the constitution the wise "constructive vote of no confidence," which obliges the opposition to agree on the chancellor's successor before being able to defeat the current cabinet. Germany has also adopted proportional representation for only half of the seats in the Bundestag and has fixed a threshold of 5 percent of the votes as a condition for a party to be able to be seated in parliament. This has excluded from the Bundestag extremists of left and right. The equilibrium so obtained has permitted all these countries to avoid ministerial instability.

In Europe, only Italy and France have been sufficiently ingenious to construct disequilibrated systems. By a combination of too much proportional representation in very large constituencies, and by the preferential vote that favors the development of factions within the parties, Italy has built a *partitocrazia,* perceived by many Italians as an illegitimate regime. This illegitimacy is also engendered, according to various surveys, by financial scandals, by clientelism, and by the inefficiency of public administration. But according to these same surveys, ministerial instability and the permanence of the governmental nucleus are not sources of concern at either mass or elite levels. Italians know how to make the distinction between illness and symptom.

As for France, it has been buffeted between the omnipotence of Parliament and the omnipotence of the president. The equilibrium of powers, and particularly that of the prime minister, is based on the hypothesis of a difference between the parliamentary majority and the presidential majority. However, many voters had until 1986 tended to vote for the same political parties, assuring in this way the coincidence of the two majorities. In addition, France had adopted, in reaction to previous experiences, an excessively long presidential tenure, almost twice that of the United States. The permanence of the governmental nucleus has been replaced by an alternation of teams. With only 1 or 2 percent difference between majority and minority, all power has been allocated to the winner, the loser having no real influence on political outcomes. When one looks at the perverse effects of "presidential monolithism," as it functioned until March 1986, one recognizes some merit in yesterday's ministerial instability.

It is an ethnocentric view on the part of some American political scientists to believe that a multiparty system accompanied by ministerial turnover is "condemned" to instability. There is a relative instability of ministers even in Britain because of the frequent reshuffling: "A Prime Minister effectively doubles the number of appointments made by reshuffling posts every two years rather than once after an election" (Rose 1987, p. 79). It suffices to note that the United States is today the only existing two-party system in the world (since the appearance in Britain of the Social Democratic Party) in order to determine where the exception is.

If it is true that to govern is to foresee, ministerial instability does not allow politicians to plan long-term governmental policy, no matter what their personal virtues may be, and despite some politicians' quasi-immovability. The consequences of their decisions, or the absence of decision, will usually appear much later, at a moment when those responsible for the decisions are no longer present in the political forum, at least not at the front of the stage. But this is true to varying degrees in all political regimes, including the most stable democracies.

Despite the existence of a core, ministerial instability can still have detrimental effects. Time horizons of U.S., Austrian, or Swedish cabinet officials when formulating policy are significantly longer than those of Italian, Finnish, or Danish ministers, who may be removed unexpectedly. Two ministers, one whose position is insecure, as in Italy, and one who knows that he has a good chance of remaining in power until the next elections, do not usually behave in the same manner. Nevertheless, it is a historical fact that in Italy, despite its ministerial instability, economic planning was, over the last three decades, more coherent and sustained than it was in Britain during the same period. The French Fourth Republic, despite ministerial turnover, had perhaps the most planned economy in the Western world at that time. If one had to choose between the political efficiency of the regime and its economic efficiency, many in the 1950s and 1960s would have preferred Italy with its ministerial dance, achieving an "economic miracle," to Britain with its solid and stable government, experiencing a relative economic decline.

NOTES

Kathleen Schwartzman from the University of Arizona was very kind to provide me with a manuscript list of ministers of all 45 cabinets in the Portuguese First Republic. Klaus Tornudd from the University of Helsinki updated the list of ministers in Finland. Robert Pahre, from the University of California, Los Angeles, helped me analyze the ministerial nucleus in interwar

Czechoslovakia, Poland, and the Austrian First Republic. I would like to express to them my warmest thanks.

REFERENCES

Arraras, Joaquin, *Historia de la Segunda Republica Espanola,* Madrid, Editora Nacional, 1970, Vol. 4.

Beyme, Klaus von, "Party Systems and Cabinet Stability in European Parliamentary Systems," in *Festschrift fur Karl Loewenstein,* Tubingen, 1971, pp. 51–70.

Bianchi, Leonard (ed.), *Dejiny Statu a Prava,* Bratislava, Slovensky Akademie Vied, 1973.

Bobbio, Norberto, "La Crise Permanente," in *Pouvoirs,* 1981 (special issue on Italy).

Bracher, Karl Dietrich, *Die Auflosung der Weimar Republik,* Villinge, Ring-Verlag, 1964.

Clissold, Stephen (ed.), *A Short History of Yugoslavia,* Cambridge, Cambridge University Press, 1966.

Dogan, M., and Campbell, P., "Le personnel ministeriel en France et en Grande Bretagne, 1945–1957," *Revue Française de Science Politique* (April-June and October-December 1957). The figures given there have since been slightly modified because they did not cover the entire Fourth Republic up to June 1958.

Dogan, Mattei, and Scheffer-Van der Veen, Maria, "Le personnel ministeriel hollandais: 1848–1958," *L'Année Sociologique,* 1957-1958, 2, pp. 383–409.

Duverger, Maurice (ed.), *L'influence des systemes electoraux sur la vie politique,* Paris, Colin, 1950.

Fenske, Hans, *Wahlrecht und Parteiensystem; Ein Beitrag zur deutschen Parteiengeschichte,* Frankfurt, Athenaeum, 1972.

Germains, Victor Wallace, *Austria of To-Day,* London, Macmillan, 1932.

Giraud, Emile, *Le pouvoir executif dans les democraties d'Europe et d'Amérique,* Paris, Sirey, 1938, p. 289.

Gulick, Charles A., *Austria from Habsburg to Hitler,* Vol. 1, *Labor's Workshop of Democracy,* Vol. 2, *Fascism's Subversion of Democracy,* Los Angeles, University of California Press, 1948.

Hakovirta, Harto, and Koskiaho, Tapio, *Suomen hallitukset ja hallitusohjelmat 1945–1973,* Helsinki, Oy Gaudeamus AG, 1973.

Hamilton, Richard, *Who Voted for Hitler?* Princeton University Press, 1982, particularly Chapter 14, "Theories of the Catastrophe."

Herman, V. M., and Alt, J. E., *Cabinet Studies,* London, Macmillan, 1975.

Hermens, Ferdinand, *Democracy or Anarchy, A Study of Proportional Representation,* South Bend, Ind., University of Notre Dame Press, 1941.

———, *Europe between Democracy and Anarchy,* South Bend, Ind., Notre Dame University Press, 1951.

Keesing's Contemporary Archives, 1930–1938.

Klemperer, Klemens von, *Ignaz Seipel, Christian Statesman in a Time of Crisis,* Princeton, Princeton University Press, 1972.
Kitchen, Martin, *The Coming of Austrian Fascism,* London, Croom Helm, 1980.
Knight, Maxwell E., *The German Executive 1890–1933,* Stanford, Stanford University Press, 1951.
Legg, Keith R., *Politics in Modern Greece,* Stanford, Stanford University Press, 1969a.
──────, "Political Recruitment and Political Crisis: The Case of Greece," *Comparative Political Studies,* January 1969b.
Lepsius, Rainer, "From Fragmented Party Democracy to Government by Emergency Decree and National Socialist Takeover: Germany," in J. Linz and A. Stepan (eds.), *The Breakdown of Democratic Regimes,* Baltimore, Johns Hopkins University Press, 1978, pp. 34–79.
Lijphart, Arendt, *The Politics of Accommodation,* Berkeley, University of California Press, 1968.
──────, *Democracy in Plural Societies: A Comparative Exploration,* New Haven, Yale University Press, 1977.
Linz, Juan, "Spanish Cabinet and Parliamentary Elites," Paper given at a symposium on "Political Elites and Social Structures in Parliamentary Democracies," Belaggio, Italy, 1975.
──────, "From Great Hopes to Civil War: The Breakdown of Democracy in Spain," in J. Linz and A. Stepan (eds.), *The Breakdown of Democratic Regimes,* Baltimore, Johns Hopkins University Press, 1978.
Lipset, Seymour Martin, *Political Man* (expanded edition), Baltimore, Johns Hopkins University Press, 1981.
Markert, Werner (ed.), *Osteurope-Handbuch: Jugoslawien,* Koln and Graz, Bohlau Verlag, 1954.
──────, *Osteuropa-Handbuch: Polen,* Koln and Graz, Bohlau Verlag, 1959.
Mavrogordatos, George Th., *Stillborn Republic, Social Conditions and Party Strategies in Greece, 1922–1936,* Berkeley, University of California Press, 1983.
Pavlowitch, Stevan R., *Yugoslavia,* London, Ernest Benn Ltd., 1971.
Rae, Douglas W., *The Political Consequences of Electoral Laws,* New Haven, Yale University Press, 1971.
Roos, Hans, *A History of Modern Poland,* London, Eyre and Spottiswoode, 1961.
Rose, Richard, *Ministers and Ministries, A Functional Analysis,* Oxford, Clarendon Press, 1987.
Schmidt-Jortzig, E., "Die Parlamentszugehorigkeit der Weimarer Reichsminister," *Zeitschrift für Parlamenten,* September 1972, pp. 343ff.
Schwartzman, Kathleen, "Contributo para a sistematizacao dum aparente caos politico: o caso da Primeira Republica Portuguesa," *Analise Social* 17 (65) 1981, 1, pp. 153–162.
Soulie, A., *L'instabilité ministerielle en France 1871–1938,* Paris, Sirey, 1939.
Tamames, Ramon, *La Republica. La Era di Franco,* Madrid, Alianza Editorial, 1973.

Taylor, Michael, and Herman, V. M., "Party Systems and Government Stability," *American Political Science Review* 65, March 1971, 1.
Tornudd, Klaus, "Composition of Cabinets in Finland, 1917–1968," *Scandinavian Political Studies,* 1969, pp. 57–70.
Weinzierl, Erika, and Skalnik, Kurt, *Osterreich 1918–1938: Geschichte der Ersten Republik,* Graz, Verlag Styria, 1983, Vol. 2.
Wheeler, Douglas L., *Republican Portugal: A Political History 1910–1926,* Madison, University of Wisconsin Press, 1978.
Wiatr, Jerzy, *The Soldier and the Nation: The Role of the Military in Polish Politics, 1918–1985,* Boulder, Colo., Westview Press, 1988.
Woodhouse, C. M., *Karamanlis, The Restorer of Greek Democracy,* Oxford, Clarendon Press, 1982.
World Almanac, The New York World, 1919 et seq.
Yrjola, Pentti, "Hallitusten poliittinen kokoonpano," in Hakovirta and Koskiaho, *op. cit.,* 1973, pp. 13–23.

ABOUT THE EDITOR AND CONTRIBUTORS

Mattei Dogan is a scientific director at the National Center for Scientific Research in Paris and professor of political science at UCLA. He chairs the research committee on political elites (International Political Science Association) and the committee on comparative sociology (International Sociological Association). Dogan's most recent publication is *Le Moloch en Europe* (with D. Pelassy). He has edited recently *Comparing Pluralist Democracies: Strains on Legitimacy* (Westview, 1988); *A World of Giant Cities;* and *Mega-Cities* (1988).

C. Fred Alford is Associate Professor of Government at the University of Maryland, College Park. In 1987 he was a Senior Fulbright Research Fellow at the University of Mannheim. He is author of *Narcissism: Socrates, the Frankfurt School, and Psychoanalytic Theory.*

John Coakley is Lecturer in Politics at the National Institute for Higher Education, Limerick, Ireland. His research interests include Irish and comparative politics and the emergence of nationalist movements. He has contributed chapters to several books in these areas and has published articles on the same themes in many journals.

Brian Farrell is Associate Professor of Government and Political Science, University College, Dublin. His recent publications include *Sean Lemass* (1983) and, as editor, *De Valera's Constitution and Ours* (1988), and (with H. Penniman) *Ireland at the Polls* (1987). He is a leading current affairs presenter on Irish national television.

Hiromitsu Kataoka is Professor of Public Administration and the Dean of Student Affairs, Waseda University, Tokyo. As a member of the

Agency of Management and Coordination, he has recommended the introduction of an ombudsman system in Japan.

Donald R. Matthews is the Bloedel Professor of Political Science at the University of Washington, Seattle. He has also taught at the University of Michigan, University of North Carolina, and Smith College and has been a Senior Fellow at the Brookings Institution. Matthews's interest in the politics of Norway began in 1980–1981 at the University of Bergen. His works on U.S. politics include *U.S. Senators and their World; Negroes and the New Southern Politics* (with J. Prothro); *The Party's Choice* (with W. Keech); and *Perspectives on Presidential Selection*.

Donald D. Searing is Professor of Political Science and Director of the Program in European Studies at the University of North Carolina at Chapel Hill. He writes on comparative politics and political behavior and has published articles in leading journals. His forthcoming book, *Roles in Parliament,* is based on extensive interviews of members of the British House of Commons.

Richard Sisson is Professor of Political Science and Acting Dean of Social Sciences at UCLA. His publications include *The Congress Party in Rajasthan: Political Integration and Institution Building in an Indian State; Social and Economic Development in India: A Reassessment;* and a forthcoming study, *War and Secession: Pakistan, India and the Creation of Bangladesh.* He is currently engaged in a comparative study of the democratization of colonial regimes.

Margaret Jane Wyszomirski is a member of the Senior Faculty of the Government Executive Institute of the Office of Personnel Management in Washington, D.C. She has been a visiting guest scholar at the Center for Public Policy Education of the Brookings Institute. From 1985 through 1988 she was Director of the Graduate Public Policy Program at Georgetown University. She has written extensively on the American presidency and presidential staffing and advisory systems. She is author of *Staffing the Presidency: Roosevelt to Reagan* (forthcoming) and is coeditor of *The Executive Establishment and Executive Leadership: A Comparative Perspective* and *Becoming President: The Transition of 1988–89.*

INDEX

Ambition, 2, 7, 21, 127, 141, 146, 162, 166
Apprenticeship, 30, 92, 141, 151, 159, 161–165. *See also* Career ladder
Athens, ancient, 15–16, 219–238
  Council of Five Hundred, 220
  orators, 229–232
  rotation of office, 224, 227, 228, 231
  selection by lot, 15, 219–238
  See also Oligarchy
Australia, 1
Austria, 111, 256–259

Backbenchers, 8, 148–152, 162, 164, 166. *See also* Parliamentarian, "average"
Baronages, 12, 120
Belgium, 10
Britain, 10, 141–167
Businessmen, 14, 52, 89, 170, 173–175, 186, 187, 203

Cabinets
  appointments to, 243, 244(table), 247, 250, 251, 253, 254(table), 257–266
  extraparliamentary, 263
  inherited, 55
  newcomers to, 22(table), 172, 193, 194, 246, 248
  pools of eligible candidates for, 5, 51–52, 54
  reshuffles of, 17, 169, 172, 179, 180, 249, 272
  resignation from, 53
  shadow, 8, 10, 11
  size of, 4, 48, 178, 200
  staffing procedures (U.S.), 45, 54, 56–58, 68
  structure of (U.S.), 47–51
Canada, 17, 211
Capital, political, 46, 52, 57, 58, 62, 63, 68, 69
Career, longevity of, 42
Career ladder, 141, 142, 162. *See also* Apprenticeship
Cartel, 255
Central Intelligence Agency, 48
Centrism (as ideology), 33, 94
Civil servants, 8, 9, 14, 19, 24, 34, 35, 88, 89, 155, 158, 165, 170, 173, 174, 175, 209, 229, 232, 249, 253, 263, 269
Clientelistic chain, 128
Coalitions, 81, 93, 100, 213, 214
Cognoscenti, 12
Companionship, 26(fig.), 37, 38, 40, 213. *See also* Ministers, selection of
Co-optation, 36, 37, 108, 123. *See also* Ministers, selection of
Corporations, 42
Corporatism, 160, 270, 271
Corruption, 226, 227
Council of Economic Advisers (U.S.), 69

279

Czechoslovakia, 253–255

Democracy
  consociational, 1, 10, 270
  direct, 219
  prerequisites for, 262
  ruled by teams, 3–4, 6, 15, 31, 199
Democracy, breakdown of
  in Austria, 256–260
  in Czechoslovakia, 253–255
  in Greece, 266
  in Poland, 263–265
  in Portugal (First Republic), 259–263
  in Spain, 259, 260(table)
  in Weimar Republic, 255–256
  in Yugoslavia, 265–266
Departments, 48–50
Deputies, promotable, 34, 36, 40, 115

Ecole Normale Supérieure, as greenhouse, 43
Economy, planned, 272
Education, 166, 185–186, 203–205
Electability, 76
Electoral margin, narrow, 55–57
Electoral "parachuting," 34
Elites
  circulation of, 119
  counter, 202
  immature, 262
  revolutionary, 206
  super, 1, 111
Ethnocentric view, 272
Experience, political, 80, 82–86, 190–191, 209, 211
Expertise, experts, 5, 56–58, 67, 112, 121, 129, 156, 157, 165, 253
Extraparliamentary cabinet. *See* Cabinets, extraparliamentary

Factions, political, 2, 11–14, 101, 119, 122–125, 127–131, 169, 170, 175, 211–214
  loyalty to, 127–129, 213

Finland, 252–253
France, 19–44
  Fourth Republic, 246–250
  Senate, 27–29
  Third Republic, 243–246
  vice president of council, 248
Freemasonry, 37
Friendship, 36, 37, 67, 129, 210, 213. *See also* Ministers, selection of
Friends-rivals, 39, 40, 155
Front-bench, 164
FUCI (Italy), as greenhouse, 110

Gaelic Athletic Association, as greenhouse, 203
Germany (Fed. Rep.), 10
Governmental nucleus. *See* Ministers, core of
Governors, 59–61
Greece, 266
Greenhouse of politicians, 43, 110, 113, 203, 264. *See also* Resistance movement, as greenhouse
Gross National Product, 255

Hegemonic parties, 1, 100, 102–107, 128, 169, 178, 250, 251
Heirs, political, 35
High flyers. *See* Ambition
Historical phases, 20, 31

Ideological cleavages, 257
Immovability, 101, 250, 252
Incompatibilities, 5, 119, 125
India, 14, 181–198
Inner circle, 4, 36, 37, 48, 49, 59, 67, 241. *See also* Ministers, selection of
Intellectuals, 113
Interest groups, 49, 52, 58, 64, 159, 269
Interlocking directorates, 242
Ireland, 199–218
  Senate, 211, 212
Irremovable leaders. *See* Leaders, irremovable

INDEX

Italy, 99–139, 250–252
   presidents of the republic, 130, 131, 132
   Senate, 112

Japan, 11, 14, 169–180
Journalists, 31, 37, 173
Journeymen, 142–146, 160, 164
Junior ministers, 4, 10, 20, 35
   in Britain, 141–167
   in Ireland, 200, 203, 210, 212
   in Italy, 115, 117–119, 122
   in Japan, 171
   role of, 143
Jury duty, 24

Key men. *See* Leaders, irremovable

Law schools, as greenhouse, 43
Lawyers, 31, 43, 65, 68, 88, 186, 204, 205
Leaders
   charismatic, 38
   irremovable, 239–275
   recurrent, 240
   selection of, 13, 90–97, 266–267
Legitimacy, 27, 68, 70, 134, 136, 256, 271,
Limelight effect, 178
Linguistic parity (Belgium), 10

Machiavellian spirit, 118
Majority, 246
Mandarins. *See* Civil servants
Mexico, 14
Military coup, 261, 262, 265
Military officers, 43, 113
Ministers
   age of, 41–42, 145(&table), 146, 166, 186, 205–206, 207(fig.), 215, 216
   careers, 86, 143, 144
   core of, 16, 101, 108, 239, 240
   duration of careers, 244(table), 247
   health of, 51
   "hemorrhage" of, 261
   hierarchy of, 4, 48, 178, 241
   junior. *See* Junior ministers
   mobility of, 190, 191–194, 267–269
   occupational background, 43, 172–176, 186–187, 204–205
   post-ministerial career, 42
   social status of, 186, 204(table), 205, 206, 207(fig.)
   tenure, 78, 243
   turnover of, 47, 62, 76, 172, 239–275
   See also Education
Ministers, selection of, 2, 7–9, 13–14, 39, 41, 114
   channels of, 8, 11, 35, 36
   and competence, 2, 31, 120, 121, 122, 210, 212
   criteria for, 209–216
   and lateral entry, 164
   and self-designation, 124, 125
   See also Companionship; Co-optation; Friendship; Inner circle; Patronage; Preselection, of ministers; Sponsorship
Minister's staff, 34, 37
Minority government, 79, 81, 116, 117
Minority interests, 66–68
Monarchy, nonhereditary, 41

Nationalist movement, 182, 188, 199, 203
National Security Council (U.S.), 69
Netherlands, 17
Newspapers, and preparation for political careers, 111
New Zealand, 1
Norway, 11, 75–98

Office of Management and Budget (U.S.), 48
Oligarchy
   of blood and wealth, 221, 222
   as camerilla/coterie, 230, 231, 232
   of expertise, 221, 231, 232
   iron law of, 15, 120, 220, 221, 225, 227, 230–234, 241

of knowledge and skills, 221
as organization, 220, 230
Omnipotence
of parliament, 271
of president, 271
Opinion leaders, 205
Opinion polls, 16, 78, 97

Parenthood, 215
Parliamentarian, "average," 7, 31, 241
Parliamentary committees, 1, 2, 9, 19, 24, 30, 32, 59, 87, 116, 122, 127, 175, 192
Parliamentary legitimation, 19, 24, 27, 30, 211. *See also* Legitimacy
Parliamentary spectrum, 32, 33
Party conversions, 64
Party hierarchy, 19, 24, 32, 33, 40, 92, 119, 172, 173, 175, 209, 253
Patronage, 26, 55. *See also* Ministers, selection of
Permanent secretary (Britain), 158
Placemen, 142–146, 164
Poland, 263–265
Polarization, 259, 262
Politicians
"ephemeral," 117, 125, 239–275
new generation of, 15, 90, 108–111, 118, 208, 251
professional, 110, 147, 173–176, 186, 187, 195
See also Greenhouse of politicians
Pool, recruitment, 5, 7, 61, 188, 205, 216. *See also under* Cabinets
Popularity, 79, 134, 135
Populistic method of choosing leaders, 95
Portugal, 259–263
Postmaster General, 61
Power
apex of, 2
personalization of, 2, 245
Preselection, of ministers, 5, 42–43. *See also* Ministers, selection of
Presidential nominees, 80, 84

Presidential system
semi, 17, 41, 252
super, 12, 41, 271
Presidents. *See under individual countries*
Promotion
as reward, 41, 166
rules of, 101
Protocol-visitors, 130, 132

Religious minority (India), 184, 185, 195
Representation
proportional, 7, 9, 122, 123, 256, 259, 262, 263, 270
regional, 120, 184, 208, 211
"Republic of Dukes" (France), 20
Resistance movement, as greenhouse, 15, 20, 21, 24, 27, 34, 38, 39, 108–111, 114, 115, 210, 249
Revolving government. *See* Ministers, turnover of
Ruling class, 101, 182, 196, 252, 257, 265

Selection of leaders, 90–97
Senate. *See under individual countries*
Seniority rule, 9, 13, 14, 28, 29, 51, 59, 61, 86, 118, 170–174, 193, 210, 241, 244
Skills
administrative, 16, 22, 46, 58, 59, 61, 62, 68, 232
of persuasion, 232
rhetoric, 162, 222, 230
of statecraft, 90, 229
"Snipers," 117
Sortition. *See* Athens, ancient, selection by lot
Spain, civil war, 259
Sponsorship, 36, 37, 111. *See also* Ministers, selection of
State governors, 85, 86

"Talent Hunt," 56
Teachers, 204, 205

INDEX

Television, 85, 93, 96, 97
Terrorists, 251
"Tetrarchy" (Italy), 125–126

Under-secretary of State. *See* Junior ministers
Unemployment, 256
Union leaders, 65
Union of Polish Youth, as greenhouse, 264
United States, 45–73, 75–98
　Executive Office of the President, 47, 62, 69
　Senate, 85
　uniqueness of U.S. presidency, 75, 86
　vice-presidency, 83, 85
Unrest, political, 256, 261, 262

Veto power, 127, 128, 214
Vocabulary, 100, 124

Whips, 10, 162
Women, 66, 67, 113, 204, 205, 215
Working class, 88, 89

Yugoslavia, 265–266